Family Ties

Family Ties

Living History in Canadian House Museums

ANDREA TERRY

McGill-Queen's University Press

Montreal & Kingston • London • Chicago

© McGill-Queen's University Press 2015

ISBN 978-0-7735-4561-8 (cloth)
ISBN 978-0-7735-4562-5 (paper)
ISBN 978-0-7735-8412-9 (ePDF)

Legal deposit third quarter 2015
Bibliothèque nationale du Québec

Printed in Canada on acid-free paper

McGill-Queen's University Press acknowledges the support of the Canada Council for the Arts for our publishing program. We also acknowledge the financial support of the Government of Canada through the Canada Book Fund for our publishing activities.

Library and Archives Canada Cataloguing in Publication

Terry, Andrea, 1978-, author
Family ties : living history in Canadian house museums / Andrea Terry.

(McGill-Queen's/Beaverbrook Canadian Foundation studies in art history)
Includes bibliographical references and index.
Issued in print and electronic formats.
ISBN 978-0-7735-4561-8 (bound). – ISBN 978-0-7735-4562-5 (paperback). –
ISBN 978-0-7735-8412-9 (ePDF)

1. Historic house museums – Canada – Case studies. 2. Historic buildings – Canada – Case studies. 3. Dundurn Castle (Hamilton, Ont.). 4. Sir George-Étienne Cartier National Historic Site (Montréal, Québec). 5. Mackenzie House (Toronto, Ont.). 6. Dwellings – Canada – History – 19th century. 7. Material culture – Canada – History – 19th century. 8. Canada – Social life and customs – 19th century. I. Title. II. Series: McGill-Queen's/Beaverbrook Canadian Foundation studies in art history

FC161.T47 2015   971.03   C2015-902420-X   C2015-902421-8

Book designed by Pata Macedo

Contents

Illustrations

Unless otherwise stated, all photographs were taken by the author.

Acknowledgments

If it takes a village to raise a child, it most certainly takes a village to support an emerging academic determined to publish her manuscript. I owe many debts to a community of valued, trusted, and loving supporters. First and foremost, I thank Lynda Jessup who believed in me even when, at times, I did not believe in myself. I find mere words insufficient to fully express the depth of my gratitude, so please know I consider you to be one of the most inspiring and kind people I have ever had the pleasure of knowing.

My field research required me to work directly with intelligent, capable, and dedicated people. I would like to thank Ken Heaman of Dundurn Castle, Nancy Reynolds, Fiona Lucas, and Rita Russell of Mackenzie House, Isabelle Chalifoux and David Ledoyen of the Sir George-Étienne Cartier National Historic Site of Canada, and Margaret Houghton and Jennifer McFadden in the Local History and Archives Department at the Hamilton Public Library. Each of these people graciously took time out of their busy schedules, particularly during the Christmas season, to answer my questions and point me in directions that I might not have pursued on my own. I am also grateful to all the unnamed interpreters who permitted me to attend and record their tours, all enthusiastic and highly skilled museum workers who imbue the tours with both energy and insight. In respecting your choice for and right to privacy, I hope you know who you are. My thanks to Jessica Wurster and

Sharon Murray who hosted me while I conducted research in Montreal and to Ken Terry, Hannah Morgan, and Michelle Bauldic who provided some pivotal images featured in this study. Also, I truly appreciate Iris Haüssler for granting me permission to feature her compelling work as the book's cover image and in the concluding chapter.

Over the course of my studies, I have been incredibly fortunate to have such wonderful teachers, mentors, and colleagues such as Blaine Allan, Jeffrey Brison, Anne Dymond, Michele George, Janice Helland, Kristina Huneault, Martha Langford, Hayden Maginnis, Alison McQueen, Clive Robertson, Joan Schwartz, Anne Whitelaw, and the late Warren Tressider. As an itinerant academic, I have had the pleasure of working at a number of different institutions during the production of this manuscript. Accordingly, I thank my colleagues at: the School of Canadian Studies at Carleton University, including Eva Mackey, Peter Hodgins, Anne Trépanier, Donna Fitzpatrick, and John Osborne; the Fine Arts Department at Mount Allison University, including Anne Koval, Thaddeus Holownia, Kirsty Bell, Morgan Poteet, and Andrew Nurse; and the Visual Arts Department at Lakehead University, including Kristy Holmes, Roland Martin, and Julie Cosgrove. It has been my privilege to maintain profound and meaningful friendships with my grad school peers who are all successful academics in their own right – Carla Taunton, Taryn Sirove, Debra Antoncic, Erin Morton, Julia Skelley, and Sarah E.K. Smith all provide inspiration on so many fronts.

At McGill-Queen's University Press, I am grateful to and for my editor Jacqueline Mason for first approaching me and then guiding me through the editorial and publishing process, and to Kaarla Sundstrom who kindly shared her expertise while leading me through the copyediting process. I thank the editors of the McGill-Queen's Beaverbrook Canadian Foundation Studies in Art History – Martha Langford and Sandra Paikowsky – for including my work in this series. Finally, I am also truly appreciative for the financial support of the Social Sciences and Humanities Federation of Canada and the Ontario Graduate Scholarship program, and I am grateful to Queen's University for their role in the development and completion of this book.

The title of this book signals the importance family has played in my life. I thank my aunt and uncle Marge and George Alkema, as well as the entire G. Alkema family, particularly my cousin/sister Vanessa Alkema, her husband Tom Christmas (and my Christmas presents, Josh, James, and

Sophia), Dan Miller, Erin Brodie, Deborah Scott, Andrea and Hugo Kruyne, Wendy Norman, and Jeff King. My father Ken Terry, my stepmother Marsha Terry, and my mother Mary Ormerod all supported me in their unique and special ways. One person made me laugh so much throughout this process, sometimes through tears – Andrew Scott has weathered this storm, showing me love, kindness, honesty, consideration, and respect. I love you – without you, none of this would have been possible.

Family Ties

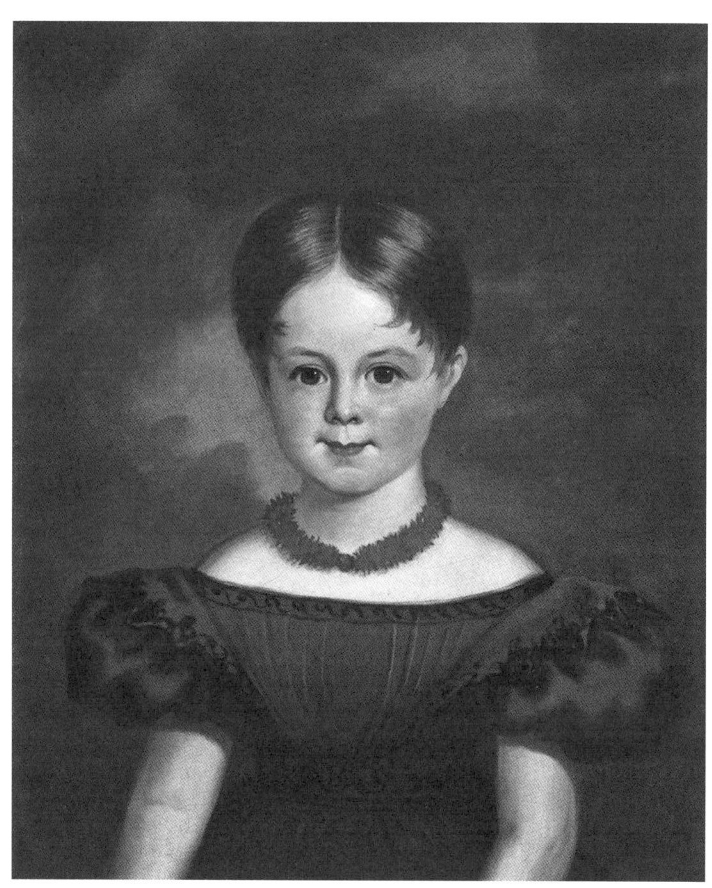

0.1 *Portrait of Sophia MacNab*, n.d.

Introduction

After over two decades of house museum visits, what stands out most prominently in my mind is the time my father took me, at eleven years old, to the Dundurn Castle Christmas Candlelight tour. It marked the start of an annual family tradition. Since 1967, Dundurn Castle has functioned as a living history house museum showcasing the life and times of the last pre-Confederation prime minister (1854–56) and Family Compact leader, Sir Allan Napier MacNab (1798–1862). It was the early 1990s and I recall standing in the drawing room transfixed by the childhood portrait of Sophia, MacNab's daughter. While the Victorian-era garbed interpreter pointed out the gifts lying underneath the decorated table-top tree in the centre of the room, I stared off to the side at the painted girl (Fig. 0.1), not much younger than myself. I wondered what it would feel like to wear that coral necklace hanging around her neck; to be (as the interpreter described) encased in a corset underneath that beautiful midnight blue off-the-shoulder dress at such a young age; to emerge from that sitting and race throughout the forty-plus rooms of this enormous Italianate-style villa. What would it be like, I pondered, to have servants answer your every beck and call, to grow up in a residence as lavish as this one?

Together, my father and I toured the home, soaking up the sights, sounds, and smells of the Victorian Christmas. We both felt we had been transported back in time, despite the invasion of obvious time-lapses. For instance, in the dining room, I turned to look out the French doors, gazing at the lights of the highway running alongside Burlington Bay. My father broke with period convention in the kitchen, helping himself to second and third servings of seasonal treats in the kitchen (claiming to me that he skipped dinner to make the tour on time). People smiled at each other, watching others' faces, others' children, others' reactions, oftentimes lamenting, "Why can't Christmas be like this today?" There were, however, some notable absences. For example, being a first generation Canadian – my mother having immigrated to Canada from Holland as an infant with her parents and two older siblings – I noted the lack of any discussion of Sinterklass (the Dutch Saint Nicholas, whom my uncles dressed up as every year to give out gifts to my sixty-plus cousins in the church basement). If anything, Dundurn reflected how, in the Victorian time period, immigrants from Britain brought with them various traditions, such as decorating evergreen conifers, over to Canada. And so I wondered, how, where, and why do I fit into this legacy? Over time and subsequent visits, I began wondering how or even if this representation might resonate with more recent immigrants. After all, locating oneself within MacNab's own home – restored though it may be – and touring it encourages one to experience the past so that physical, mental, emotional, and spiritual encounter(s) with a decisively domesticated type of public history stirs up personal memories.[2] House museums have (been) adapted to address present-day values, priorities, and concerns.

They are both sources and suppliers of history.[3] These institutions, over the course of their existence, have functioned as private residences, commemorative monuments, and in some cases, fully-restored state-sanctioned living history museums offering theme-based programs. Strategic choices made in different times and places give rise to their institutionalization. As sources of history, houses routinely undergo museumification based on their architectural merits and the socio-political primacy of the historical figures represented by them. As suppliers of history, house museums re-present the so-called "private" lives of historical figures, their families and servants. While the owner's political accomplishments routinely recommend a home's museumification, the original structural purpose determines its interpretive aim – to portray domestic culture.[4] Costumed interpreters guide visitors through restored period rooms identifying particular objects and delivering stories spun around those objects, anecdotes that iterate the household routines and customs prevalent during the time period represented.[5] Given living history practitioners' keen awareness that "the past in *all* its detail can never be recovered," and that they can never know "all the facts," they routinely use objects and facts available to them to construct a semblance of "narrative coherence."[6] Drawing on art historical discourse, I treat house museums as objects that act as vehicles designed to foster a collective sense of cultural history.[7]

Family Ties explores how house museums anchor and transmit mythic histories, providing a physical, material, and visual connection with the past.[8] It connects the artifact to the performance of history at three house museums – Dundurn Castle in Hamilton, Ontario; the Sir George-Étienne Cartier National Historic Site of Canada in Montreal, Quebec; and the William Lyon Mackenzie House in Toronto, Ontario – which, like so many heritage sites in Canada, taken together deploy "founding nations" mythologies. Both the homes and artifacts located within them, I suggest, function as representational signs – objects that, by virtue of their provenance, conservation, and subsequent institutionalization, authorize each museum's interpretation. In my view, the credibility of performative house museums relies on the deployment of what I call "artifactual accuracy," which is to say the calculated deployment of historical objects designed to sanction the site's period representation. To see how each house's museological practice connects to its performance of history, I examine the annual "Victorian Christmas" program. These programs are examples of "living history" in action; period rooms are decorated to represent a historical seasonal celebration, interpreters discuss activities associated with the occasion, such as kissing under the mistletoe, and visitors eat festive treats. My study explores the implications of institutionalized interpretations of the past that privilege bi-national mythologies, despite the fact that each site I have chosen is located in the midst of a large urban centre's ethnically diverse (multicultural) population, and in the case of the Cartier Houses in Montreal, within a constituency informed by contemporary *souverainiste* issues. I examine how the character and re-animation of these sites encourage visitors to "live history" as personal – rather than political – experience. At its heart, this book interrogates how house museums in Canada function as hegemonic cultural tools.

Taking into account how they came to be, I explore how Canadian house museums perform for domestic tourists in the twenty-first century. Sustaining visitor attendance has become *the* primary concern for both cultural administrators and politicians. Take the case of Toronto's historic museums. In September 2011, City Manager Joe Pennachetti issued a report recommending various public service "adjustments" to manage the city's 2012 $774 million budget shortfall, such as the closure of city-operated museums (one being Mackenzie House) with the "least attendance, and revenues compared to costs."[9] In effect, he characterized heritage sites as passengers on the "gravy train" (to use Toronto mayor Rob Ford's conceptualization touted in his 2010 campaign), suggesting that their value is not as much ideologically determined as it is market-driven.[10] But when one analyzes how these museums came to be, it becomes apparent that these two aspects are inextricably linked. Moreover, the Victorian Christmas programs generate the highest attendance rates in a five- to seven-week time period, thereby establishing the selected house museums as active tourist destinations during the harsh Canadian winters. These sites lure their local constituencies – their target demographic – out of their homes on a cold winter's night.[11]

Popularized constructions of Christmas conventionally portray the home as the hub of family life during the festive season, thereby advancing the primacy of the familial unit.[12] James Tracy explains further, writing:

> Christmas summons images of family gathered around a decorated tree, of music and light and the comforting smell of a special dinner cooking on a snowy winter day ... These images are appealing and powerful ... [People] feel obliged to go through the motions of preparations for what they have been socialized to believe are Yuletide necessities, spending large portions of their income on obligatory gifts and long hours of increasingly limited leisure time fighting for parking spaces ... The ... Dickensian Christmas that is sought never actually existed.[13]

In other words, people perform ritualistic activities that seemingly recall but, in effect, *imagine* an earlier time.[14] And heritage practitioners take advantage of the appeal of this historicized, romanticized, and ethnicized ideological construction, making a concerted effort to "authenticate" the decisively familial (and thus familiar) period representation.[15]

Former Dundurn curator Bill Nesbitt suggests that contemporary festivities encourage public interest in the historical celebration. People, he states, "seem to be naturally interested in tradition at this time of year, and appreciate such long standing ones. Because our secular society still largely accepts the idea of celebrating the Christmas season, the topic is of interest to a much wider audience than many of the interpretive themes of the site."[16] But, as Mackenzie House Programs Officer Rita Russell points out, historic site workers are oftentimes "torn between historical accuracy and the marketing and interest of the museums."[17] In this study's three cases, there is a marked lack of historical evidence that demonstrates how – or even if – the respective homes' original owners celebrated the Christmas season; as a result, the Victorian Christmas programs convey highly speculative accounts of what might have transpired in these spaces. According to Russell, the museum represents the way "a good number of people would have celebrated Christmas in Toronto during the mid-Victorian era," showcasing examples of traditions, activities, and events that, as she puts it, "can help link us all together." My analysis therefore considers examples used across all three sites and as such is based on extensive field research,[18] which included my having observed and carried out audio-recordings of tours as well as conducted interviews with both interpreters and site administrators. All recordings were transcribed. The duration of the research period took place over, on average, six to seven weeks at each site – Dundurn Castle (2004), Mackenzie House (2006), and the Cartier Houses (2008). The thematic focus and limited duration of the Victorian Christmas tour underscores the museums' intentions to appeal to a "wider audience." It differs significantly from those offered year-round at each site, which conventionally discuss the owner's political accomplishments, household management, and nineteenth-century Canadian material culture.

My analysis of each historic site's programming takes into account three common facets of a house museum's layout and operation: first are commemorative plaques to greet the visitor upon their arrival on the house grounds; second are object-based exhibitions composed of both text panels, images, and historical artifacts that address various themes or events pertaining to the home owner's life and the house's institutional history; and finally, there are period rooms through which costumed interpreters tour visitors. I examine how the plaques' texts characterize the original homeowners and, by extension, set the stage for the visitor, identifying historical figures, facts, events, and features they will come to learn about more in-depth while on tour inside the respective home. I also consider the object-based exhibitions within which text panels articulate the themes, events, and people that play essential roles in the house's commemoration and operation. It is only the Cartier Houses, however, that contain fixed object-based exhibitions – Dundurn and Mackenzie House use their exhibition spaces to mount temporary exhibitions that change based on a wide array of factors (such as impending anniversaries of significant events pertaining to the home or homeowner, the discovery of research that sheds new light on old perspectives, or trends in popular and mass culture, such as the prolific fascination with PBS's Masterpiece Theatre Series "Downton Abbey" and subsequent interest generated in period costumes, manners, and dioramas). Both the plaques and exhibitions function to set up the tour of the house and its interior as the zenith of the visit. Accordingly, this study focuses on ways in which house museums ground and project mythologized representations of the past, thereby encouraging visitors to "live history." My analysis therefore concentrates on in-house representations. I identify the function of restored period rooms on conventional tours (based on the furnishings located within) and then interrogate – by virtue of the holiday décor and interpretive delivery – how this function is augmented or highlighted in the context of seasonal tours.

The material culture in situ or, more precisely, the "artifactual accuracy" validates the interpretation of the rooms' historical function. The "core" furniture – the largest objects that signal the primary function(s) of each room, such as the table in the dining room – remains in place *permanently* throughout the year; during the Victorian Christmas tours, interpreters lay décor out, such as the garlands strewn around the perimeter of the dining room table and place settings for both family members and esteemed guests and iterate to visitors that the layout signals preparations for a holiday feast. I interrogate the combined effect of the artifactual displays in the period rooms, their interpretation and themes in order to explore the dynamics and implications of the sites' performances. In so doing, this book probes what house museums say about and with Victorian material culture in Canada's contemporary multicultural context.

My work thus brings a new perspective to existing studies of living history museums, which focus largely on US sites and historic homes.[19] Significant in this context is the work on Colonial Williamsburg undertaken by Eric Gable and Richard Handler. US historical sites frequently commemorate the origins of the Republic.[20] Gable and Handler contend that, at Colonial Williamsburg, "teaching history to the public" represents a "social encounter,"[21] one that aims to valorize the nation's past and present, in that the site seemingly stands as a testament to the survival of freedom, patriotism, and self-government, ideological principles upon which US national identity bases itself. Simply put, despite their location in a "heterogeneous" state, historical sites such as Colonial Williamsburg – those that identify and champion the nation's past – advance a distinctively "American" patriotism. In the absence of the sort of heroic conflicts that distinguished both the French and American Revolutions, as well as the American Civil War, historian Arthur G. Neal explains, Canadian identity is "less sharply defined."[22]

Canada, as a political state, has made a strategic effort instead to cultivate a distinctive nationalism based on a multiculturalism policy, located within a bilingual framework. Canada's multiculturalism policy, instated in 1971 and formalized in the Canadian Multiculturalism Act (1988), is understood on a popular level as "unity-in-diversity." Its national culture is positioned as being open-ended and provisional or, in Jon Stratton and Ien Ang's words, as "permanently unfinished business."[23] This claim ostensibly frustrates the need for a unifying Canadian identity. As Richard Day explains, the rhetoric of multiculturalism posits the "possession of a national Thing" as desirable. "This Thing," he writes, "is universal, it is every Thing. But, as *every*thing it is also *no*thing at all."[24] In characterizing cultural pluralism as that which defines Canada's national identity, the Multiculturalism Act, in effect, provides the foundation for a flexible Canadianism.[25] Accordingly, my study examines the regeneration of Canadian historic sites, investigating how they manage national narratives.

Chapter 1 of this book sets forth the primary organizing idea of this study, namely, the concept of the house museum as an *artifact* used as a civic instrument in the practice *and* performance of history. Using Pierre Nora's concept of the "site of memory" as a theoretical marker,[26] I make the case that the house museum's credibility and attractiveness relies – as does disciplinary art history – on its calculated deployment of objects to naturalize its interpretation of the past, representing it so that the present appears as the natural outcome.[27] The "burden of authenticity" typically falls on the historical residence, and so interpreters typically showcase that which "*authenticates* over that which is authentic, a culturally congenial deceit."[28] Moreover, their performances indicate a desire to concretize and project an "authentic spirit" of the nation. The institutionalization is an expression of nationalism. Nationalism, according to Anthony D. Smith, functions as a type of political religion that projects shared historical experiences through the veneration of formative myths and symbols, and it requires a place, space, or site for the nation to inhabit.[29] House museums encourage visitors to experience a "contextual departure" from the present and, subsequent to that, develop a communal identification with and appreciation of Canada's past. They act as the foundation(s) for national identity, setting up the nation as an "ancestral homeland."[30] "[T]he conviction of common kinship ties," Smith explains, "need not, and usually does not, accord with real biological descent and what we know of factual history. But then, what is important in the study of nationalism is not what is, but what is *felt* to be the case."[31] *Family Ties* therefore demonstrates how house museums in Canada address the politics of place, adapting narrative(s) to fulfill their mandates and ensure sustained operation.[32]

Bearing foremost in mind the politics of place, I explore how the concerns of the respective local constituencies informed the restorations and, consequently, how the sites currently address the priorities of their respective communities in their programming to shore up visitation rates. Dundurn Castle exists today as an outcome of the Hamilton community's efforts. The Cartier Houses in Montreal, on the other hand, reflect the priorities of the federal government as they are owned and operated by Parks Canada. Finally, Toronto's Mackenzie House has been managed so that it portrays the region's cultural diversity, validating the municipal government's efforts to brand the region as a multicultural "global city." Divided into three sections, this study considers how perspectives that prioritize local, national, and global interests (respectively) affect how house museums portray the past.

The first section of this book documents communal commitments to the past, focusing on Dundurn Castle. Chapter 2 explores how Dundurn's reincarnation stands as the consummation of related developments during its stint as a community museum. From 1901 to the 1960s, a host of local "women volunteerists" worked to establish the home as a historic house museum.[33] Their efforts ultimately recommended the possibility of the site's restoration as Hamilton's Centennial project and so I explore hegemonic processes bound up in state-sponsored commemorative endeavours. Those involved in the restoration strove to reconceptualize both the home and the historical persona of Sir Allan MacNab as illustrious parts of Canada's national narrative.

In contrast, Chapter 3 explores Dundurn's Victorian Christmas tour and the types of subject positions the site's performance projects in the contemporary multicultural context. Considering both the tour's longevity and popularity, my analysis of the artifactual arrangements, activities, and thematic oral content suggests that the museum, upon reanimation, portrays the celebration of an upper-class family as one that is distinctively British. In this discussion, I draw on the work of scholars such as Erna Macleod, Eva Mackey, and Himani Bannerji, who contend that, despite Canada's federal multiculturalism policy that recognizes the existence of cultural diversity, historic sites often reproduce a core Canadianism.[34] I thus use the example of Dundurn Castle to explore how house museums act as hegemonic cultural tools, re-affirming values associated with Canada's dominant culture.

In the second section, I explore how museum workers manage the Sir George-Étienne Cartier National Historic Site of Canada to render it attractive to Montrealers, a constituency sensitive to contemporary souverainiste issues. Chapter 4 considers how the federal agency Parks Canada turned the two adjoining homes formerly owned by one of the "Fathers of Confederation" into a museum. I suggest that the houses' monumentalization, undertaken by Parks Canada in the wake of Quebec's Quiet Revolution, indicates the degree to which the federal government responded to the efforts and achievements made by Quebecers in cultivating a distinctively Québécois nationalism.

While the site commemorates a particular French-Canadian identity, upon reanimation, it reinvigorates a distinctly "Canadian" nationalism. In Chapter 5, I consider how interpreters handle the site's Christmas performance so that it deals with themes that are markedly devoid of explicit political references. Significantly, this museum is the only one of the three that uses object-based exhibitions to acknowledge the original owner's political achievements, while the "living history" portion reflects the lifestyle of Montreal's upper-middle classes, acting as an "immersive environment," one that visitors, according to Parks Canada, find more "memorable."[35] Chapter 5 considers how the site has been reanimated to project a particular version of

the past, one that presents a so-called "Canadian" lifestyle, a way of life pur-
portedly characterized by both English- and French-Canadian traditions,
customs, and ideologies.

The final section uses the example of Mackenzie House, the retirement home of Toronto's first mayor, to explore the historical and socio-
political roots of globalizing processes as they occur in Canadian heritage
sites.[36] Chapter 6 examines how nationalist agendas not only motivated
the museumification of Mackenzie House but also provided the basis of
"branding" strategies for the City of Toronto in the current global age.[37] In
fact, Canada's adoption of a multiculturalism policy – intended to cultivate nationalism based on the concept of "unity-in-diversity" – encouraged
Toronto's heritage administrators to reconsider the purpose of city-oper-
ated heritage sites.[38] The staff developed the museum so that it might
reflect Mackenzie's family life and then underscore Toronto's status as a
"multi-cultural" city. Taking into account city officials' 2003 mandate that
both the site and the region be branded as "culturally diverse" (to bolster
Toronto's reputation as a "global city"[39]), I examine how site workers use
multicultural discourse to reflect a particular image of the region.

By way of extension, Chapter 7 considers how heritage practitioners
strive to imbue Mackenzie House with a sense of cultural diversity. I examine the Victorian Christmas program, taking into account how site administrators redeploy the museum's narratives to not only commemorate the
region's past but also advance present-day values by displaying "culturally
diverse" exhibitions in the gallery space appended to the historic residence,
while using the "house proper" to make the past "come alive" for visitors.[40]
I evaluate the inferences of these "soft" temporary displays – dedicated to
the representation of ethnic diversity – compared to those of the "hard"
object-based displays permanently installed in the period rooms. More
broadly, this chapter considers the deployment of, to paraphrase George
Yúdice, heritage-as-resource in the global marketplace.[41]

I find house museums to be intriguing cultural institutions, particularly
when one takes into account not only what they do but also how they came
to be. While one might visit a house museum and assess the merits of (or
problems inherent in) live interpretation, such an approach fails to take into
account the larger picture – the fact that these sites have been "recycled"
over the course of the past century and a half.[42] As Patricia West argues
in her seminal analysis of the American house museum movement, "the
history of American historic homes demonstrates that their missions, far

from being neutral and far from meriting the status of inviolability, were manufactured out of human needs bound by time and space."[43] My analysis evaluates not so much "human needs" but rather the ways in which the formation of Dundurn Castle, the Cartier Houses, and Mackenzie House, as well as their current operations, capitalizes on the flexibility of both state-managed historical narratives and associated ideologies. Accordingly, this study approaches house museums as agents of Canadian cultural politics.

CHAPTER ONE

Artifactual Experiences: The Interplay of History, Objects, and Memory

Home is where the heart is.
Pliny the Elder (24 August 79 AD)[1]

The house museums discussed in this study are alike in that they all act as material evidence of the nation's eminence, designed to generate loyalty to that which is represented. With the restoration of each of the three sites – Dundurn Castle, Mackenzie House, and the Cartier House – the federal government designated Dundurn and the Cartier House national historic sites while, in the case of Mackenzie House, designated the museum's namesake a "National Historic Person" following the restoration of the house. Their state-sanctioned veneration, bestowed by the Historic Sites and Monuments Board of Canada (established 1919 – hereafter HSMBC), demonstrates that the federal government recognized each structure – along with a plethora of others – as reflective of the nation's past. The processes and politics inherent in HSMBC's recognitions, negotiations, and designations have been examined by scholars such as Charles Taylor, Yves Pelletier, and Thomas Symons, to name a few. Taylor, for example, interrogates Canada's official tradition of marking persons, events, and places of national significance, ultimately concluding that the Board's achievements depended upon members' personalities rather than its bureaucratic structure and its accountability to Parks Canada, the office to which the Board reports.[2] Such assessments reveal motivations and claims to objectivity and authoritative experience underlying the designations bestowed by granting bodies or organizations.[3] Similarly, this study takes into account the ideological associations bound up in the sites' designation and pushes it further. I explore how the state's designations informed the operations of the respective heritage sites, as well as their performance in the twenty-first century or, more broadly, how the state heritage policies affect localized heritage practices.

Individually, Dundurn Castle, Mackenzie House, and the Cartier House rely upon their architectural style, restored period rooms, and interpretive programs to deliver speculative representations and nullify competing interpretations of the nation's past.[4] Reconstituted as institutionalized residences, interpreters lead visitors throughout the various chambers, identifying artifacts and delivering stories spun around them to buttress the museum's account of the time period portrayed. The dwellings' respective performances encourage visitors to experience the past so that their private memories of the visit might foster physical, mental, and emotional connections with a larger (ancestral) community. This type of reanimation turns "public history into private memories."[5]

Accordingly, these homes, I suggest, function as "repositories of national narratives."[6] *Family Ties* approaches these institutions as evidentiary artifacts that have been reanimated expressly to draw in large numbers of people so that they might experience "what it felt like to live back then" or, simply put, as artifactual tourist destinations.[7] This chapter investigates the roles of both the house and the artifacts located within it, comparing them to the use of objects in disciplinary art history and museum studies. In my view, the credibility of house museums relies on the belief that the architecture and period rooms operate as "evidence" of the time, culture, nation, and people that produced them. I then examine how and why such vestiges of the past are redeployed as national symbols in the context of the harsh Canadian winter months. As I see it, because the performance underscores each museum's domestic character, local citizenry is offered the opportunity to experience and understand a past framed by the primordialism of both a decisively ethnicized family unit and belonging itself. By tying the past to the present (with decorative paper and bows), interpreters of these reanimated homes reveal the malleability of national narratives.

Houses of historical repute that have been reincarnated as "living history" sites depend upon the artifactual nature of both the architecture and the restored interior spaces to make history "come alive." Only in the last four decades have such sites been subjected to extensive critical analysis, although such analyses have primarily concentrated on those in Western Europe and the United States of America, such as Colonial Williamsburg.[8] Initially, some scholars regarded performative heritage sites as opportune venues within which to learn from and about historical material culture, upholding the pedagogical aspects of the place. For instance, in 1982, American folklorist Jay Anderson first defined the living history movement for academic audiences. Describing it as an idea familiar to "lay historians" and interpreters, he characterizes the movement as "an attempt by people to simulate life in another time." Put on either to test archeological hypotheses, the validity of interpretive tools, or for recreation, Anderson ultimately defines living history as "essentially ... the intrusion of the *past into our present* ... a fascinating and threatening experience."[9] Expanding on his definition, Anderson went on to publish the book *Time Machines: The World of Living History*, in which he traces the formative development of the living history movement, describing only those sites that adhere to his conceptualization.

The living history format originated in Stockholm, Sweden, with the 1891 opening of Skansen, the first open-air museum – a 75-acre outdoor museum staffed with costumed guides, farm animals, musicians, and folk dancers all designed to, as Anderson puts it, "exhibit the folk life in living style."[10] Following Skansen, other institutions were established in Europe, and in the 1920s and 30s, the format became more common in North America. Prominent industrialists began sponsoring what went on to become the largest and most popular living history museums, such as Colonial Williamsburg, whose 79 million dollar restoration was funded by corporate capitalist John D. Rockefeller Jr.[11] Significantly, the restoration and reanimation of Colonial Williamsburg indicates the degree to which objects are redeployed to represent the native conceptualization of "the facts," which corresponds to a mimetic and literalistic understanding of history.[12] Material culture functions to represent those who might have owned and used the objects; this definition of cultural ownership reproduces the logic of possessive individualism and the private property characteristic of capitalist society.[13] To that end, up until the late 1980s and 90s, black history at Colonial Williamsburg was often seen as "conjectural" and impoverished compared to other histories displayed at the site, what with the perceived lack of "slave culture material."[14] Furthermore, this conceptualization has dominated the epistemology of other museums since their inception, sites such as Greenfield Village and Mount Vernon, the house museum dedicated to the life and times of George Washington.

By the early to mid-1990s, studies had begun to approach these same institutions as theoretical networks of symbolic signifiers, as well as physical sites or objects.[15] Such analyses typically reference Pierre Nora's analytical paradigm outlined in his seminal 1989 article "Between Memory and History" to underpin their arguments. Nora's "Between Memory" draws on his multi-volume series *Les Lieux de Mémoire* that traces the deployment of memorials intended to codify France's national memory, such as the museumification of the Château de Versailles, the restored palatial residence of Sun King Louis XIV (1638–1715). Notably, the article provided an English theoretical introduction to the French compendium within which Nora explains that he uses the term *lieux de mémoire* – a term that, prior to his publication, did not formally exist in the French language – to mean "sites of memory."

Sites of memory are so called based on their materiality, symbolism, and functionality, aspects that "always" coexist. These memorials represent, for Nora, the "play of memory and history."[16] He goes on to explain that, "if we accept that the most fundamental purpose of the *lieu de mémoire* is to stop time, to block the work of forgetting, to establish a state of things, to immortalize death, to materialize the immaterial – just as if gold were the only memory of money – all of this in order to capture a maximum of meaning in the fewest of signs, it is also clear that lieux de mémoire only exist because of their capacity for metamorphosis, an endless recycling of their meaning and an unpredictable proliferation of their ramifications."[17] While the concrete nature of house museums denotes permanence, my study's selected residences came into being in and around the Confederation time period and have been recycled time and time again over the ensuing decades. Confederation conventionally describes the "political reorganization of 1864–67" that ultimately resulted in the formation of Canada as a federal state.[18] Key events that aided in the reorganization of the disparate colonies include the Charlottetown Conference (1–9 September 1864) and the Quebec Conference (10 October 1864), which resulted in the adoption of what is conventionally known as the Seventy-two Resolutions or the Quebec Resolutions. In the winter of 1866–67, colonial delegates from the United Canadas, New Brunswick, and Nova Scotia met with the British House of

Commons and refined the resolutions, which constituted what is known as the British North American Act. On 1 July 1867, the Dominion of Canada came into being as Confederation "went into effect."[19]

Since 1867, a great many factors, both actual and ideological, have transformed Canada's socio-political landscape. In the twentieth-century, for example, certain actions reveal decisive moves toward the founding of an individualized Canadian nation, one notably distinct from that of the mid-nineteenth century. Such actions include, to name a few: the Canadian Citizenship Bill (1946); the adoption of a Canadian national flag (1965); the creation of the Royal Commission on Bilingualism and Biculturalism (1967); the creation of the Canadian national anthem (1975), which was instigated by the independence movement in Quebec; and the 1971 federal multiculturalism policy located within a bilingual framework, later formalized in the Canadian Multiculturalism Act (1988), which fosters the idea that diversity is a national virtue.[20] Accordingly, reflections on the past – be they textbooks, treatises, or edifices – are habitually reinvented to reflect new presents.[21] Such objects are thus hardly objective.

Because heritage sites and living history museums use objects to ground interpretive representations of the past, I explore how house museum performances first and foremost depend upon the architectural permanence of the structure, but also on the flexibility of historical narratives. The setting typically includes a historically designated structure that houses period artifacts; both the building and artifactual arrangements located within it function as material evidence. According to cultural historian Stephen Mills, the building functions not only as a "very large [artifact]" but also as "signified and signifier, an unmediated image that is no image at all, being the clearly authenticated structure, as real as the day it was built in the old country."[22] The architectural context "authenticates" the artifactual representations located within it.[23] Situated within house museums, restored period rooms showcase artifactual arrangements, representing a "system of signs."[24] These systems are thus re-positioned within a "landscape that is greater than the sum of its parts," which serves to suppress the fact that objects have been strategically placed to convey specific values, concepts or convictions.[25] Such designs located within a particular architectonic context re-present material culture – both the home and the artifactual arrays in the case of this study – as evidence so that they might construct and naturalize the "truth of what is intended."[26] The role of objects, be they architectural or artifactual, in performing house museums relates directly to the use of objects in disciplinary art history and museum exhibitions. Both the architecture and artifacts function as representational signs – objects that, by virtue of their existence, documented provenance, and subsequent museumification authorize the site's interpretation. Over the past four decades, art historians have argued that the "object" does not have inherent meaning, making the case that its meaning is constructed in the interplay between the object, exhibition, and visitor.[27] The concept of the object as a representational sign, art historian Donald Preziosi explains, stems from the historical development of disciplinary art history. Since its establishment in the mid-nineteenth century, art historical discourse has upheld the object as being inherently meaningful. The most prevalent theory in art history has been the conception of the object as a medium of communication or expression, "a vehicle by means of which the intentions, values, attitudes, messages, or emotional state(s) of the maker ... are conveyed (by design or chance) to targeted or circumstantial beholders."[28] In Preziosi's view, disciplinary art history privileges both the existence and communicative values of the object. What these objects communicate is determined by those who select, designate, and interpret their significance.[29] What is more, the selection, location, and merit of objects included in museum exhibitions is buttressed by a "willed fiction" – a belief that they collectively stand together as "signs or surrogates" of their producers or consumers.[30] According to curator and literary scholar Caterina Albano, art historical objects assume a specific role in exhibitions; they assume evidentiary value that can, in turn, be adopted by or applied to historical artifacts. Albano explains further: "Extending the notions of authenticity identified for artworks – nominal authenticity as the correct identification of the origins, authorship and provenance of an object, and expressive authenticity as the 'value possessed by works of art' or an object – we can argue that the evidential force of an artefact constitutes part of its expressive authenticity, that renders it culturally, historically and ... biographically 'true.'"[31] In house museums, the "burden of authenticity" falls upon the historic building – acting as an artifact – which, in turn, validates the period portrayal. The architectural structure constitutes the setting so that the heritage site acts as an embodiment of authenticity; when a house is turned into a museum and period objects are placed within it, an "aura of authenticity pervades" the site.[32]

Living museums turn assemblages into events. In other words, as Hillel Schwartz puts it, "living Museums tend to choose that which *authenticates* over that which is authentic, a culturally congenial deceit."[33] Interpreters guide visitors through the historic site delivering an authoritative oral interpretation, one validated by the appearance and location of individual artifacts that are documented as being from the same time period as that depicted. Such compilations function as evocations of what Edward Bruner calls a "historically accurate" environment, one based on research and scholarship that is relayed orally to visitors so that they will in turn find it artifactually credible and, by extension, appealing.[34] The materiality reinforces the representation's authority, thereby allowing the house to, as museologist Tamar Katriel points out, "sustain the fiction that the past is told 'as it really was.'"[35] This approach grounds the museum's discourse, a practice that typically conceals its "rhetoric of history" and thus naturalizes ideology. Both art history *and* history are appealed to and transcended through the deployment of what I call "artifactual accuracy," thereby allowing memory to carry out its ideological work.[36]

On one level, the museumification of historic houses, particularly those designated as national historic sites, demonstrates a desire to concretize an "authentic spirit" of the nation. On another, their performance aims to promote among visitors opportunities for communal and, by extension, national bonding. In short, the institutionalization is an expression of nationalism. As Anthony D. Smith explains it, nationalism is a type of political religion that seeks to cultivate a unified national populace, "all to create nations in the 'authentic' spirit and image of earlier ethnic and religious communities, but transformed to meet modern geopolitical, economic and cultural conditions." Thus, nationalism manifests itself in the choice and (re)interpretation of not only formative myths but also in symbolic physical structures that make it possible for those myths to come alive.[37] It requires a place to inhabit so as to reconceptualize the nation's terrain as an ancestral homeland, one that provides both emotional and physical security for its citizenry.[38] Such communal identification of land is carried out in practice by attaching ancestral memories to places or objects. "Across the landscape," Smith writes, "lie the 'sites of memory'; the fields of battle, the monuments to the fallen, the places of peace treaties, the temples of priests, the last resting places of saints and heroes, the sacred groves of spirits and gods who guard the land."[39] Now while Smith's assertion here applies to military places not domestic ones, he makes the point that heritage sites acquire meaning. Drawing on Smith, I argue that a house museum's reanimation gives it a more positive and active role. Cultivated cultural resources thus act as foundational to national identity.[40] House museums utilize particular strategies

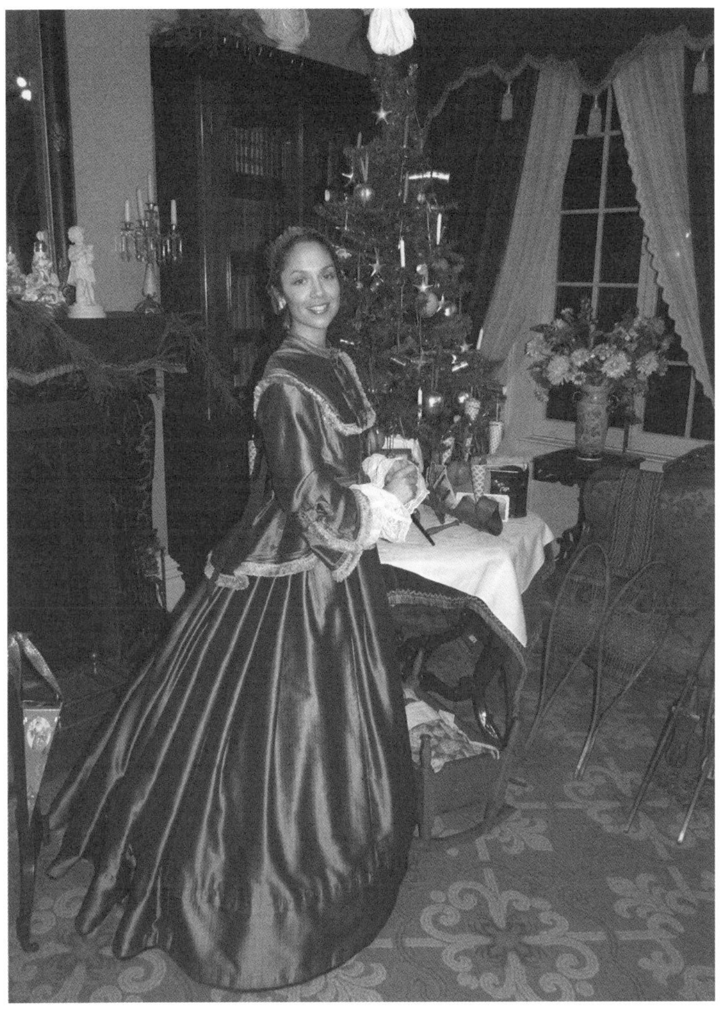

1.1 Interpreter Isabelle Chalifoux, Sir George-Étienne National
Historic Site of Canada, Montreal, Quebec, 2008.

to render the past appealing to visitors, and so their institutional histories
and programs, upon critical investigation, reveal more broadly how they
negotiate and manage relationships between the past and present, fact and
fiction, history and memory, and objects and performance.

While the artifactual nature of state-sanctioned heritage sites indicates the advancement of a national memory system that is "transcribed in
stone" (to use historian Christine Boyer's conceptualization), such "didactic

artifacts" not only commemorate but also communicate national mythologies.[41] They provide a "should have been past," thereby advancing a historical fiction that emphasizes "narrative cohesion."[42] I approach house museums as evidentiary artifacts that perform. These seemingly "dumb" objects – ones that have been designated as illustrative of the nation's achievements – do in fact "speak for themselves"; in the context of the guided tours, the "real site" acts as both setting and stage for a fictionalized performance of the past in the present.[43]

Such events provide lived experiences that become, as Alan Gordon puts it, "an essential part of the public socialization of individuals as members of their society. When this happens, public history becomes internalized by individuals and shared as public memory."[44]

Thus, these re-enactments, to my mind, portray the past in a rational, orderly manner that makes the present state of the nation appear natural (or inevitable). They champion "narrative coherence" – they naturalize their "story of the nation."[45] While they offer micro-narratives of family routines, lifestyles, mysteries, scandals, and intrigue over the course of guided tours, the narrative thrust champions the present state of the nation, as well as potential opportunities for the future. In other words, they urge visitors to take part in a shared historical metanarrative, an event that ultimately culminates in the contemporary lived experience. They promote one's appreciation for the "imagined community" (as Benedict Anderson terms it), encouraging individuals to perceive themselves as part of a constituency with shared goals, ideals, and "family values."[46]

The implications of this shared narrative, one evoked within a museumified familial home, is underscored by recent findings in the project "Canadians and their Pasts," an alliance of seven supervisory researchers together known as The Pasts Collective, as well as nineteen collaborators, six universities, and fifteen community partners. Mandated to explore the "role that history plays in the lives of Canadian citizens," the project collaborators conducted a bilingual telephone survey, interviewing 3,419 Canadians on their "general interest in and understanding of the past; activities related to the past; and trustworthiness of sources of information about the past." Touted as the "most wide-ranging survey of its kind ever undertaken in Canada," the findings regarding the particulars of one's historical consciousness demonstrate the degree to which the primordialism of the family unit informs one's awareness and appreciation of the past. No matter what memories a person embodies, The Pasts Collective write in the resultant book *Canadians and Their Pasts*, "family memory is usually central in answering the age-old question, 'Who am I?' and orients us to many of the other histories, identities, and memories that we draw upon. Indeed, it is usually in families that we first develop a sense of linear time as we learn about generations of relatives that gave rise to our being."[47] By 2009, the survey results had recorded that two-thirds of Canadians characterized the past of their family as "very" important, a figure markedly higher than that allotted to "any other past."[48] The survey findings thus reveal the degree to which citizens privilege their family as the lens through which they learn about and engage with the past.[49] Moreover, The Pasts Collective suggests, family history becomes even more significant when it intersects with group identities: "family history often serves as a foundation for a broader historical consciousness and is a fundamental building block of people's citizenship in their communities, in their country, and in the world."[50] Seemingly motivated by the dictum "a people who do not know their past will have no future," these linkages aim to unite different temporalities.[51]

In seeking to provide visitors with a "contextual departure" from the present, performative house museums act as both state-sanctioned historic institutions and tourist destinations, sites of interest which one might visit to escape from daily life. Assessing this function requires an increasingly sophisticated theoretical understanding of tourism. In house museums, the sights, sounds, smells, and often tastes of the immersive environment envelop the visitor, generating a "holistic experience." Foundational tourism studies, such as Dean MacCannell's *The Tourist* (1973, 1976) and John Urry's *The Tourist Gaze* (1990), as well as art historical and critical museum studies, however, often prioritize the visual aspect(s). In fact, in his conceptualization of the "tourist gaze," Urry argues that tourism is primarily a visual endeavour; during their excursions, tourists – motivated by socially organized and systematized forms of consumption – search sites for familiar sights to consume. Because touristic practices involve the concept of departure, a breaking with the schedule and habits of daily life, stimuli or features of the landscape that contrast with one's everyday existence direct and maintain the gaze. I expand on this argument, pointing out that visitors' experience of "living history" in house museums is contingent upon an enveloping sensorial experience that also encourages a mental one.

Engaging in tourist activities allows one to physically locate oneself in a particular destination so that the physical experience promotes a specific mental experience, thereby allowing one to reconnect with what sociologist

Ning Wang refers to as one's existential, "authentic" self. As Wang explains, people travel to tourist destinations, perform different activities in these places, experience different physical sensations and, subsequent to that, liberate themselves both physically and mentally from the perceived constraints of the urban, industrial work-a-day world. In other words, people engage in touristic pursuits in the hopes that their experiences of and in these places might allow them to temporarily transcend the stresses and monotony of modern (now post-modern) life so as to reconnect with their "authentic selves" – a person unfettered by the perceived rationality and reason that otherwise dominates contemporary existence.[52] Wang explains that "existential authenticity in its common place acceptance means that 'one is true to one's self.'"[53] In tourist settings, such as the beach for example, Wang posits that people's physical location causes them to enter what he calls an "alternative, yet intensified, experiential state"; people's experiences of bodily and, by extension, spiritual pleasure, offers relief from the boredom and stresses of modern life. People's encounters with cultural heritage thus allow them escape to not only a different place but also a different time (whether an imagined past or "off the clock"). More specifically, upon entering a house museum, people achieve a "contextual departure" from their present-day existence.[54] Therefore, one might suggest that in the context of living history sites, experiencing a different place and time constitutes a leisure activity, given the reprieve from the pressures, tensions, and strains of the contemporary age it offers.

Accordingly, house museums' reliance on the architectural permanence and the flexibility of historical narratives to evoke a particular experience for visitors makes evident how these institutions act as domestic tourist destinations. Heritage sites that venerate the Victorian time period, events, and society in Canada take on a specific role in the contemporary multicultural context in that they mythologize and naturalize the past; they represent the past such that the (multicultural) present appears as the natural outcome of it. Conceived as, to borrow Canadian historian Ian McKay's term, "nationalist myth-symbol complex[es]," these institutions demonstrate the heritage industry's inclination to provide "continuous national histories." In a country that grapples with issues related to cultural pluralism, tolerance, and equality, the existence of heritage sites that project "founding nations" mythologies makes evident the tenuous relationship between the past and present. In this ideological construction, Confederation represents a crucial moment in Canada's development as a federal state, one that stands for the unification of anglophones and francophones as the nation's "two founding peoples," which, in turn, characterizes Canada's formation as a binational achievement. They seek to act as cornerstones in the promotion of a coherent, bounded national identity, one that people can readily identify, accept, and support.

My study therefore performs what McKay refers to as a "new strategy of reconnaissance." I go beyond the parameters of conventional museological analyses and critically analyze the factors that motivated the designation and restoration of historic homes within a decisively nationalized framework that informs their ongoing operation in the current "post-national climate."[55] As McKay explains, the outcome of the 1995 Quebec Referendum, in which the motion for Quebec to secede from the rest of Canada was defeated by a slim margin, represented for Canada a "process of dissolution" signaling that the citizens of Canada already resided in a "post-Canadian terrain." In his view, the national narratives, related cultural institutions, and legends that once offered Canadians reassurance that they belonged to a unified nation had been called into question and found lacking. As he puts it, the result of the Referendum indicates quite clearly that such nationalist constructions "have had their day."[56] With this in mind, I explore how homes institutionalized in the context of nation-building perform in the contemporary climate.

My study thus offers a critical investigation of house museums that romanticize the past. In so doing, house museums perform to evoke a sense of nostalgia in visitors – a yearning for a time and place that never actually existed. As Susan Stewart explains, nostalgia "is always ideological; the past it seeks has never existed except as narrative, and hence, always absent, that past continually threatens to reproduce itself as a felt lack."[57] As a result, heritage practitioners typically select *and* omit that which they deem is important to and in Canadian history. "By romanticizing colonial history and cultivating nostalgia for lost community and family values," Erna Macleod writes, "heritage sites entrench Eurocentric attitudes and resist the change necessary to alleviate the marginalization of colonized cultures ... Museums are not neutral; their interpretations function in a hegemonic way to define the boundaries of national unity."[58] The credibility of their character and reanimation is contingent upon the utility of "artifactual accuracy" and performative stagings in order to not only attract visitors but also "authenticate" the authority of their interpretive representations. In examining the Victorian Christmas program offered at each house, I interrogate how site administrators and interpreters endeavour to make the past relevant and appealing to twenty-first century visitors in Canada, a country whose history reveals efforts to cultivate, as Richard Day writes, a "self-consciously multinational state, in which all nations can seek their enjoyment in possession of a national Thing."[59] In so doing, I consider what happens when the nation's past is rendered as being distinctly different from its present, when current political and social realities relate little or indirectly to that which is supposed to have given rise to them.

Family Ties is divided into three parts that consider how perspectives that prioritize local, national, and global interests (respectively) affect the representations offered in house museums. Each section offers first a critical account of a site's institutional history, then a detailed examination of its programming. Part one documents communal commitments to the past, focusing on Dundurn Castle, and explores how its reincarnation stands as the consummation of related developments during its stint as a community museum. In Part two, I use the example of the Sir George-Étienne Cartier National Historic Site of Canada to explore how the site commemorates a particular French-Canadian identity while, upon reanimation, reinvigorating a distinctly "Canadian" nationalism within Quebec. Part three uses the example of Mackenzie House, the retirement home of Toronto's first mayor, to explore the historical and socio-political roots of globalizing processes as they occur in Canadian heritage sites. In so doing, this study investigates how three different historic house museums – ones linked by similar representational historical periods, subject matter, and programming – work with specific facts and objects to espouse different ideological attachments.[60]

PART ONE

Communal Commitments to the Nation: Dundurn Castle, Hamilton, ON

— ‿ —

CHAPTER TWO

— ‿ —

Imperialist Idealizations and Curatorial Strategies in the Domestic Sphere

> Royal visits are always a great honour for Canadians. Given our
> deep devotion to members of the Royal family and their devotion to
> Canada, these visits are regarded as "homecomings" by Canadians.
> *Prime Minister Stephen Harper's official welcome speech to the*
> *Prince of Wales and Duchess of Cornwall, 2 November 2009,*
> *Mile One Centre, St John's, Newfoundland.*[1]

During their first tour as a married couple, Prince Charles and Camilla Parker Bowles visited Dundurn Castle in Hamilton, ON, the home of Bowles' great-great-great-grandfather Sir Allan Napier MacNab (1798–1862). Operating as a historic house and living history museum, Dundurn showcases the lifestyle and family life of the last pre-Confederation prime minister (1854–56) and Family Compact leader. Anticipating the excursion, the prince was quoted by Hamilton journalists, stating, "We both look forward to discovering those family roots and seeing her forebear's home."[2] The visit – an orchestrated event attended by roughly 500 spectators – and the press coverage promoted the conceptualization of the house as that which connects elite British culture, the Hamilton community, and more broadly, Canada as a whole. One journalist went so far as to suggest that the royal visit had a decisive "impact on ticket sales," citing the fact that, over the 2009 Christmas season, 19,000 people visited the site, compared with 11,000 one year prior.[3] There is, however, the provenance, character, arrangement, and function of the site to also consider. This section explores how Dundurn's institutionalization and reanimation endorses the monumentalization of particular aspects of British-Canadian identity in the current multicultural state. More broadly, it also considers how the museumification of historic houses not only projects but also naturalizes particular facets of "founding nations" mythologies.

Given that such naturalizations arguably authorize a particular version of the past, Chapter 2 considers factors that motivated Dundurn's rejuvenation as a performative institutionalized dwelling. Bearing in mind the fact that, first, Dundurn's current function marks the culmination of developments made during the site's tenure as a community museum and, second, its restoration was funded as part of Canada's Centennial celebrations, this chapter investigates how nation-building frameworks inform the reconceptualization of historic houses. In the case of Dundurn, these frameworks necessitated a deliberately strategic reinterpretation of both the site and the ethnic primacy of the political figure represented by it. For example, from 1901 to the 1960s, a host of "women volunteerists" worked to establish the site as a historic house museum.[4] Notably, these women took into account that Dundurn Castle was a Picturesque villa representing "essentially a British point of view" and so refurbished various rooms to depict what might have been in place in MacNab's day.[5] This curatorial move sparked a significant increase in visitor attendance, so much so over the years that the site gained a profile significant enough to warrant the attention of municipal government officials, who in the 1960s applied for federal funding to restore Dundurn Castle in its entirety.

Because Dundurn's restoration was funded as part of Canada's Centennial celebrations – celebrations that marked what Eva Mackey refers to as a "high point in Canadian state-produced national sentiment" – the site's restoration also seemingly demanded the instatement of MacNab as a historical figure.[6] In other words, those working at the site hoped that Dundurn's reincarnation might cultivate a narrative that stressed the ways in which MacNab fostered elite British culture in the Canadian colony and how his endeavours produced tangible and physical examples of that culture. As one journalist wrote in 1962, "*True* [MacNab] was a 'Family Compact' man, and member in excellent standing of a group whose class-conscious rule inevitably led to rebellion and then to democratic reform. *But* Sir Allan was a powerful, constructive statesman in his time ... [Dundurn Castle] and the man who built it have a strong claim for recognition in the history of our city and our country."[7]

People often select commemorative historical subjects and sites for specific reasons. In considering factors that motivated the decision to restore Dundurn Castle, I suggest that this choice reveals a decisive connection between commemorative endeavours and power. Such endeavours often indicate "an ongoing contest for hegemony." The types of subjects chosen for commemoration, historian Alan Gordon explains, oftentimes "illustrate and teach idealized social conventions ... Patriotism, so often the message of public commemorative monuments, may either serve as a means of edifying the population in the maintenance of an existing social structure or as a teaching tool in the construction of an ideal one."[8] Since the restoration of Dundurn Castle, executed as part of Canada's Centennial celebration, seemingly required the reinstatement of both the site and MacNab as a political figure, the house's reincarnation sought to, as I will show, concretize, monumentalize, and in effect privilege Anglo-Canadian culture. These two chapters therefore investigate hegemonic processes bound up in national ideologies that compel the reincarnation of historic sites and subjects. While Chapter 2 focuses on Dundurn's institutional history, Chapter 3 examines the longevity of hegemonic processes, particularly those that continue to infuse the site's programming.

Tactical goals routinely inform the cultural politics of heritage sites. In the case of historic house museums, the architectural structure routinely provides the ideal stage for a fictionalized performance of the past, one that represents the so-called private lives of the original inhabitants to solicit visitors' identification with particular aspects. Focusing on four particular phases of Dundurn Castle's development, this chapter charts ways in which nation-building designs informed the home's museumification. Over the course of its existence, Dundurn has acted as a private residence, historic house museum, Centennial project, and most recently as a fully-restored living history museum and national historic site offering a theme-based program. First, in my examination of Dundurn as Sir Allan MacNab's familial residence, I investigate how MacNab managed the construction of the house so that it would function as an architectural manifestation of the affluent lifestyle to which he aspired in the early years of his career. Second, I examine how women's "cultural custodianship" galvanized Dundurn's institutionalization as a house museum so that it took on a distinctly pedagogical role.[9] Cognizant of the potential Dundurn held as a tourist destination, they determined that visitor attendance might be increased by refurbishing the house so that it reflected what might have been in place during the MacNab family's residency. Accordingly, I interrogate how women curators (re)deployed the museumified dwelling to propagate particular British-Canadian cultural values. Third, in terms of Dundurn's incarnation as Hamilton's Centennial project, I chart how historians, consultants, and site workers endeavoured to reconceptualize both the home and the historical personae of Sir Allan MacNab as illustrious parts of Canada's national narrative. Finally, I take into account that, following the restoration, site workers sought to bolster the site's reputation as a living history museum by introducing "special event" programs. Such efforts make evident how nationalist ideologies compel the creation of communal monuments so as to (re)situate them, in seemingly "national" terms, as not only part of Canada's past but at the very foundations of national identity.[10]

I

While Dundurn Castle has been a familiar part of Hamilton's cultural landscape since its construction in 1832, it initially functioned as a private residence, one deliberately designed to reflect its owner's cultural predilections. Lawyer and land speculator Allan MacNab commissioned British-trained architect Robert Wetherell to design the house in the style of a Picturesque style villa. Picturesque architects in Britain drew on the foundational visual techniques of eighteenth-century Italianate landscape painters such as Claude Lorrain (c. 1604–82). Characterized as a theory of vision, the term picturesque literally means "like a picture," a theory that artists and then architects took up in their production. [11] Picturesque paintings depicted landscapes with compositions using organic means, such as trees, rolling hills and the like to format the composition. Eighteenth-century artists typically arranged organic framing devices within the works to signal the paintings' cultural resonance. The location of the trees and bushes highlight the artists' emulation of classical Italian Renaissance compositional arrangements of space; the location of the foliage typically divides the composition into distinct spatial planes, including an identifiable fore-, middle-, and background. More to the point, as art historian Anne Koval points out, English collectors began actively accruing the work of Italianate painters like Claude, Nicolas Poussin (1594–1665), and Salvator Rosa (1615–1673).

These artists had travelled throughout Italy, engaging on a touristic excursion popularly known as the Grand Tour, to enhance their cultural and artistic edification. With the advent of the Napoleonic Wars (1803–15), however, travel across Europe became increasingly difficult and prohibitive and so British collectors purchased works that either recalled their own Italian sojourns or, alternatively, provided them with the ability to visually consume such sites while remaining at home.[12]

Likewise, British architects emulated artists' accomplishments to satisfy collectors' tastes. They designed structures in the Picturesque style – architecturally eclectic buildings that would visually merge with the surrounding British countryside, thereby constructing in real time and space a physically idealized composition. The Picturesque architectural style was promoted by British architects such as John Nash (1752–1835), Uvedale Price (1747–1829), and Richard Payne Knight (1750–1824), and popularized by both aristocratic and moneyed patrons. Nash explains that the style united "freedom of form with an idealized, arcadian view of the landscape," and that "the asymmetry of these vernacular buildings lent itself perfectly to this romantic aesthetic."[13] The architectural style sets up the scenery so that the foliage frames the residences and so, as Koval puts it, the buildings "were Italianate in nature, although the landscape was no longer Italy." She explains further, writing:

> This nationalistic fervor helped to define the picturesque as uniquely British, and tours gained in popularity throughout England, Scotland and Wales. Regional landscape became a suitable subject for the painter and the tourist, helping to shape a nationalistic identity that surfaced in many guidebooks, and engraved books on regions of England, Wales and Scotland. Within the context of nationalism, the privileged concept of ownership shifted to become more of a collective conscience. The viewer of the picturesque could appreciate the merits of the 'British' landscape, and collectively 'own' or visually possess that land.[14]

By the mid-nineteenth century, the style spread beyond Britain to North America and Australia.[15] In the case of Dundurn, Wetherell designed the eclectic exterior so that the building would blend with the landscape, which overlooks the waters of Burlington Bay on Lake Ontario.

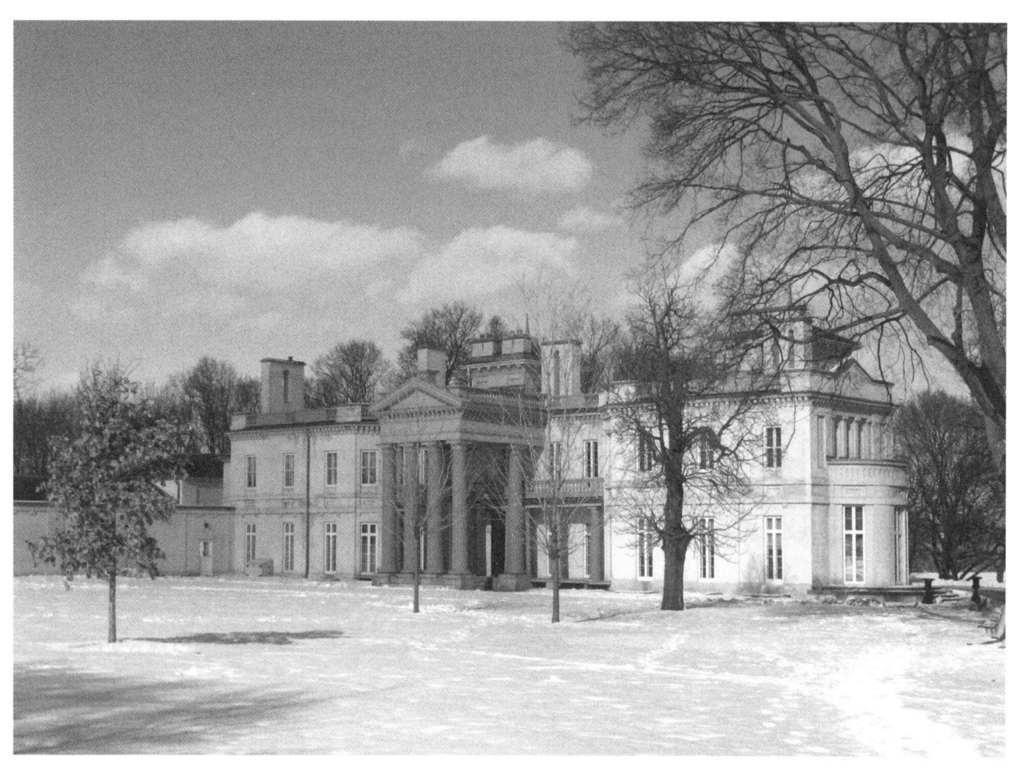

2.1 Front façade, Dundurn Castle, Dundurn National Historic Site of Canada, Hamilton, Ontario, 2014.

The eclecticism of the style – characteristic of the Picturesque – is evident in the combined use of diverse architectural elements, such as Greek mouldings, Italianate-style watch towers, Gothic details, French windows, and a Doric porch, which is located in the back of the house.[16] As a result, the house simultaneously emulated and maintained elite British architectural preferences within the colony.[17]

At the time of its construction, Dundurn also reflected its owner's personal and political preferences. Erected in the early years of MacNab's political career, Dundurn proclaimed its owner's intention to align himself with those dedicated to the Loyalist tradition of governance. However, MacNab went on to become active in the very institutions opposed by the Loyalists; consequently, historians conventionally characterize him as an "ambitious, contradictory [and] ambiguous" political figure.[18] During the late 1820s and early 1830s, he cultivated connections with members of the Family Compact, a political faction comprised of interlocking networks of wealthy individuals who maintained the Loyalist tradition of social hierarchy and

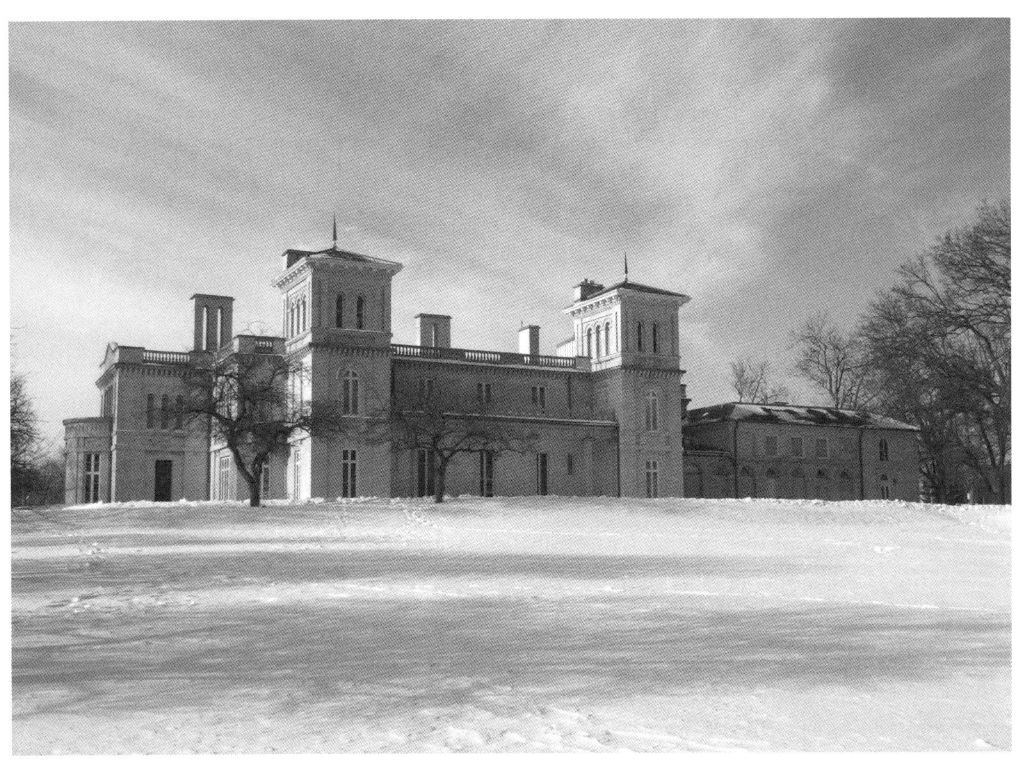

2.2 Back façade, Dundurn Castle, 2014.

opposed the importation of republican institutions. The construction of his house, MacNab biographer Donald Beer notes, came to be understood and perceived as one of MacNab's "most famous actions, [one that] reflected the attitudes of the odious so-called Family Compact."[19] MacNab went on to act as the head of this particular faction and, subsequent to that, assumed a military role in support of the Loyalist cause in the Upper Canada Rebellion of 1837. Credited with suppressing rebel forces led by William Lyon Mackenzie, who fought for governmental reform, MacNab was later knighted by Queen Victoria. His political career, however, reached its highest point when he was elected Premier of the United Canadas (1854–1856). His election, Beers argues, symbolized "Canada's colonial consensus. Threading his way through the sectarian and sectional issues that divided the province," Beers writes that MacNab "increasingly made a virtue of bowing to the wishes of the people."[20] He navigated the conflict-ridden political terrain and eventually came to support "colonial consensus," even while ultimately remaining staunchly dedicated to shoring up his personal economic resources.[21]

Despite his ambitious financial goals and "contradictory" political ventures and accomplishments, MacNab wound up depleting his finances, which, in turn, had a decisive effect on the fate of his home. Ultimately, his accomplishments provided little in terms of financial security for his dependents.[22] Following his death on 8 August 1862, the family furnishings were sold at various auctions to pay off his debts, and Dundurn stood empty.[23] As the years passed, various owners and institutions used the building for different purposes. In October 1899, the municipal government of Hamilton purchased Dundurn Castle and turned the house into a civic museum and the grounds into a park.[24]

This began a second stage in the development of Dundurn, which increasingly took on the trappings of a museum, the interests of the Hamilton community determining the arrangement of the programming so that the site remained directly related to the culture of Victorian England. Dundurn Park officially opened to the public on Queen Victoria's birthday, 24 May 1900, "to celebrate the public dedication and to do honour to Queen Victoria."[25] According to literary scholar and historian Daniel Coleman, such celebrations of "Britishness" or "pro-British view[s]" in settler colonies conventionally aimed to commemorate the achievements of liberty and equality while simultaneously maintaining "a respect for traditional monarchical ... order."[26] Accordingly, the fact that Queen Victoria was still alive at this time would have played heavily into some, if not all, of the decisions that the Hamilton authorities made.

II

During its tenure as a community-based house museum, those employed at Dundurn sought to cultivate its "Britishness." In 1901, Clementina Trenholme Fessenden (1843–1918) – an advocate of the imperial connection between Britain and Canada – was appointed curator, the first woman to hold what was described at the time as this "important position" within the public realm.

Determined to advance the British presence in Canadian life, Fessenden campaigned to bring about the observance of Empire Day in Canadian schools (1898).[27] She also acted as the founding secretary of Hamilton's first chapter of the Imperial Order of the Daughters of the Empire (1900), known as the Fessenden chapter, and soon became a councilor in the League of

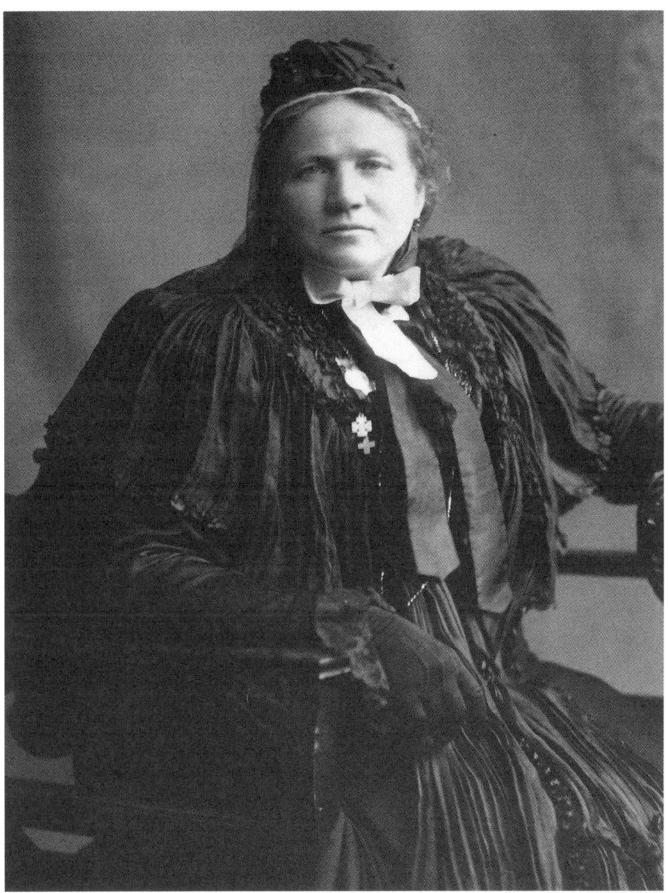

2.3 *Portrait of Clementina Fessenden*, circa 1896.

the Empire in 1903. Her propensity for historical preservationist activity is evident in her membership in both the Brome County Historical Society in Quebec and the Wentworth Historical Society, within which she acted as the recording secretary.[28] Her employment at Dundurn thus allowed her to advance her nationalist ideologies, using extant historical material culture.

Under Fessenden's supervision, the site took on a distinctly pedagogical role, one that sought to propagate a sense of devotion to particular cultural ideals. It initially operated as "a storehouse of science, art and history" showcasing "valuable relics," including an ostrich egg, Chinese coins, shells, minerals, and "Indian specimens."

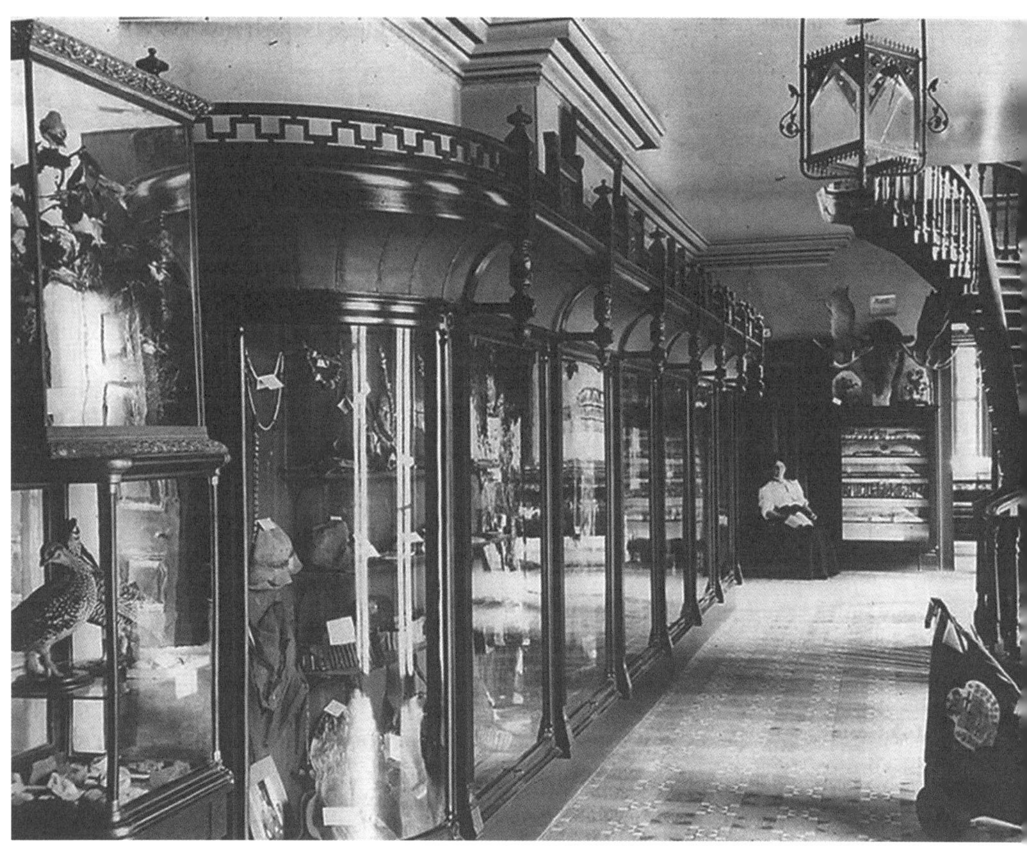

2.4 Display in hallway of Dundurn Castle, Hamilton, circa 1908–10.

Ultimately, Fessenden aimed to "repeople" certain rooms to reflect what had been in place in the 1840s and 50s, an intent inspired by what she referred to as "a century or two of museum growth."[29]

Because women typically established historic house museums, however, their work, as Patricia West points out, routinely remained "enmeshed in the 'cult of domesticity.'"[30] As Dundurn's first professional curator, Fessenden's work was often couched, particularly in popular press, in the idiom of domesticity. As one journalist wrote, "The management [at Dundurn] was fortunate in having secured the services of so capable a woman as curator … [One] important trait in Mrs. Fessenden's composition is her social and affable manner; seek her out for any information desired – it will be willingly and pleasantly imparted … The curator has been very busy lately getting her house in order and attending to the many little things incidental to the welfare of her daughters – the Daughters of the Empire."[31] In keeping with West's argument, the journalist's language not only downplays the professional aspects of Fessenden's occupation but also likens her actions to those that take place within the private sphere. Given that Fessenden herself had no biological daughters but five sons, the terminology establishes a decisive link between the curator's seemingly maternal duties – her dedication to women's welfare – and imperial patriotism. This type of characterization seemingly aimed to legitimize her occupation and activities in the public sphere.[32] Notably, Fessenden's viewpoints regarding women's agency and the state reflected her intention to uphold the patriarchal assumptions of state bureaucracy and Canadian nationhood. In 1913, she began to publically oppose women's suffrage in a series of newspaper letters, describing votes for women as "an empty promise of power, since only men were in positions to enforce legislation," even going so far as to suggest that the possibility threatened to "dismember" imperial advancement.[33]

Despite such characterizations, Fessenden's efforts were in fact frequently lauded by those bent on preserving Canada's examples of elite architectural preferences. As one local journalist explained: "The castle will always be the chief attraction, or its associations at least be the chief theme … It does not need much imagination to behold the builder of Dundurn welcoming at these hospitable doors the approved patriots of the forties and early fifties to witness him in this banquet hall, with its twin pillared sideboards, dispensing the cheer which he knew how to bestow with hearty unction … We can see the very character of the owner in the building … [and] visitors can gain more than a mere outing by making themselves familiar with the historical

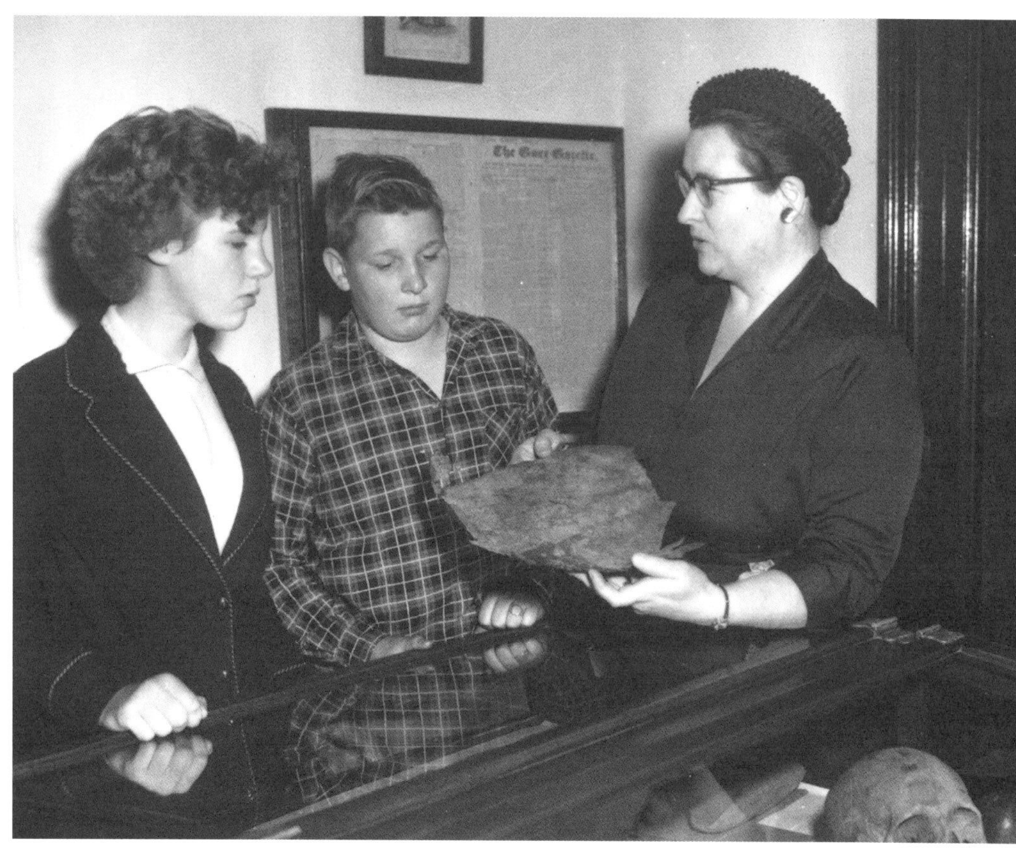

2.5 Dundurn Castle in the *Hamilton Spectator*. The caption that ran beneath this image was "this photograph shows visitors, Deanna Ellis and Larry Davenport from Bennetto Public School, being shown a piece of an Indian copper kettle by Mrs. M.G. Metcalfe, curator. The artifacts were featured especially for schools in an interesting display of the archaeology of Ontario arranged by Walter Kenyon, anthropologist with the Royal Ontario Museum," 1 May 1958.

associations of the spot."[34] Connecting the architecture – "essentially a British point of view" – with the perceived character of the owner, the writer suggests that, from Dundurn Castle, visitors might learn about and come to appreciate the history of the Hamilton area and, by extension, of Canada as a whole.[35] Moreover, as Coleman points out, such ethnicized projections maintained and promoted not only the "privileged, normative status of British whiteness in English Canada" but also the "gentlemanly code of Britishness."[36] The ensuing proliferation of women's cultural custodianship at Dundurn, as a result, posits a complex gender dynamic in relation to the male historical figure commemorated at the site.[37]

Women curators recognized not only the historical value of Dundurn but also the potential it held as a tourist destination, and they developed exhibition policies specifically to draw in visitors.

In the 1950s, for example, then-curator Gwen Metcalfe identified the one thing "most lacking" at Dundurn – the "human touch." Born in 1913 in Fort Dodge, Iowa, Margaret Gwendolyn Carley's parents moved to Hamilton, where her father worked as the Physical Director of the YMCA.[38] In 1936, she married Albert Metcalfe and went on to take a "summer job at the desk" of Dundurn Castle. She carried out various projects, training the birds in the onsite aviary, scrubbing floors, and clearing turrets[39] before taking on the curatorial post in 1954. She described the position as one she felt well-equipped to assume, writing "In doing this type of work I'm beginning to feel that either one has the ability or one doesn't. Technical knowledge is desirable of course, but no amount of technical knowledge would give one the necessary, natural inborn knowhow." And so she went on to conceive of ways in which to develop exhibition policies at the museum in order to draw in more visitors. As she explained to Dundurn's Museum Committee Chairman Dr W.S.T. Connell, "Sir Allan's political life is known but the everyday happenings and way of life in Dundurn Castle is completely lost. Those are things people are most interested in when visiting a Historical House, the whys and wherefores."[40] Having thus identified aspects of the site that might be explored and perhaps represented as a means to encourage people to visit Dundurn, Metcalfe proceeded to enact a proposal her predecessor, Agnes Mundie, made, "to refurnish the rooms in Dundurn Castle in the period when Sir Allan MacNab lived there."[41] Beginning in 1954, Metcalfe spent the next three years refurbishing various rooms so that they displayed "lived-in touches"; for example, in MacNab's bedroom she put a massive, ornate walnut dresser and other personal objects such as a portrait of MacNab hung over the fireplace and reading glasses perched beside an open book on a table.[42] The site's reincarnation as a historic house museum spurred a significant rise in visitor attendance and, subsequent to that, a third stage in its development.

City officials, cognizant of Dundurn's increasing presence in the civic landscape, proposed to consolidate the site's cultural profile within a decisively nationalistic framework by recommending that it be restored in its entirety as Hamilton's Centennial project. From 1956 to the end of 1957, Dundurn's visitor attendance had increased from 26,000 to 31,000 – Dundurn had become a major tourist destination.[43] Significantly, a 1959 article in the Toronto *Globe and Mail* credited the increase to "the new policy of more interesting fashion displays," as had been undertaken in the bedroom.[44] Later in January 1961, Mayor Lloyd Douglas announced that it might be possible to restore the site as a "period piece" as Hamilton's contribution to the Centennial celebrations.[45] Ultimately, Dundurn's restoration was due to the cultural custodianship of women,[46] with its first curator, Fessenden, who spearheaded the Dundurn's museumification in the 1890s that set the tone for its first fifty years, and then Metcalfe, who led the next major directional shift by reconfiguring the heritage site as a house museum.

III

The 1960s marked a watershed, not only with Dundurn's institutional development but also for Canada's heritage industry at large, that culminated in 1967 with the centenary of Confederation. Government officials, heritage practitioners, and local community groups alike planned projects to celebrate the history of the land in which they lived.[47] Sponsored by the federal government, the Canadian Centennial celebrations sought to stimulate a sense of devotion to the nation among the populace.[48] The celebrations therefore took on a "pedagogical role" in that various undertakings, including festivals and exhibitions such as Expo '67 and the construction or restoration of historic monuments, functioned as governmental efforts to educate citizens about Canada's national identity.[49] Governmental investment in historic site development indicates how new roles (and values) were assigned to heritage properties in and around this time. Using the example of the 1960s reconstruction of the eighteenth-century Fortress of Louisbourg in Cape Breton, Nova Scotia, Christina Cameron explains that when the site reopened to the public, the government came to recognize ways in which heritage sites could be reconfigured and act as "key factors in economic renewal," drawing in not only visitors but also domestic tourism revenue. As Cameron points out, "No longer were historic places merely conserved for the benefit of the nation, education was a necessary element" of such projects.[50]

In keeping with this, those vested in restoring Dundurn determined that, in order to secure funding for the project, the site would serve a didactic function. In 1961, Anthony Adamson, who had been retained by the city of Hamilton as an architectural consultant the year before, recommended that the municipal government apply for a grant offered under the National Centennial Projects Act to finance the restoration.[51] The restoration would require the city's financial involvement as well; grants were provided on the condition that the provincial and municipal governments each contribute one-third of the funds required for the project, with the federal government providing the remaining third. To receive funds, however, the project would have to be of a "lasting nature" and completed by 1967.[52] Adamson therefore advocated that the house be restored "to show its original condition when in use by Sir Allan MacNab," and that a terminal date of 1856 be established; 1856 "is thought the most suitable date on which to base an application for a grant under the National Centennial Projects Act," Adamson wrote at the time, adding, "The heyday of Dundurn was probably in the 1850's when Sir Allan, though a widower, was not only a Prime Minister but wealthy and a baronet."[53] In other words, he thought that funding for the restoration might be secured by emphasizing MacNab's contributions to the nation, an approach that would in turn set the house up as a concrete example of MacNab's accomplishments.[54] It was a successful strategy; on 18 August 1964, the federal government announced its approval of the application and, with it, financial commitment to the restoration project.[55]

Given that the project represented Hamilton's contribution to the Centennial celebrations and had to be of a "lasting nature," those involved in the 1960s restoration had to determine how to make both the dwelling and the persona of the original owner attractive to potential visitors. Because information relating to MacNab's family life was scant at the time and there were no visual records documenting the interior as it had been in MacNab's day, a so-called "authentic recreation" was impossible and so Adamson advocated that newly-formed Restoration Committee use whatever historical sources it could find to "interpret the house" as a heritage site.[56] Over the next three years, committee members conducted extensive searches to procure both primary documents and architectural evidence that shed light on MacNab's family life, tastes, and character. Researchers, historians, and scholars alike surveyed, excavated, and examined the house's infrastructure to determine what wallpaper, paint, carpets, curtains, or room layout had been in place. Artifacts and furnishings placed in the various rooms had not belonged to the MacNab family but were chosen, as historian Marion MacRae explains, because "they were consistent with the social pattern of the city in their day."[57] In short, they strove to construct what Edward Bruner calls a "historically accurate" environment; based on research and scholarship, they worked to establish the castle as an alluring tourist destination by creating a site that visitors would find artifactually credible and, by extension, appealing.[58] Notably, this intention required they not only confront but also strategically manage the "contradictory [and] ambiguous" aspects of MacNab's life.

Dundurn's museumification demanded a restoration of both the house and the personae of MacNab as a historical figure. Scott Symons, Curator of Canadian Art at the Royal Ontario Museum, articulated the relationship that was being established between the two and explained that there were mythologizing aspects to the restoration process. As he put it to Metcalfe, "Old Sir Allan MacNab represented all that was good and walrus-hopeless in the Family Compact. He has been maligned; and I feel is due for a 'restoration.' Whatever the compacters may or may not have done, they did establish here in Canada a cultivated, dignified rich life. *Their homes* show it. Very few Canadians are aware of the Regency culture in Canada, or think of it as Canadian. When they do awake to it, they may then no longer feel it a sin to read, to think, or wish to improve themselves."[59] As Symons suggests, those involved in the restoration endeavoured to rework the negative associations commonly drawn in historical studies of the Family Compact. One might suggest that the restoration project represented, as Coleman puts it, "the formulation and elaboration of a specific form of whiteness based on a British model of civility" made manifest in the architecture of the site and the perceived conduct of its owner.[60] Those involved in the restoration aimed to cultivate a narrative that stressed the ways in which a figure such as MacNab cultivated elite British culture in Canada and how his efforts resulted in concrete examples of that past, thereby enhancing the cultural status of a city such as Hamilton in the present.[61]

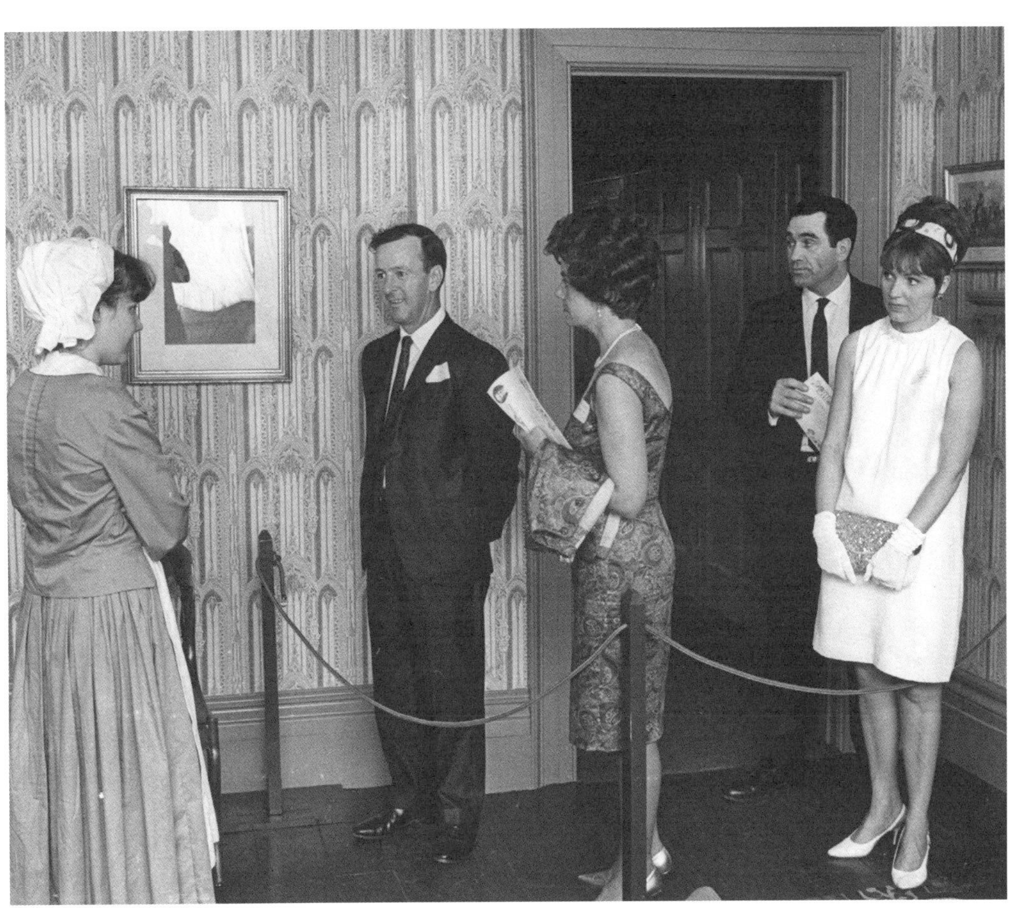

2.6 Visitors on a tour of Dundurn Castle. Photograph, *Hamilton Spectator*, circa 1967–69.

The reincarnation of Dundurn Castle as a national historic site sought to portray the site as emblematic of the nation's past, even as it advanced the site's function as a tourist destination.[62] When Dundurn reopened to the public on 18 June 1967, offering guided tours by young women posing as Upper Canada housemaids, government officials characterized the site as representative of Hamilton's contribution to nation-building efforts and achievements. At the opening-day reception, Solicitor-General Larry Pennell praised the project and identified what he perceived to be the site's primary purpose. He stated that "one of the difficulties in finding national identity [stemmed] from a lack of understanding [of Canada's] history," declaring that, as a product of that history, Dundurn would make Hamiltonians "better citizens and richer human beings."[63] According to Pennell, touring the museum represented a "civilizing ritual," to use art historian Carol Duncan's term.[64] His commentary suggests that in visiting Dundurn, the museum visitor performs the role of citizen, thus making evident that the restoration project represented, as Jill Vickers terms it, a "Canadianisation project": visitors might, upon entering and touring the site, learn about the history, culture, and values that would unite him or her with other Canadian citizens.[65] This characterization of the restoration project *and* the resultant house museum is reiterated by the commemorative text panels installed at the site by both the Ontario Archeological and Historic Sites Board (hereafter OAHSB) and the Historic Sites and Monuments Board of Canada (hereafter HSMBC).

Both the provincial and federal bodies erected commemorative plaques, thereby capturing in sculptural text the purpose of the restoration and the role of the site. As Sandra Barry explains, such monuments are visible "indelible markers … public texts documenting what was, and what continues to be considered important about our heritage, at least officially, as most of these plaques were erected by federal, provincial, and municipal governments."[66] Notably, the provincial body set their plaque six years before the inception of the restoration effort, while the federal government put two in place in 1985, seventeen years after the re-opening of Dundurn upon completion of the restoration. Such timely decisions had a definitive effect on the ideological inflections espoused in the respective texts. In July 1958, then-Hamilton mayor Lloyd D. Jackson dedicated the plaque erected by OAHSB (founded in 1956, now the Ontario Heritage Trust).

Situated at the start of the gravel path leading from the site's parking lot to the house, the plaque, entitled "Dundurn Castle / 1832," focuses explicitly on the life and accomplishments of the home's owner. The inscription reads:

> This mansion was built 1832–35 by Allan Napier MacNab (1798–1862) and named after the family ancestral seat in Scotland. Enlisting at fifteen, MacNab distinguished himself by his bravery in the War of 1812. He subsequently entered politics and was noted for his support of the Family Compact. During the Rebellion of 1837 he was one of the government's most active military supporters and was knighted for his services. Leader of the Tory-Conservatives, MacNab was speaker of the Legislative Assembly on several occasions and Prime Minister of Canada 1854–56.[67]

The text sets MacNab up for visitors – who take the time to read it – as a war hero, a celebrated politician "noted for his support of the Family Compact" and one knighted for his services during the 1837 Upper Canada Rebellion. Since MacNab, born in 1798, was "only" fourteen years old when the War of 1812 broke out, historians have debated the degree to which he distinguished himself among British troops, while others are quick to point out that he sup-posedly earned the reputation as a "boy hero."[68] And then there is mention of MacNab's support of what came to be characterized by historians in the 1980s (and thereafter) as the "odious" Family Compact.[69] Finally, and prob-ably most notably, the panel identifies MacNab as the "Prime Minister of Canada 1854–56." Given that Canada did not come into being as a state until Confederation on 1 July 1867, there was no official state-sanctioned post as Prime Minister at this time.

In 1840, British Parliament, heeding the recommendations of Lord Durham, the parliamentarian who investigated the causes of the twin 1837 rebellions and subsequently authored the 1839 *Durham Report*, passed the Act of the Union, thereby officially uniting the provinces of Upper and Lower Canada (now the provinces of Ontario and Quebec) as the Province of Canada or, more colloquially, the United Canadas. MacNab went on to assumed headship of the Legislative Assembly of the Province of Canada in 1854. According to Don McIver, during this period, references to MacNab's post used the titles "premier" and "prime minister" interchangeably.[70] And so while the terminology is "technically" accurate, the plaque's phrasing delib-erately positions MacNab as a historical figure on par with the accomplish-ments and veneration afforded John A. MacDonald, the first Prime Minister of Canada, following Confederation (1867).

While, at the time of its construction, Dundurn's architectural designs proclaimed MacNab's alliance with the Family Compact, the OAHSB's plaque and the subsequent restoration sought to merge – in the minds of the public – MacNab's cultural predilections with his political achievements, in par-ticular his election as Canada's last pre-Confederation "Prime Minister." This fusion, monumentalized in the establishment of Dundurn as a nation-al historic site, suggests the promotion of particular aspects of "founding nations" mythologies. In this ideological construction, Confederation rep-resents a crucial moment in Canada's development as a federal state, one that stands for the unification of the anglophone and francophone as the nation's "two founding cultures."[71] Furthermore, as McKay points out, treatises that celebrate the "Birth of the Nation" do so in order to provide citizens with a sense of belonging.[72]

Notably, thirty years later, the HSMBC aimed for a greater degree of precision in its monument description of MacNab's place in Canadian politics, while still heralding the homeowner's cultural predilections. In 1937, the federal body first designated MacNab a "National Historic Person," venerated in a commemorative plaque installed some forty-eight years later. Characterizing MacNab as a "successful lawyer" and land speculator whose profitable enterprises allowed him to build the home in front of which the panel sits, the text identifies the politician as Premier. It reads, in its entirety:

SIR ALLAN NAPIER MACNAB
1798–1862

Politician, businessman, land speculator and soldier, Allan MacNab enjoyed a very public life. He was a successful lawyer and was appointed Upper Canada's first Queen's Counsel. In 1838 he was knighted for his role in suppressing the rebellion in Upper Canada. The profits from his extensive land speculation were fed into a variety of projects, including construction of his monument, Dundurn. He was influential in establishing the Gore Bank and in promoting the Great Western Railway. During a political career spanning three decades, he was three times Speaker and, from 1854 to 1856, Premier.

Homme politique, home d'affaires, spéculateur foncier, officier militaire et avocat, Allan MacNab eut une longue vie publique. Premier conseiller de la reine au Haut-Canada, il fut créé chevalier en 1838, en récompense de son role répressif lors de la Rébellion. It contribua à l'établissement de la *Gore Bank* et du *Great Western Railway.* Il investit les profits de ses spéculations dans divers projets dont la construction de ce château, Dundurn, qui devait prolonger sa mémoire. Au cours de ses quelque 30 ans de carrière politique, il fut président de la Chambre à trois reprises et premier ministre de 1854 à 1856.[73]

Significantly, any reference to the Family Compact has been abandoned, as has any mentioning of MacNab's role in the War of 1812. When HSMBC erected this plaque, they put up an accompanying one that testifies to Dundurn's designation as a National Historic Site, notably coming 48 years after the recognition of the owner and 17 years after the site's reopening as a fully restored period house museum. It reads:

DUNDURN CASTLE
LE CHÂTEAU DUNDURN

This villa was completed in 1835 for Allan Napier MacNab. Incorporating an existing farmhouse, it was designed by the local architect, Robert Wetherell, as a statement of its owner's place in Hamilton society. The house features an eclectic blend of classical and Italianate motifs, French windows, broad verandahs and a panoramic view of Burlington Bay. With its outbuildings and grounds, Dundurn Castle stands as an important example of the Picturesque Movement in Canada. After years in private hands, the property was purchased by the city and from 1964 to 1967 restored to its former splendour.

Achevée en 1835, cette villa fut construite pour Allan Napier MacNab. Pour son concepteur, Robert Wetherell, elle devait témoigner du statut social de son propriétaire. Incorporant une ancienne maison de ferme, elle affiche un amalgam éclectique de lignes classiques et de motifs à l'italienne, des portes-fenêtres, de grandes vérandas, et offer une vue splendide sur la baie. Avec ses dépendances et ses parcs, elle constitue un important exemple du style pittoresque au Canada. Résidence privée pendant de nombreuses années, elle a été achetée par la ville de Hamilton, qui l'a restaurée de 1964 à 1967.[74]

Here, the text identifies the owner, describes the eclectic nature of the architectural fixtures, and thus characterizes it as "a statement of the owner's place in society," as well as "an important example of the Picturesque Movement in Canada." In such a construction, as art historian Carol Duncan explains, the museum stands as a "keeper of the nation's spiritual life and guardian of the most evolved and civilized culture."[75]

The HSMBC cites Dundurn's representation as the "most comprehensive statement of the Picturesque values of Canadian Architecture" as the source of its "heritage value" and, by extension, its national historical significance. Architectural historian Janet Wright underscores this connection in her 1984 study *Architecture of the Picturesque in Canada* (produced and published by Parks Canada) which notably sold out its first edition printing, thereby indicating the degree to which Wright communicated this association to the Canadian public at large.[76] In her study, she characterizes MacNab as a "wealthy gentleman patron who was determined to build a house of great distinction to reflect his noble Scottish ancestry and his perceived position in society ... When completed in 1835, it surpassed in scale and lavishness and sophistication of design anything previously known to the young colony. Dundurn has changed little over the years."[77] Elsewhere, she articulates the connection between the architecture and Anglo-Canadian culture, labeling the Picturesque style – notably in the introduction – as "essentially a British point of view."[78] Dundurn's construction, preservation, restoration, and textual commemoration collectively sought to commemorate particular aspects of a distinctively class-based British-Canadian identity. As Veronica Strong-Boag pointedly states, the effects of "all official commemoration are of course a natural product of the dominant agenda of national institutions such as the HSMBC ... [its] very mandate seeks to emphasize cohesive, even unitary, collective identity. Differences, and attendance grievances, among subjects and citizens of the state can threaten the very object of celebration, Canada itself."[79] Moreover, one might suggest that Dundurn's institutional history, assessed above in the form of three particular phases of development, monumentalizes a certain type of historical narrative and that, moreover, the programming, installed in connection with Dundurn's incarnation as a living history museum, transmits and advances it.[80]

IV

Dundurn's restoration as Hamilton's Centennial celebration project brought forth the site's reconstitution as a state-sanctioned living history museum, offering programs designed to make the past "come alive" for visitors. As a living history museum, site workers developed programming that took into account the architectural style of the site, the identity, political accomplishments, and cultural predilections of the house's owner, as well as his "private" life. As of 2014, Dundurn offers a host of "special event" programs catering to a diverse range of people, including families, domestic and international tourists, as well as local school groups and military history enthusiasts. The standard program is the conventional tours offered at the site year-round. Interpreters greet visitors in the main hall and begin the tour, identifying Sir Allan Napier MacNab – pointing to the portrait hanging on the wall – as not only the home's original owner but also as Canada's last pre-Confederation Prime Minister. They proceed to guide visitors throughout the residence's 40 plus rooms, so that they might "experience life in a grand country home of the MacNab family and the servants working below stairs."

"Special event" programs include workshops, events, and themed object-based exhibitions. For example, Dundurn Castle – currently part of the Hamilton Civic Museums' network and in conjunction with the city's War of 1812 Bicentennial celebration – hosted two object-based exhibitions, complete with historical artifacts and illustrative text panels, one located in the Coach House gallery (formerly MacNab's stables) and the other in the Hamilton Military Museum, which was originally Dundurn's gate house and later turned into a museum in 1976. Unlike MacNab's home, however, this museum lacks full-time staff to maintain its operations year round and so closes for months on end when those working in-house set about mounting new exhibitions. Moreover, its architecture is reflective of a part of a larger assemblage of buildings, the home being the foremost site of socio-political recognition, interest, and funding.

Within the home, staff offers educational programs for elementary and secondary school groups and community programming for groups, such as five different themed-based historic cooking programs. The site is also available for rental for wedding ceremonies, receptions, and photography, as well as for family gatherings, children's birthday parties, and corporate rentals with optional programming available. Certain programs are offered in accordance with the seasons, such as historic garden tours offered during the summer months, July to mid-September, and the Victorian Christmas tours. Significantly, Dundurn's Victorian Christmas tours are not only a "special event," site workers also offer five different variations of this program, including free admission during the first Sunday of the tour's duration, two Christmas themed workshops where visitors tour the house and are taught how to make their own period treats in the historic kitchen, using mid-nineteenth century technologies, implements, and recipes, evening tours and finally, a special "Ring in the New Year" tour where interpreters take visitors throughout the home on the last Saturday of the year.

From its inception up to the present day, Dundurn's character and function(s) have sought to reflect the cultural capital of the Hamilton community. Its construction initially signaled its owner's socio-political affluence, and its Picturesque design in turn necessitated its location in a landscape that might effectively frame it, one found in the Hamilton area on the shores of the Burlington Bay. As a community-based museum owned by the municipal government, its operations depended upon those invested in living and working in the area, such as Fessenden and Metcalfe. Moreover, the restoration reflected choices made by Metcalfe, as well as the municipal government, given that the latter put forward the application for Dundurn to be Hamilton's centennial project. Its restoration reflected how a communal monument might be reconfigured so as to connect the history of the Hamilton area to Canada's national narrative. Ultimately, however, the restoration project benefited the region as it propelled the site's ability to act as the community's chief tourist attraction.

Given that the city of Hamilton owns and manages Dundurn Castle, the city tourism marketing strategies indicate how it aims to attract Hamilton's key tourist demographic: local day-trippers. In 2004, the year in which I conducted onsite research, Tourism Hamilton distributed pamphlets to the city's key geographic markets, among them Hamilton, Eastern and Western Ontario, the Greater Toronto Area, and New York, all areas that are generally within an hour's driving distance of the city.[81] The guide contains a list of activities, festivals, and events held in the city throughout the year. The Christmas program at Dundurn is one of eight events listed for the months of November and December, where it is described as "Victorian Christmas at Dundurn National Historic Site."[82] In terms of site visitation statistics, Dundurn currently uses a combination of an electronic ticketing system and in-person ticket purchase onsite; current records for the electronic system are overwritten day-to-day, and no one has – as yet – calculated day-to-day numbers based on the cash register readings. As a result, definitive statistics pertaining to visitation rates remain unknown at this time.

There is, however, research indicating who in fact tours museums in the Hamilton area, which underscores the merits of the city's tourism marketing strategies. In 1996, a study conducted by the provincial Ministry of Economic Development, Trade and Tourism found that Canadians accounted for 89.4 per cent of tourists to Hamilton that year and that 99.3 per cent originated within Ontario. Same-day trips remained the most popular type, as 75.7 per cent of all visits fell within this trip duration.[83] In 2000 and 2001, domestic tourists generated 84 per cent of the city's tourism revenue.[84] Such statistics reveal how the home might speak to those in the region and how they in turn benefit from the house.

CHAPTER THREE

"Deck the Halls": Performing Dominance in Multicultural Canada

In living history museums, the setting conventionally sets the stage for the performance, which in turn animates the site – and Dundurn Castle is no exception. Dundurn's history as an artifactual object determines how interpreters choose to make the house "come alive" for visitors. In order to effectively interrogate the types of historical narratives privileged in this museum and their implications, I explore Dundurn's Victorian Christmas program and consider how interpreters deploy the house as a living history museum so as to frame visitors' engagement with the past. First, I look at how Dundurn interpreters utilize the architecture, the artifactual arrangements, and historical research to authenticate the representation.[1] In other words, I investigate how interpreters coordinate particular elements – the architectural context, decorated period rooms, and interpretation – to (re)construct Dundurn as a performative site that conveys, for visitors, a sense of what it "felt like to live back then" or, more precisely, the lifestyle, habits, and customs of Canada's anglophone gentry.[2] Second, I review what facts, objects, events, and activities interpreters routinely discuss over the course of the tours, using the 2004 season as my case study. This chapter, as a result, considers not only how site workers reanimate Dundurn's portrayal of the seasonal celebration of an upper-class family in nineteenth-century Canada, but also what such performances reveal about the function of this particular living history museum in the contemporary multicultural context.

Restored as a Picturesque villa representing "essentially a British point of view," Dundurn Castle provides the ideal stage to host specific interpretive performances of the past.[3] The "object permanence" of the site itself (to use art historian Donald Preziosi's conceptualization) works to validate the implementation of a Victorian Christmas tour.[4] In 1968, to consolidate the site's operation as a living history museum, the curatorial staff produced Dundurn's first Christmas program, a program that has been offered every year since and, to this day, remains the site's longest running special event. Because the restoration included installation of a proper heating system, the site remained open in the winter months, allowing Dundurn staff and volunteers to design "special event" programs and to decorate the house in accordance with the season.[5] Moreover, from 1993 to 2003, according to then-curator Bill Nesbitt, the site's annual attendance averaged 50,000 paid admissions and the Christmas program generated 25 per cent of the annual attendance in the six-to-seven-week period that defines the Christmas season, thus making it the top attendance-getter.[6] Reanimating Dundurn in the guise of a Victorian Christmas suggests that site workers take into account public perceptions of both the contemporary and historic celebration to encourage site visitation. As historian Adam Kuper explains, the contemporary performance of festive rituals marks the Christmas period with a "special quality ... It tends to freeze history, to associate this Christmas with [the Victorian celebration]."[7] The ritualistic nature of contemporary activities, as a result, advances a utopian version of the past so that the Victorian Christmas becomes an ideological reality.

Interpreters conduct historical research and arrange artifacts dated to the period that is being depicted, thereby constructing speculative object-based representations of what might have been in place in these rooms during the MacNab family Christmas. Individual staff members develop a thematic exhibitionary premise for a particular area of the house; each produces a decorating plan and, from that, arranges artifacts within that area based on research derived from primary documents, such as diaries, letters, newspapers, and drawings.[8] Significant among these sources is the diary of Sophia MacNab, Sir Allan's daughter. Dated 1846, it describes in detail the daily life and activities of the family. The diary, however, begins just after Christmas on 20 January 1846 and ends on 8 July the same year and so there is no primary evidence that sets out how the MacNabs and their servants celebrated Christmas. Consequently, interpreters also rely on evidence that pertains to the lives of others – primarily British immigrants – as well as on material related to the type of event that was most common in Victorian England. During the one-hour tour offered as part of the program, visitors experience period rooms decorated in the style of a Victorian Christmas, hear about activities associated with the festive celebration, sing carols, and eat festive treats. In the context of guided tours, interpreters validate the speculative arrangement of the period rooms for visitors discussing the nature and significance of such artifactual arrangements, as well as research undertaken by either themselves or their colleagues.

Dundurn's conceptualization of the past is consistent with the scholarly assertion that Victorian Britain both inspired and shaped sentiments and activities that are a part of the Christmas celebration in Britain and many of its former colonies today. In fact, Russell Belk argues that Christmas traditions were dying out in Europe in the seventeenth and eighteenth centuries, but that Charles Dickens's 1843 publication of *A Christmas Carol* renewed interest in the holiday. Among other things, Dickens's work stressed the importance of social equality, sentimentality, family, and generosity, and made the family dinner the hallmark of the celebration.[9] Following its initial, serialized publication in London, serialized reprints of Dickens's work became available in Canada, appearing in the colony as early as 1844.[10] With the advent of interest inspired by Dickens's secularized version of the Christmas season, upper-class Victorian society incorporated specific activities into its holiday celebration, among them Christmas dinner and the decoration of the Christmas tree (a German import introduced by Queen Victoria's consort, Prince Albert).[11]

Interpreters at Dundurn relay particular facts to endorse the institutionalized interpretation of the MacNab family Christmas; critical analysis of their espousal of research findings and subsequent speculative arrangements and discussions can reveal the ideological underpinnings of their narrative constructions of the past. Obscuring this ideology is the decisively object-based nature of these constructions, which, as Tamar Katriel explains, "allow[ ] the museum to sustain the fiction that the past is told 'as it really was.'"[12] The result of living history sites routinely privileging artifactual histories is what Eric Gable and Richard Handler describe as an "uncritical retailing of some old ... myths and dreams."[13] Accordingly, I suggest that the popular Dundurn Castle Victorian Christmas tour offers a representation of an upper-class Canadian family's holiday celebration that favours, to adapt Gable and Handler's phrase, an uncritical retailing of some old Canadian myths and dreams.

Moreover, following David Lowenthal, I would stress the degree to which this type of interpretation is deliberate. In re-constructing concrete representations of the past so as to emphasize certain aspects, heritage workers reshape not only the site but also conceptualizations of the nation's past. Lowenthal points out that such reconstructions aim to render the past "easy [for visitors] to embrace. And just as heritage practitioners take pride in creating artifice, the public enjoys consuming it."[14] Dundurn interpreters therefore redeploy the site as an institutionalized setting – with its attendant historical research, decorated period rooms, and particular interpretation – to privilege particular subject positions[15] and, ultimately, to entice visitors, especially local families, during the winter season. In catering to the Hamilton public, interpreters at Dundurn conduct unscripted tours, a pedagogical approach that lets them not only gauge but also cultivate visitor interest; over the course of the tours, the interaction between interpreters and visitors oftentimes determines the content discussed. The interpreters I interviewed agreed that the unscripted approach allows them to take into account comments and questions posed by guests so that they might determine what information to relay to pique visitor interest. As one interpreter explains, "The tours are the best and most intimate way to deal with the specific desires of the public and are the most successful way to tailor information, given the diverse nature of our visitors and group structure." Another proposes that the lack of a script creates a more relaxed atmosphere because interpreters are given "the freedom to discuss and to talk and to interact ... If it was a presentation ... I think mentally it would just be a bust ... These people can always talk about the dynamics, there is non-stop dynamic in dealing with people." The tour content, as a result, conventionally reflects the concerns of both site workers and visitors. My analysis of Dundurn's Victorian Christmas tour content therefore examines common themes, activities, and traditions discussed by interpreters in 2004 to examine how interpreters "reshape" or "tailor" the past in deference to visitors' expectations or desires.[16]

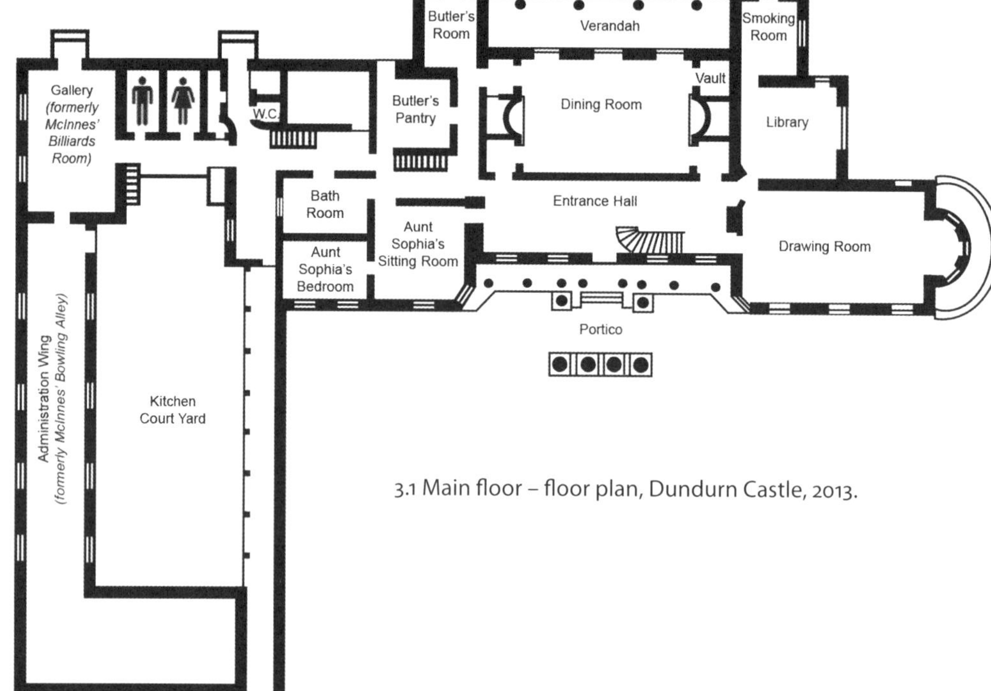

3.1 Main floor – floor plan, Dundurn Castle, 2013.

Main Floor

The Christmas tour starts in the main hall where staff welcome visitors to the house and invite them to sing carols. In contrast to regular tours, in which interpreters begin by emphasizing MacNab's political achievements, such as his election as Canada's last pre-Confederation Prime Minister, the Christmas tour introduction (re)conceptualizes MacNab as a major political figure with a number of different entrepreneurial interests whose fortune allowed him to build the house. He is also positioned as the head of both a prestigious family and household. This type of interpretation of the historical figure of Sir Allan MacNab represents what historian Michael Kammen refers to as the "depoliticization of memory." The interpreters downplay MacNab's political roles, actions, and pursuits in order to re-present him as a financially successful entrepreneur, an avid socialite, and the quintessential "family man," aspects that might render him "acceptable to as many people as possible."[17] In linking MacNab's professional and personal achievements as those which ultimately culminated in the house's museumification,

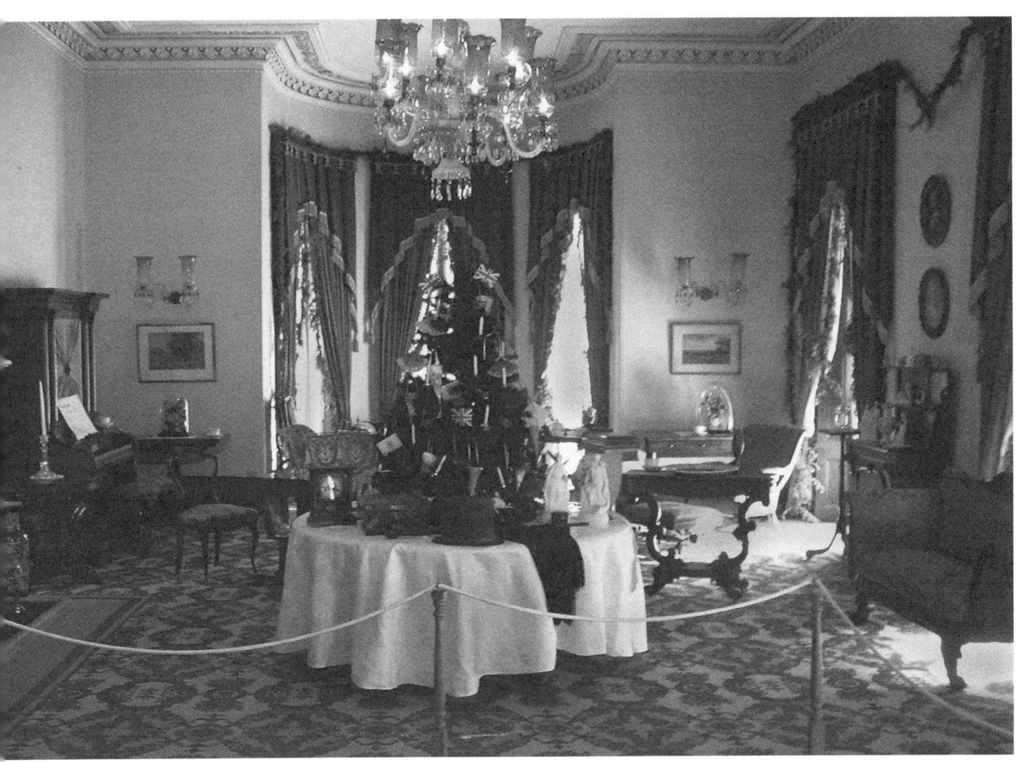

3.2 Drawing room, Dundurn Castle, 2004.

staff encourage visitors to appreciate and, by extension, identify with the ways in which MacNab provided for his family. Furthermore, according to the introduction given in the front hall, the Victorian Christmas was "not [celebrated] exactly the way Christmas [is] today" in that it was "not as commercial" as the contemporary celebration, although the event was starting to become quite popular during the period portrayed in Dundurn.[18]

Over the course of the tour, the three floors, which include the main floor, the upper floor, and the downstairs, are distinguished as three separate areas where three different types of celebrations took place. The main floor, which includes the drawing room, MacNab's library and smoking room, the dining room, and Sophia's suite (MacNab's sister-in-law's room), is positioned as a place in which a formal celebration for adults would have taken place.

On this floor, elaborate decorations demonstrate the MacNab family's intention to maintain the appearance of wealth. The interpreters refer to the drawing room and dining room as two of the home's most impressive rooms in terms of their architectural character, design, and decoration.[19]

The drawing room displays one of the two Christmas trees in the house. On a round table in the middle of the room stands a small tree decorated with cornucopias, miniature musical instruments, miniature flags of the Royal Rampart, one of the flags of Scotland, and the Union Jack. Unwrapped gifts that would customarily have been given to family members surround the base of the tree. The tree stands as an example of what one interpreter refers to as "the adult tree with adult gifts under it."[20] It is also introduced as a German tradition that was imported to England with the marriage of the German Prince Albert to Queen Victoria. In order to justify the type of Christmas that is represented, the historical interpreters emphasize the characterization of MacNab as a Loyalist who maintained close ties with the British Empire. In other words, this type of Christmas is one that follows the British Royal tradition promulgated by the English aristocracy and transported to the Canadian colony, which was, according to one interpreter, "still a British colony [that copied] everything British."[21]

Various interpreters recognize different means through which the popularity of the Christmas tree was established, but, overall, ties to the British upper-class celebration are central to the explanation of its presence in the Castle. One interpreter, for instance, states, "[Victoria and Albert] aren't the only source of tradition, though, because it's a German tradition that comes to North America quite independently with German settlers in Pennsylvania and, of course, here in Ontario as well, with the Loyalists coming up ... And they brought the evergreen, the Christmas tree with them, so that would have been known to the MacNabs. I suspect that it was the Royal tradition of the Christmas tree that MacNab would have been following because he was very much a Loyalist."[22] In other words, the interpreters position the MacNab family Christmas as one that would have followed the standards set by the Victorian British monarchy.

Following the visit to the library and smoking room, the interpreters lead visitors into the dining room, decorated to impress. A crystal chandelier hangs in the centre of the room, and garlands, interwoven with the MacNab tartan, extend out from the chandelier to the four corners of the long rectangular space. The elaborately decorated table is also adorned with garlands lining the perimeter, and in its centre sits a fantastic silver centerpiece given to MacNab by the citizens of Hamilton in thanks for the role he played in bringing the Great Western Railway to the area.[23] Set for the Christmas dinner to begin, twelve place settings indicate that the meal will be an "intimate" one for friends and family.[24] The interpreters explain that, although an adult celebration would have taken place on the main floor, the family would have had Christmas dinner in this room and included the children. The children, however, had to remember their manners in order "to be fit for adult society, which was generally considered to be about the age of twelve and up."[25]

Following their tour of the dining room, visitors walk into Aunt Sophia's suite, another room in which the artifactual arrangement and interpretation emphasize the MacNab family's social affluence. The interpreters explain that Aunt Sophia, following the death of MacNab's wife Mary Stuart in 1846, became the "lady of the home," responsible for instructing and caring for MacNab's daughters, Sophia and Minnie. The round table in the middle of Aunt Sophia's sitting room has been set to receive friends for tea. Pointing out evidence that Aunt Sophia is gathering things, such as used clothing, preserves, and assorted oddities, they state that these items were intended to be donated to the local parishes for Boxing Day. Such performances of charity, they explain, represent the social obligations of the upper-classes at the time. "This is one of your responsibilities," says one interpreter. "If you have money, you were expected to give charity. If you didn't, then people started talking about you, and that would be a social disgrace."[26] The interpretation, as a result, positions the MacNab family members as "good" and "generous" people, but the act of giving itself is interpreted as a social obligation, a demonstration of wealth, power, and prestige.[27]

Significantly, this interpretation is stridently connected with historical cultural constructions of the Victorian Christmas. Looking around the room, one interpreter explains that Charles Dickens's *A Christmas Carol* "[advocated] charity work for the wealthy ... Boxing Day, in 1855, had nothing to do with good bargains at the mall."[28] Set in this room, the interpretation thus serves to explain the origins of Boxing Day, linking its function to generosity and good will, both of which are promulgated in Dickens's work. At the same time, the interpreters play upon the public's inherent familiarity with the nineteenth-century work of fiction – a familiarity generated in an age of mass communications.[29]

Once visitors have seen both the public and private rooms, the interpreters call attention to the importance of functional rooms, such as the ablutions room and the flushing water closet. Given that Dundurn Castle was the only house in Hamilton to have indoor plumbing, the building, according to interpreters, stands as an example of the most modern house of its time. Characterizing these rooms as "impressive," interpreters point

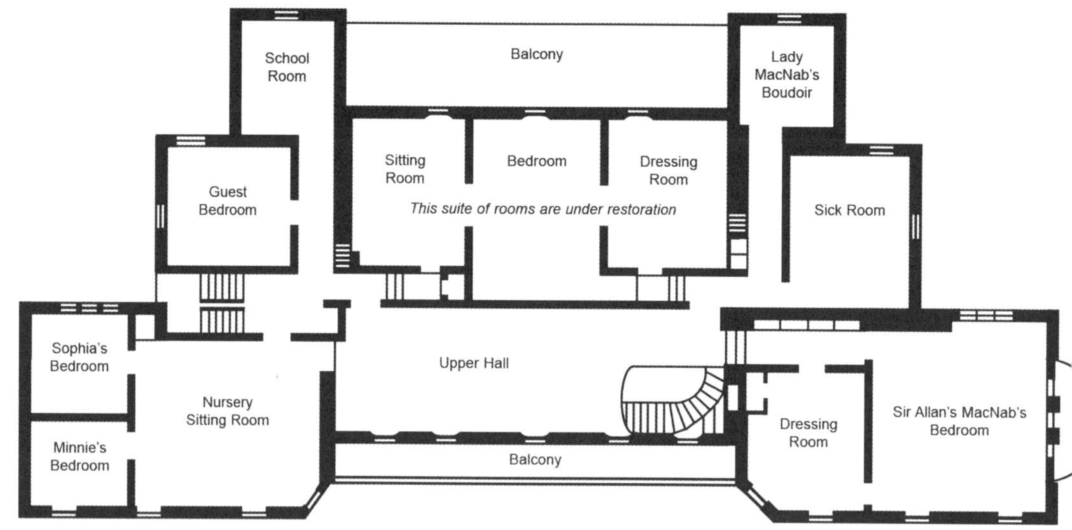

3.3 Second floor – floor plan, Dundurn Castle, 2013.

out the technology they contain, rather than their aesthetic qualities – qualities that render rooms such as the drawing and dining rooms "impressive." As a result, these rooms reflect a distinct tension between what is perceived to be an "old-fashioned" Christmas and the technology within the home that rendered it "the most modern house" of its day.[30] Progress is linked to the presence of "modern" technological advances that, by way of extension, reflect MacNab's socio-economic standing.

Upper Floor

The upper floor, which hosts bedrooms for family members and overnight guests as well as the children's nursery, is characterized as the floor on which a more informal type of Christmas celebration occurred. On this floor, it becomes most apparent that historical accuracy has been sacrificed in an attempt to present a familial Christmas celebration.

The sitting room of MacNab's two daughters, who were ages 23 and 21 in the year 1855, has been transformed into a children's nursery, complete with a children's Christmas tree with "just children's toys" arrayed around the base. The idea, as one interpreter puts it, is to show visitors "a traditional children's Christmas, so we have the children's tree set up in this room."[31] This interpretation privileges the intimacy of the immediate family's celebration.

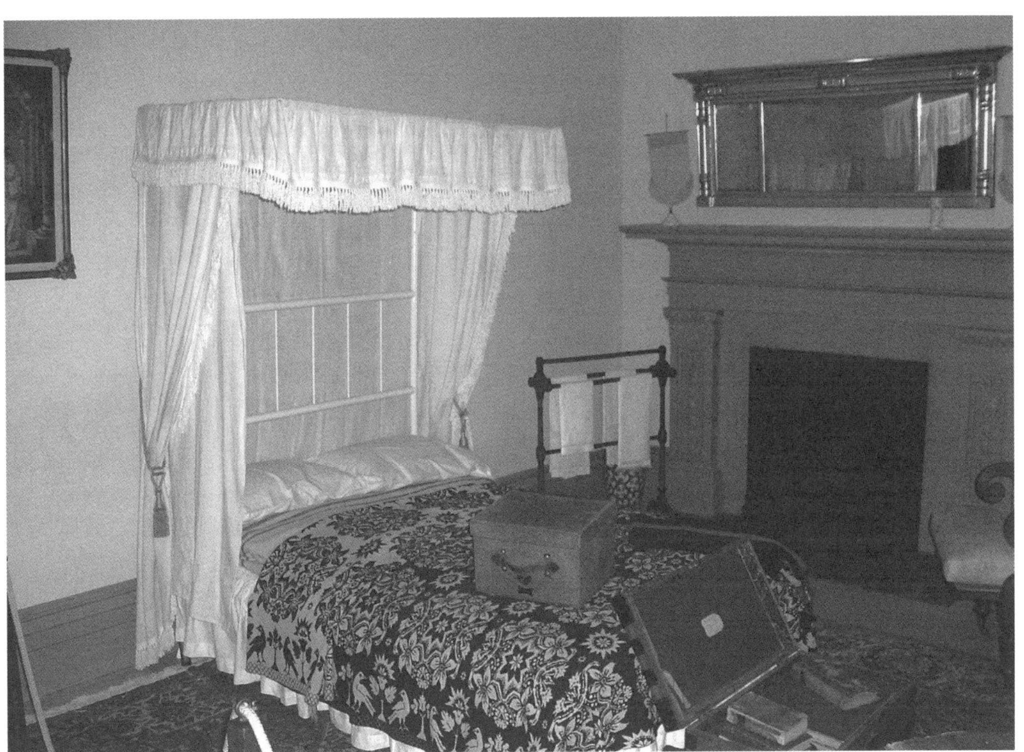

3.4 Guest Room, Dundurn Castle, 2004.

Interpreters then lead visitors from the upper hall to MacNab's bedroom and dressing room and to various guest rooms around the corner.

Consideration of the artifactual arrangement and interpretation of Lady MacNab's sickroom during the Christmas season, makes evident how history is both appealed to and transcended to reflect cultural memory. The room that functions on regular tours as Lady MacNab's sickroom – the room in which she died – has been changed and stands as a guest room, specifically for a military man, a recasting of the room's function made apparent by the brigadier pants lying on the bed.

While serving to avoid reference to an ailing beloved family member in the context of the holiday season, this representation also recalls MacNab's military affiliations, as well as his connection to Britain, for he was knighted by Queen Victoria for the military position he assumed in the Rebellion of 1837. One interpreter explains as well that MacNab's daughter, Sophia, was married in the home in 1855, and "the best man at her wedding was in the Royal Brigadiers, which is why we've got that pair of pants here. That's an army pair of pants with the red stripe on them, and the idea is that he

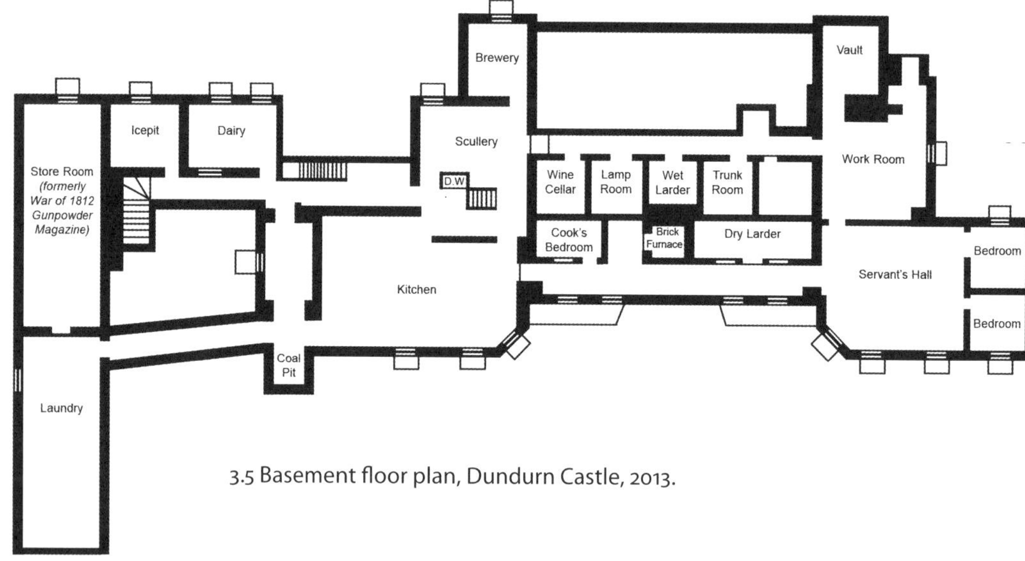

3.5 Basement floor plan, Dundurn Castle, 2013.

stayed for the Christmas season."[32] While the interpretation suppresses any associations of the loss of a loved one, based on the location of the pants/ artifact, the interpreter grounds the interpretation of the room in historical fact. At the same time, however, by referring to the interpretation of the room as an "idea," the interpreter situates the visitor as both an active viewer who "lives" history by physically gazing upon the room and a passive witness. This type of oral interpretation makes evident the degree to which interpreters encourage visitors to "suspend disbelief."[33] Thus, the performance both reinforces and undoes the illusion of the museum.

Basement

In contrast, the interpreters introduce the basement as the floor where visitors might bear witness to how the other 98 per cent of the population of the time worked and lived. (MacNab and his family were counted among the top two per cent of the population in terms of wealth.) In showing how the "other half" laboured and lived, interpreters aim to re-present the home as a representation of what Nesbitt refers to as a "microcosm of Hamilton society." They describe the lives and duties of those who worked "behind the scenes," rendering what was intended to be, in its day, invisible visible.[34] Despite such efforts, the interpreters, in the context of the Christmas tour,

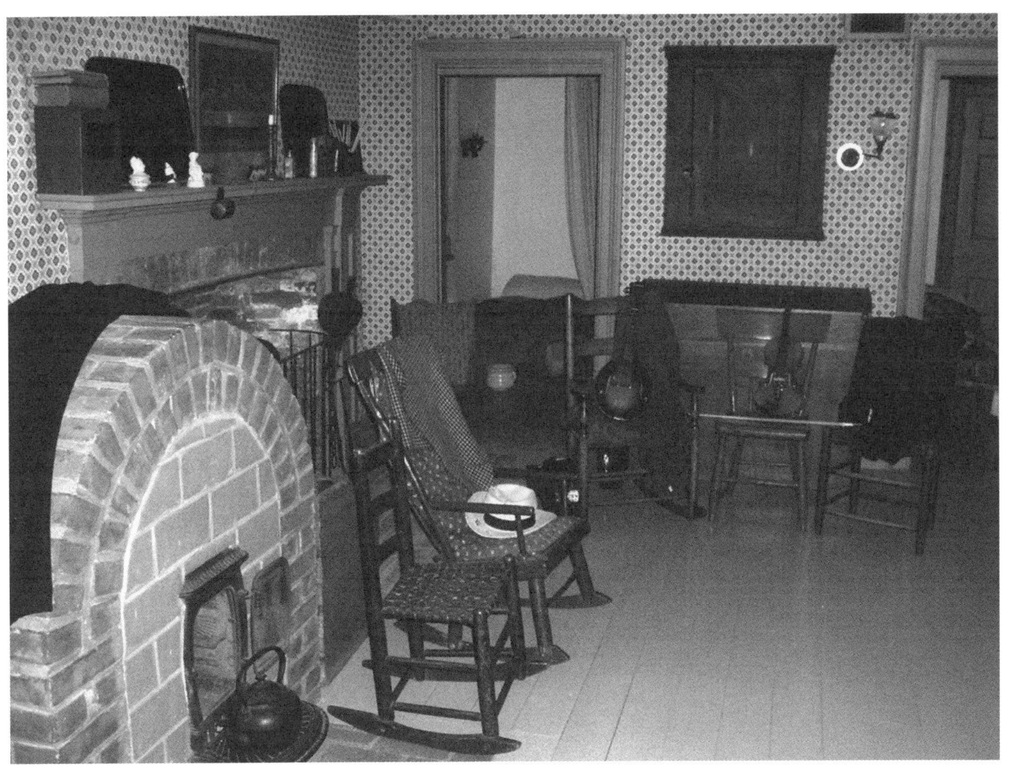

3.6 Servants' living quarters, Dundurn Castle, 2004.

routinely recall whom those on this particular floor were there to serve, thereby reinforcing in the minds of visitors the prominence of the so-called dominant "half."

The basement offers visitors an impression of the servants' employment as they tour the various spaces within which the staff performed their duties, rooms such as the dairy, ice pit, laundry, kitchen, scullery, and well room. MacNab, interpreters explain, provided his servants with the modern amenities of the time, including indoor plumbing, heating, and gas lights; he also constructed the basement so that the surroundings facilitated their relative comfort and thus ensured prolonged employment.

For instance, the servants' living quarters have wood floors and large windows, which provide natural light during the day; most one-room houses in Hamilton, could any of these servants afford one, would have had dirt floors. As a result, the interpreters explain, "In its own way, [the basement] is as luxurious as the upstairs."[35] While they do discuss the extra work that the servants were expected to perform during the festive season, what with so many extra guests presumably visiting the family, the interpretation in fact privileges MacNab. Pointing out conveniences that MacNab put in place for his servants and comparing them with other domiciles, interpreters characterize the home's patriarch as a man who treated his servants very well, thereby advancing his paternalism in terms of the charity and good will commonly bound up with both the Victorian and contemporary Christmas celebrations.

Furthermore, the factual account given of the duties servants performed suppresses the reality of the work involved; the dry, hard facts gloss over the physical labour involved and the long hours worked. According to historian Louisa Blair, for instance, nineteenth-century servants' lives were "arduous, lonely and restrictive. Working for fifteen to eighteen hours per day was the norm, and they had to do everything themselves. There was water to carry, fires to lay, water to haul, chamber pots to empty, children to care for, meals to prepare, pots to scour, silver to clean, clothes to wash, iron, and starch, candles to light and replace."[36] The context of the Victorian period must also be carefully considered in that, as Blair argues, for servants, "the Victorian equation of cleanliness with godliness was a nightmare: yet more water had to be hauled up and down the stairs, and more laundry. Homemaking turned into an academic discipline known as "domestic science," and servants now had to undergo training that went into fierce detail about their duties ... [Servants became] more involved in the arcanely complex maintenance of the home."[37] Immigrants, orphans, illegitimate children, and poverty-stricken often found themselves forced into servitude. When the demands of the serving-class lifestyle became more involved as the scope of their responsibilities increased, some sought out other types of employment, such as factory work, to escape their "domestic" hardships, both physical and emotional. In the context of Dundurn's Christmas tours, however, interpreters' recollections of the effort that goes into, for instance, preparing the festive feast seems to revere both the family unit and the home as iconic hallmarks of the celebration.[38]

In the kitchen, the male or female cook (whichever historical cook is working on that particular night), introduces visitors to the period goodies, savouries, and sweets that would have been served at the MacNab family Christmas dinner. The historical cook invites visitors to partake of both the treats and hot cider. Prior to this invitation, however, the cook identifies each of the items that visitors see laid out before them.

For the purposes of this study, what is of particular interest is the fact that the historical cooks make a point not only to mention but also to explain

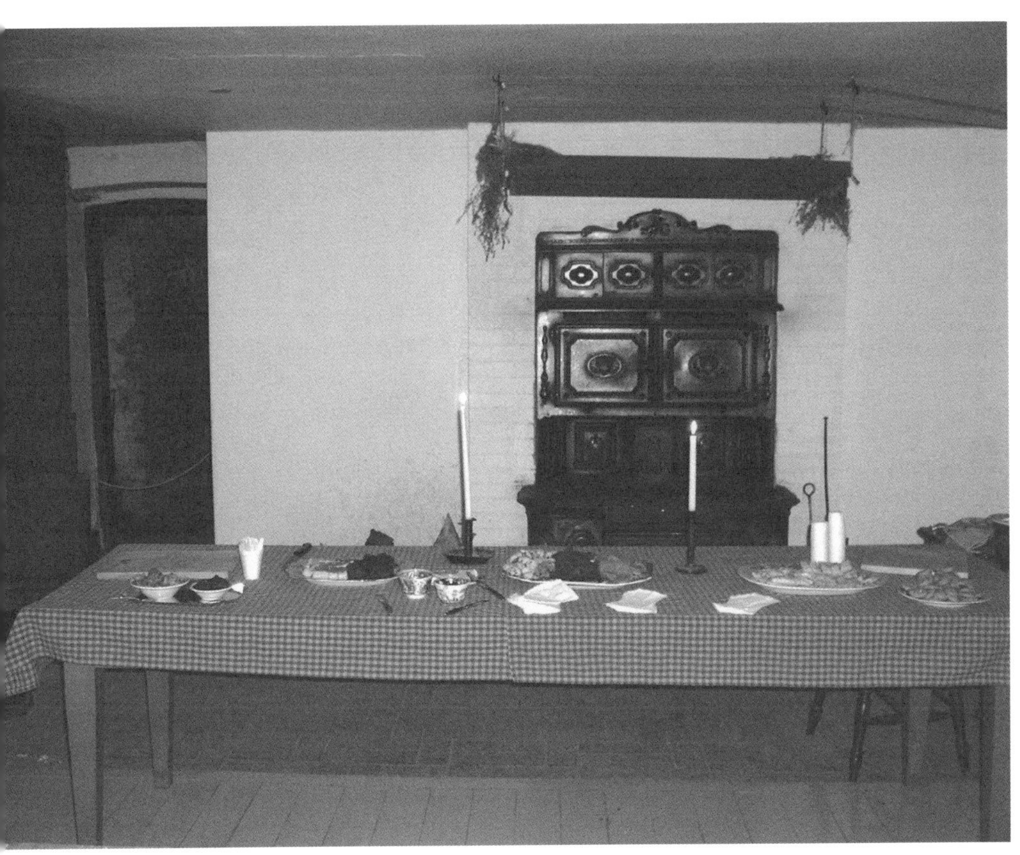

3.7 Kitchen, Dundurn Castle, 2004.

the ethnic origins of each of the foods placed on the table. Some examples include Indian chutney and Indian pickles, which allow the visitor to, in the words of one cook, "see the influence of India, sub-continental India, on British cookery," even as the cook underscores the position of India as a colonial possession in the British Empire. There are also puffed pastries with Cajun spices and cheese and some "Irish soda bread." The cooks also point out biscuits they describe as "Another Christmas Cookie." One cook explains, "These are actually American ... You can always tell if they're American recipes because they call them cookies rather than biscuits or cakes." The most interesting example, however, is the pound cake made according to a recipe taken from Catharine Parr Traill. The cooks position this particular pound cake as a "nice example of a *Canadian* recipe." They proceed to describe the ingredients in this recipe, thereby denoting its national qualities: "It's typically Canadian, in that it's very British – a British pound cake with lots of butter and lots of eggs, [and] a bit of alcohol made for flavouring. And included in this is a distinctively North American ingredient, cornmeal. So, it's a bit like all of us, I think, a hybrid version, a mix of North America and the British past."[39] The interpretation of food, therefore, also privileges a British past, the cook assuming as well, it seems, that every Canadian on the tour is of British descent, or at least should be of British descent to be Canadian.

Overall, the tour emphasizes the elite "Britishness" of the Victorian Christmas so as to suggest that contemporary Christmas activities retain or maintain specific classist or, more particularly, ethnicized qualities, characteristics further reinforced by the visitor's experience of "living history." In light of the original purpose, structure, and design of the restored domestic structure, the interpretation focuses primarily on the celebration and associated activities that may have been performed by the MacNab family, activities drawn from historical sources written primarily by British immigrants. Furthermore, the decorated atmosphere, interpretation, and associated participatory activities encourage visitors to experience a sense of what it "felt like to live back then" so that they experience "contextual departure," thereby facilitating visitors' achievement of what Ning Wang and others refer to as an "authentic experience."[40] The program thus connects the contemporary Canadian celebration to an ethnicized ideological construct, one that allows visitors to step "out of time" and seemingly gain a greater appreciation of the history of the contemporary celebration.

Given my analysis of how the site's performance ethnicizes Canadian history as distinctively British based, I would suggest that Dundurn's reanimation endeavours to naturalize "founding nations" mythologies. Therefore, in the following section, I consider the implications of such an operation in the contemporary multicultural context. This consideration is necessary, particularly in light of changes that have occurred within Canada's political framework over the course of the twentieth century. As Yasmeen Abu-Laban and Christina Gabriel explain, in the nineteenth and early twentieth centuries, the policies of the Canadian state promoted a "two nations" vision – one that characterized and thus privileged the British and French as "founding peoples."[41] In the 1970s, however, multiculturalism emerged as a "uniquely Canadian policy, a new approach to nation-building." In granting federal recognition to Canadians who were not of British, French, or Aboriginal descent, it sought to reconfigure ideas and ideals of Canadian identity and, subsequent to that, include ethnocultural minorities.[42] As a result, the relationship between present-day social, economic, and political realities in Canada and national mythologies – particularly those espoused in state-sanctioned house museums – is complex, tenuous, and strained.[43] In light of this tension, I explore the implications of national mythologies put forth in Dundurn's Christmas program that re-construct the past as distinctly separate from the present.[44] The sustained projection of such ethnicized constructions, I suggest, signals the tense negotiation of past and present, history and memory, and ethnicity and diversity in not only Canada's historical homes but also, more broadly, in the nation's heritage industry.

❦

Dundurn Castle's Victorian Christmas tour encourages visitors to associate the contemporary celebration with a distinctively aristocratic British one and, subsequent to that, identifies Canadian history in general with elite British colonial culture. How do then such representations of the nation's past operate in Canada, a state with a federal multiculturalism policy that has fostered the popular idea among Canadians that ethnic diversity is a national virtue? Given Dundurn's dual function as a house museum and national historic site – a state-sanctioned institution – one might suggest that, upon reanimation, it reproduces what scholars, Eva Mackey among them, refer to as the unmarked whiteness of a core "*Canadian*-Canadian identity" in the face of the Canadian state's cultural policy.[45]

Canada's multiculturalism policy, as sociologist Richard Day explains, is symbolically dependent on the fantasy of national unity.[46] In the 1960s, several factors, including the post-Second World War decline of the British Empire, the perceived threat of American cultural imperialism, and the federal government's effort to expand Canada's labour force with non-European immigrants led politicians to posit that the cultural and, by extension, symbolic character of Canadian institutions needed to be renewed and thus redefined.[47] Accordingly, on 8 October 1971, the day the White Paper on Multiculturalism was released, the Canadian government officially adopted a multiculturalism policy, and then in 1988, adopted the Multiculturalism Act, which included establishing Canada's two official languages. The multiculturalism policy, which is understood on a popular level as "unity-in-diversity," positions Canada's national culture as being open-ended and provisional.[48] As a result, the policy's rhetoric, as Day puts it, "says that

Canada is attempting to become, not a nation-state, but a self-consciously multinational state, in which all nations can seek their enjoyment in possession of a national Thing."[49]

While the policy aims to set Canadian identity up as that based on a seemingly universalized national identity, this flexibility in fact legitimizes ambiguity and, in doing so, facilitates the implementation of hegemonic processes that define and construct a core culture. Canada's multiculturalism policy, as Mackey explains, functions as part of a nation-building exercise, a hegemonic process based on Western principles of progress, liberty, tolerance, equality, reason, and human rights. "In this framework," Mackey writes, "the *construction* of culture and difference, and not simply its erasure, is an integral part of the flexible Western project, practices and procedures."[50] As she puts it, "power is not essentially repressive, but rather constructive and constitutive."[51] The policy allows those defined as "real" or "true" Canadians to define the limits of difference. While multiculturalism, as official state policy, promises civil, legal, political, and socioeconomic rights and equality to all, regardless of a citizen's country of origin or distinguishing ethnic traits, multiple cultures become subordinate, and the unmarked core remains dominant. Liberal values and strategies that prioritize inclusion are fundamental elements in designs aimed at sustaining dominant power and buttressing Western cultural hegemony. Evidence of the hegemonic processes bound up in Canada's multiculturalism policy can be found in the Canadian Multiculturalism Act.[52] Through its employment of ethnicity as a broad and all-encompassing political concept, as opposed to a referent to a specific group(s), to mark or distinguish Canadian identity, the bill nullifies ethnicity and the minority status of ethnic groups through its normalizing rhetoric.[53] "Defining the ethnic subject by normalizing it," Smaro Kamboureli writes, "stresses those elements of its subjecthood that conform to 'Canadianness' rather than those about which it begs to differ." Ethnicity becomes an "all-embracing" concept characterizing Canada and attests to the diversity that "Canada" has come to signify.[54]

But if cultural diversity has become a national signifier, biculturalism in terms of language and multiculturalism in terms of culture coexist as contradictory institutions whose viability is contingent upon nullifying each other.[55] Because the multiculturalism policy is located within a bilingual framework, "only the collective rights of Canada's two founding peoples," Evelyn Kallen explains, "have been constitutionally secured."[56] English and

French function as Canada's "official" languages, an epithet that is synonymous with legal endorsement.[57] Furthermore, because the use of these languages in governmental ministries, departments, programs, and services follows as a result of state legislation, a citizen's access to and engagement in federal bureaucracy – for example, the judicial system – is contingent on his or her mastery of what Kamboureli calls the "mother tongues of the two 'heritage' groups."[58] Moreover, as proponents of multiculturalism declare, language and culture are indivisible; multiculturalism, as a result, is "meaningless without multilingualism."[59]

The public sphere is thus envisaged as an "Anglo or Franco cultural monolith" where participation in public institutions is based on acculturation to established bi-cultural practices, conventions, and so-called norms.[60] It is only in the private sphere that multiculturalism affords minority Canadians any kind of social legitimization in terms of collective rights. In their private lives, peoples of ethnic minorities are free to preserve and perform their respective cultural heritage, but there is no provision of governmental institutions that allows them to convey their cultural traditions to future generations. So, on the one hand, the policy legitimates the right of ethnocultural communities to preserve and maintain their difference; on the other hand, it assigns no political or legislative rights to those ethnicities, as such.[61] Multiculturalism thus "grants ethnicity subjectivity ... without ... agency."[62] What is more, as Tony Bennett explains, multiculturalism "constructs and organizes cultural diversity from a position of whiteness" to simultaneously manage and promote cultural diversity as a "national possession, a sign of its own tolerance and virtue."[63] What role then do cultural institutions that allow Canadians to "live history" play in this context?

Living history practitioners conventionally select and interpret specific objects and facts to construct representations of the past that are marketable. Because practitioners determine how these institutions might simultaneously represent and perform particular aspects of Canadian history, more often than not such sites enshrine the values, perceptions, and priorities of the dominant culture. As a result, such culturally determined representations, as Erna Macleod aptly puts it, "function in a hegemonic way to define the boundaries of national unity."[64] Accordingly, it might be suggested that, when interpreters reanimate Dundurn Castle in the guise of a Victorian Christmas celebration, the site functions as a hegemonic cultural tool that not only performs but also entrenches the values of Canada's dominant culture. To push the point further, I would argue that the program stands as an example of what historian Anthony Smith calls the "territorialization of memory."

Based on his definition of nationalism as a type of public religion that aims to cultivate a decisive sense of unity among citizens through the designation and veneration of formative myths, symbols, and traditions, Smith contends that nationalism consistently involves a struggle for control, more specifically for control of and over land.[65] The cultivation of nationalism thus requires the state's land be reconceptualized as a bonded community.[66] In cultivating a distinctly identifiable patrimony, such requirements help to not only determine but also to shape communal memories and experiences.[67] The practice of identifying land with community – achieved by attaching ancestral memories to territory – functions so as to mobilize and consequently privilege particular ethnic collectivities.[68] Smith's analysis suggests that memories dedicated to the testament of ethnic survival in a national context have not always existed but are deliberately cultivated or contrived. Likewise, as Alan Gordon explains, "Public history constructs a narrative of the past in support of the present. Public memory, in turn, relies on public history, but it conscripts aspects of pubic history, further enshrining them in defence of present power relationships ... in order to aid the ongoing negotiation of hegemonic control."[69]

In the case of the Dundurn's Christmas Evening Tour, it could be argued that the site reproduces what Mackey, Kallen, and Macleod have identified as core Canadianism. What is more, the work of Smith and Gordon reveals how, because the program essentializes Canadian history as being distinctively British-based, the Christmas Evening Tour represents the "territorialization of memory." While the house functions as a venue or historical artifact that contains and, by extension, authorizes the interpretive performance, interpreters manage various aspects of the site itself, including the decorated period rooms, artifactual arrangements, and oral interpretation, to not only illustrate but also emphasize the "Britishness" of the historic festive season. In other words, the site has been reanimated in such a way – through historical research, decorative schemas, artifactual arrangements and live interpretation – so that this home's fictionalized, performative representation conjures up what appear to be "memories" attesting to ethnic survival. As a result, one might suggest that Dundurn, in the context of the Christmas program, concretizes, projects, and naturalizes a given hegemonic "social" – one that seemingly upholds the primacy of "founding nations" mythologies in Canada.[70] Also, the fact that, over the last four decades, this particular tour is not only the museum's longest running but also most popular "special event" program makes evident the degree to which this type of performance appeals to members of the Hamilton community. Year after year it seems, they corral their loved ones into cars, vans, and suvs and brave the treacherous conditions of the region's serpentine roads surrounding the bay on which Dundurn is located, all ostensibly in the hopes of achieving a "contextual departure" from the present.

PART TWO

Personalizing Canadian Nationalism: Cartier House, Montreal, QC

CHAPTER FOUR

Tactical Pacts: Parks Canada, the Québécois, and Confederation

House museums developed to showcase the lifestyles of politicians active in the Confederation period indicate the desire of heritage practitioners to promote a collective appreciation of Canada's past, particularly in the case of those located in Quebec. As was argued in the previous section, the house sets the stage for a fictionalized performance of the past, a version ultimately informed by its domestic character. Curators and interpreters develop programs encouraging visitors to identify with particular values, such as the primacy of family ties and communal bonds and the relevance of the past in the present. Such underpinnings can be seen in the staging of the Sir George-Étienne Cartier National Historic Site, a museum composed of two adjoining homes formerly owned by Cartier, one of the "Fathers of Confederation" who, as attorney general of Lower Canada (1858–62), shared leadership of the United Canadas with John A. Macdonald.

Taking into account the site's location in Montreal, Quebec, a major urban centre with a large souverainiste constituency, and the fact that it is owned and operated by the federal agency Parks Canada, I use this case study to explore how cultural administrators work to make the museum appealing and thus marketable to the local populace. In the early 1980s, while planning the site's development, Parks Canada determined that site's "special target group" would be the Montreal public and so developed a "dual approach" to expose visitors to "both the man and the time in which he lived."[1] The agency turned the east house into a visitors' centre that contains object-based exhibitions and text panels illustrating various socio-political changes that Cartier helped bring about; in contrast, the west house was restored so that interpreters might guide visitors through the period rooms and evoke the environment in which Cartier lived. The site is arranged so that it acknowledges Cartier's political achievements but ultimately, upon reanimation, focuses on the lifestyle of Montreal's upper-middle class.

Because nationalist agendas put forward by the Québécois in the latter half of the twentieth-century arguably stimulated the federal government's institutionalization of the Cartier House, I suggest that the federal government reconstituted the homes to reinvigorate the authority of federal heritage policies and, by extension, the Canadian national project. For example, in the early 1960s, Quebec's Quiet Revolution transformed the provincial government into a bureaucratic welfare-state, allowing it to, among other things, implement heritage legislation and develop historic sites that would inspire a distinctly Québécois nationalism.[2] This particular nationalist ideology sought to eradicate any pejorative implications of the term French-Canadian – with its connotations of cultural minority within the Canadian federation – and distinguish the Québécois as a territorial majority living within a specific geographic domain.[3] Moreover, the legislation pitted Quebec's heritage, as Richard Handler puts it, "in competition" with the federal government's national policies and historic sites.[4] Significantly, in 1964, the federal government mounted a program to honour those pronounced to be "Fathers of Confederation," which resulted in the purchase, commemorative designation, and restoration of Cartier's Montreal residences. The monumentalization of the Cartier House, initiated in the wake of the Quiet Revolution, indicates the degree to which the federal government responded to the energies and actions of the Québécois.[5] Given that the federal government developed the site so that it might re-deploy particular historical narratives, it ultimately aims to venerate not only a distinctly French-Canadian identity but also Canada's "founding nations" mythologies.

Parks Canada employees have arranged the site so that the east house operates as the visitors' centre containing a plethora of exhibitions detailing the original owner's political achievements, and the west house, with its living history format, serves as a "contextual departure" from the present for people residing in Quebec. How interpreters work to "depoliticize" the experiential atmosphere of this house museum is particularly interesting.[6] As historian Michael Kammen explains, heritage practitioners often minimize or suppress contentious political issues so that portrayals of the past might help unite the citizenry.[7] This impulse becomes evident with the Cartier House where the past is represented so as to selectively remember (or forget) particular historical figures or events in order to urge Montrealers to not just "live" but "remember" history as personal experience[8] and to foster a collective sense of cultural history.[9] More specifically, I explore how interpreters encourage members of the local populace to experience the lifestyle of Montreal's mid-nineteenth century bourgeoisie within the museumified dwelling so that their engagement with and memories of the site might cause them to feel connected to the larger community of the nation itself. In short, this section investigates how Parks Canada manages the homes so that the reanimation of Cartier's "home" life might perpetuate the authority of Canada's national project.

Historic monuments typically commemorate the ideologies of those who develop them.[10] In examining how the priorities of the federal government informed Parks Canada's museumification of Cartier's former homes, this chapter concentrates on three specific phases of the site's development and, subsequent to that, aspects of each phase that aided in the determination of both the site's design and its current function as a national historic institution. Over the course of their existence, Cartier's houses functioned as private residences and celebratory monuments before becoming the current state-sanctioned heritage site offering educational and theme-based Noël victorien/Victorian Christmas tours. Part I of this chapter deals with the history of the building and considers how Sir George-Étienne Cartier's ownership of the two Neoclassical London-style townhouses broadcast his cultural preferences, specifically his "anglophilism," thereby challenging his self-professed political role as champion of a working-class French-Canadian constituency.[11] Part II considers the site's provenance and institutional history and how the federal government came to identify Cartier as a "Father of Confederation" in the 1960s and subsequently designate his houses as being of "national historical importance."[12] Part III concerns the museum's institutionalization. I examine how Parks Canada determined that the site showcases the themes "Cartier the politician" and "Cartier the

Montrealer, a representative of the *bourgeoisie* of his era."[13] For example, in June 1982, two years after the first referendum in which the motion to grant Quebec sovereignty was defeated by a margin of 59.6 to 44.4 per cent,[14] Parks Canada mounted a public consultation program to help decide how it might "promote the harmonious integration of the historic [site] into its environment." Taking into account concerns expressed by Montrealers, historians, and local and provincial heritage organizations, the agency resolved to "avoid any form [of] political partisanship."[15] I thus explore how government workers have organized the houses so that the site recognizes Cartier's political career while reanimating a particular lifestyle so as to "depoliticize" the past. Such efforts make evident ways in which nationalist ideologies not only compel the commemoration of history but also shape the character of historic monuments. And finally, bearing in mind such tense negotiations, I examine how the museum is employed as a pedagogical instrument shaped by both ideological and market-driven concerns.

I

Each townhouse initially functioned as Cartier's familial residence. He purchased the east house as he embarked on the fulfillment of his political ambitions and the adjacent house years later – a sign of his achievements in that domain and his resulting social prominence.[16] In February 1848, lawyer and aspiring politician George-Étienne Cartier purchased the first of two semi-detached houses on Rue Notre Dame at the corner of Rue Berri.[17] His decision to reside in Montreal makes evident the extent of his determination to enter politics, given that the city, as of 1844, was the Canadian capital and seat of government at the time.[18] Two months later he was elected as a member of the United Canadas assembly.[19] In 1855, Cartier rented his house out so that he could live and work in Quebec City when the Canadian Parliament relocated there.[20] His political career reached its highest point when he became Attorney General of Lower Canada (1858–62), sharing leadership of the country with John A. Macdonald. In June 1862, he returned to Montreal and bought the residence adjoining the house he had rented earlier.[21] His family lived in the west house from 1862 until 1871, during which time Cartier travelled extensively, taking part in key political events like the Charlottetown Conference (1–9 September 1864) and the Quebec Conference (10 October 1864), and helping to bring the disparate colonies together within a unified federal state. In the winter of 1866–67,

Cartier, along with other colonial delegates, travelled to London and met with the British House of Commons. Together, the delegation and the House refined the Quebec Resolutions and produced what became known as the British North America Act. On 1 July 1867, the Dominion of Canada came into being and Confederation went into effect.[22]

Cartier's choice of Neoclassical London-style townhouse residences reveals his desire to proclaim not only his political successes but also his class-standing as a member of the French-Canadian bourgeoisie. While he was a political representative of French Canada's working-class constituency, Cartier also sought to portray himself as a "confirmed anglophile who ... turned to London for his clothes, his status symbols, and his ideology." Historian Brian Young explains further, writing, "Cartier and many of his [French-Canadian *bourgeoisie*] peers ... sought legitimacy and security in British values and institutions ... They used 'Britishness' to ... guarantee their social position."[23] As a result, they looked to purchase residences that might act, by virtue of their architectural style, as status symbols.[24] To accommodate these desires, architects and builders often looked to building designs in places like London and used smooth-finished grey stone from Montreal and the surrounding areas to produce houses with "a sober classical style," characteristics that are hallmarks of the British Neoclassical style.[25] In terms of Cartier's houses, both erected in 1837, the builders used cut stone to build flat, linear exterior walls to enhance the visual symmetry and regularity of each house; the Neoclassical façade of both houses thus replicated the appearance of a nineteenth-century London-style townhouse.[26] The structural aspects of Cartier's homes, however, also denote "des influences françaises" or, more particularly, measures put in place to accommodate urban living conditions in Quebec.[27] For example, both houses border the public walkway alongside the street as the lot size would not allow for the integration of an English-style courtyard.[28] Following Cartier's death in 1873, the family retained ownership of both houses up until 1951. In 1893, the city of Montreal extended the width of Rue Berri, which required that the size of the east house be reduced three metres. As a result, structural changes were made to the house that not only altered its size and façade, but also required that a new roof be installed on both houses; builders replaced the pitched, tin plate roof with a Second Empire style curb roof or "French roof."[29] Ensuing social and political developments would bring about more changes in the houses' purpose, structure, and design.

II

In the 1960s, nation-building frameworks developed on the provincial and national levels encouraged both groups to commemorate their respective pasts. This impulse not only inspired but also helped shape the second stage in the house's development since the residences had come to be venerated as monuments of Canada's past. At the outset of the decade, the push by Francophone Québécois against the colonized aspects of governance and identity came to be known as Quebec's Quiet Revolution.[30] People worked to empower and subsequently "modernize" Quebec's government so as to advance a more secularized, urbanized Québécois identity, one that promoted a "more civic, territorially-based nationalism."[31] Proponents of the Quiet Revolution brought about the establishment of Quebec's Ministry of Education, which transferred control of mass education from the church to the state, and the creation of Hydro-Québec, which allowed the state to manage electricity production. It also saw the development of the Charter of the French Language (1977), otherwise known as Bill 101, which designated Quebec a "French-language society" so that Francophone Québécois constituted the territorial majority.[32] The Quiet Revolution also inspired the creation of a provincial Ministère des Affaires culturelle (1961), a governmental bureaucracy that classified, restored, and maintained Quebec's heritage properties and, in doing so, developed historic sites that would inspire Québécois nationalism.[33] Notably, it was in this particular decade that the Canadian federal government also mounted commemorative programs designed, according to Richard Handler, to assert "its own nationalism in response to the claims of Quebec."[34]

In the wake of the Quiet Revolution, the federal government decided to mount a series of programs designed to honour those it determined to be "eminent Canadians," seemingly in order to revive the primacy of Canadian nationalism.[35] Such endeavours demonstrate that commemorative activities are, as historian John Gillis explains, "by definition social and political ... [and] involve the coordination of individual and group memories, whose results may appear consensual when they are in fact the product of processes of intense contest [and] struggle."[36] Significantly, the coordination of public memories within heritage sites typically requires modifying classifications of historical figures such as Sir George-Étienne Cartier. For example, in May 1959, Canadian historian Donald Creighton submitted what he considered to be an "official and correct" list of "Fathers of Confederation" to Canada's

Historic Sites and Monuments Board so that it would be held in trust by the Public Archives of Canada (now Library and Archives Canada).[37] Board members then turned their attention to Cartier's Montreal residences. In October 1964, as part of a developing federal policy to commemorate the Fathers of Confederation, the Board designated Cartier's houses as being of "national historical importance."[38] Moreover, Board members moved that the Canadian government purchase and restore both houses so that they might operate as a national historic site.[39] Notably that same year, the Quebec Ministère des Affaires culturelle, along with City of Montreal, granted "historic district status" for the region in which Cartier's houses were located, formally establishing the historic district of Vieux Montréal/Old Montreal.[40] In June 1973, Parks Canada, charged with the Board's 1964 recommendation, purchased the houses and instituted a research program devoted to Cartier to "learn more about the times, life and work of this illustrious figure and the features of his Montreal residences."[41]

III

In the early 1980s, Parks Canada began exploring how it might turn the houses into a museum, which activated the third stage in the residences' development – their incarnation as a national historic site. Taking into account the socio-political strain roused by Quebec's 1980 referendum campaign and the federal government's subsequent advancement of the 1982 Constitution Act – viewed by the Québécois as the government's legislative obfuscation of Canada's "constituent duality"[42] – Parks Canada proposed in May 1982 to develop the site so that visitors might "become acquainted with Sir George-Étienne Cartier and ... his contribution to Canadian political life."[43] The agency went on in its development concept to suggest that the site use "exhibitions and furnishings" to explore two primary aspects of the original owner's life, "Cartier the politician and legislator, the statesman and architect of Confederation" and "Cartier the Montrealer, a representative of the *bourgeoisie* of his era."[44] Because the east house's façade had been shortened by three metres in 1893, the agency determined that it would be "almost impossible to restore it to its original state" and so recommended that it be rehabilitated and set up to house a series of thematic exhibitions on both the ground and first floors that traced Cartier's political career and achievements.[45] As far as the west house was concerned, Parks Canada suggested that, because "it would be almost impossible to create an understanding of Cartier 'the man' without evoking the environment in which he lived ... [it was advisable] to decorate and furnish various rooms in the 'west house' according to the style of the era."[46] Moreover, the agency stated that the interpretive programs would be "aimed particularly at the Montreal public, considered to be the park's special target group"[47] and would show Montrealers that Confederation represented "the system which still shapes our political institutions." By portraying the lifestyle of the mid-nineteenth century Montreal bourgeoisie, the agency also hoped to "provide visitors with a more concrete means of visualizing various facets of the past."[48]

The federal government advanced the Constitution Act (1982) to confirm Canada's existence as a political federation, but the Québécois perceived this legislation as evidence of the Canadian government's desire to eclipse the "two founding nations" ideal.[49] The Constitution Act, signed into law by Queen Elizabeth II on 17 April 1982, formally transferred the control of Canada's constitution from British Parliamentary jurisdiction to the Canadian government. The Act consisted of the renamed British North America Act, the Charter of Rights and Freedoms, and an amending formula, which allowed the federal government to make changes to the constitution so long as the changes met with the approval of Parliament and seven provinces representing a combined total of 50 per cent of the Canadian population; because previous legislation required the unanimous consent of all provinces, the 1982 Act effectively stripped individual provinces, such as Quebec, of their right to veto.[50] On the day the Act was signed, the Québécois demonstrated their opposition in various ways. The Quebec government proclaimed its opposition to the Act by flying the provincial flag at half-mast on all government buildings, while in Montreal over 25,000 people marched down the streets in protest.[51]

One month after the publication of the agency's "development concept," Parks Canada mounted a public consultation program to make the Montreal public aware of the federal agency's objectives. This disclosure demonstrates the extent to which Parks aimed to work with and ostensibly for the Quebec public, involving them in the formative stages of the museumification project. Up until the 1950s, Historic Sites and Monuments Board of Canada (hereafter HSMBC) members "freely" selected sites, events, and individuals for designation "without public consultation or political influence."[52] Following the approval of the 1953 HSMBC Act, however, the legislation required the Board submit nominations to the federal Minister of the Environment who would, in turn, approve the selection. The explosion of "state-produced national sentiment" propelled by centennial celebrations revealed to Board members and Parks Canada how citizens' interests might be stimulated and included in the designation and museumification process.[53] For instance, Dundurn's restoration came about by the city's application to the National Centennial Projects Act and subsequently was co-funded by all three levels of government as Hamilton's centennial project. The 1960s restoration of the Fortress of Louisbourg, Nova Scotia was another significant Parks project. In the early to mid-1980s, Parks made a pointed effort to tap into citizens' historical consciousness, concerns, and priorities, holding public consultations as part of their sites' development process, a step that went on to become part of the agency's planning procedures and operating policies that were codified and published in 1994.[54] According to David Neufeld, during the early 1980s, both Parks Canada and HSMBC became increasingly cognizant of the "cultural imbalance of the country's national historic sites," recommending consultations be held with First Nations people to determine "their interest in the commemoration of their history."[55] As a result, the Cartier House consultation represents a formative step in determining the federal government's place and reception, following the decades that witnessed the formulation and proliferation of a distinctly secularized, urbanized Québécois identity.

The public consultation program allowed the public to make recommendations concerning the site's development.[56] On the evenings of 16 and 17 June 1982, Parks Canada presented the scope of the project to various parties, including interested members of the Montreal populace, historians and local heritage agencies, as well as historical societies.[57] The agency stated that it intended to develop the site in order to "provide visitors with an opportunity to become acquainted with Sir George-Étienne Cartier and to highlight his contribution to Canadian political life," an approach that would be "aimed particularly at the Montreal public."[58] Members of La Fédération des sociétés d'histoire du Québec pointed out that recent developments in Canada's political framework might require that Parks Canada take a more nuanced approach in its interpretation so as to appeal to the local citizenry. More specifically, according to the Fédération, because the federal government had patriated Canada's constitution earlier that year, Parks Canada's proposal to commemorate Cartier as a "Father of Confederation" could be perceived as a "political gesture," one that Montrealers might oppose. It advised Parks Canada that the site's interpretation "should go beyond the political element" to attract visitors, advising that "the interpretation center should not be too oriented to the man, and thus too specialized. The period and the political, economic, social, cultural and religious conditions should be emphasized to interest a greater group of people."[59] Likewise, historian Brian Young recommended that "the site should emphasize [Cartier's] contribution to Montreal, Quebec and Canadian society rather than to 'Canadian political life.'"[60]

The public consultation program encouraged Parks Canada to take into account the contemporary socio-political context so that it provided a "more rounded" representation of the historical figure within the site.[61] Various participants, including members of the public, La Fédération des sociétés d'histoire du Québec, and historians like Brian Young, advocated that the agency avoid, to use Parks Canada's term, "hero-worship." The agency therefore stated that it would design the site so as to "go beyond the political element ... [and] situate Cartier in relation to his time and social environment."[62] In other words, it determined that, in order to avoid allusions to "political partisanship" or the presentation of Cartier through what might be perceived as a "tendentious prism," it would follow "the essence of historical analysis as it is practiced today."[63] Parks Canada further explained, "More and more, historians are developing the reflex, a good one in our opinion, of analyzing people or events in relation to their economic, social, cultural and political environment, making them more rounded. Studies done by Parks Canada on George-Étienne Cartier reflect this 'whole' view, which will orient the communications we present."[64]

As a result, when the Sir George-Étienne Cartier National Historic Site of Canada officially opened to the public in 1985, the agency developed both the houses and the commemorative plaque text so that the museum might give people "an opportunity to discover Cartier and his work, life in Montreal in his era, and the habits and customs of the time."[65] Significantly, the original plaque, installed by the HSMBC in 1985, is no longer extant, having been stolen in 2006. The original 1985 plaque's text began by calling the visitor's attention to the building, rather than the owner – as was the case with both Dundurn plaques. The Board's sensitivity of and to the provincial context (Quebec is the only province where the majority of inhabitants claim French as their first language[66]) can be seen in the order of languages on the plaque – the French text is stacked upon the English. In the case of Dundurn, the opposite is true.

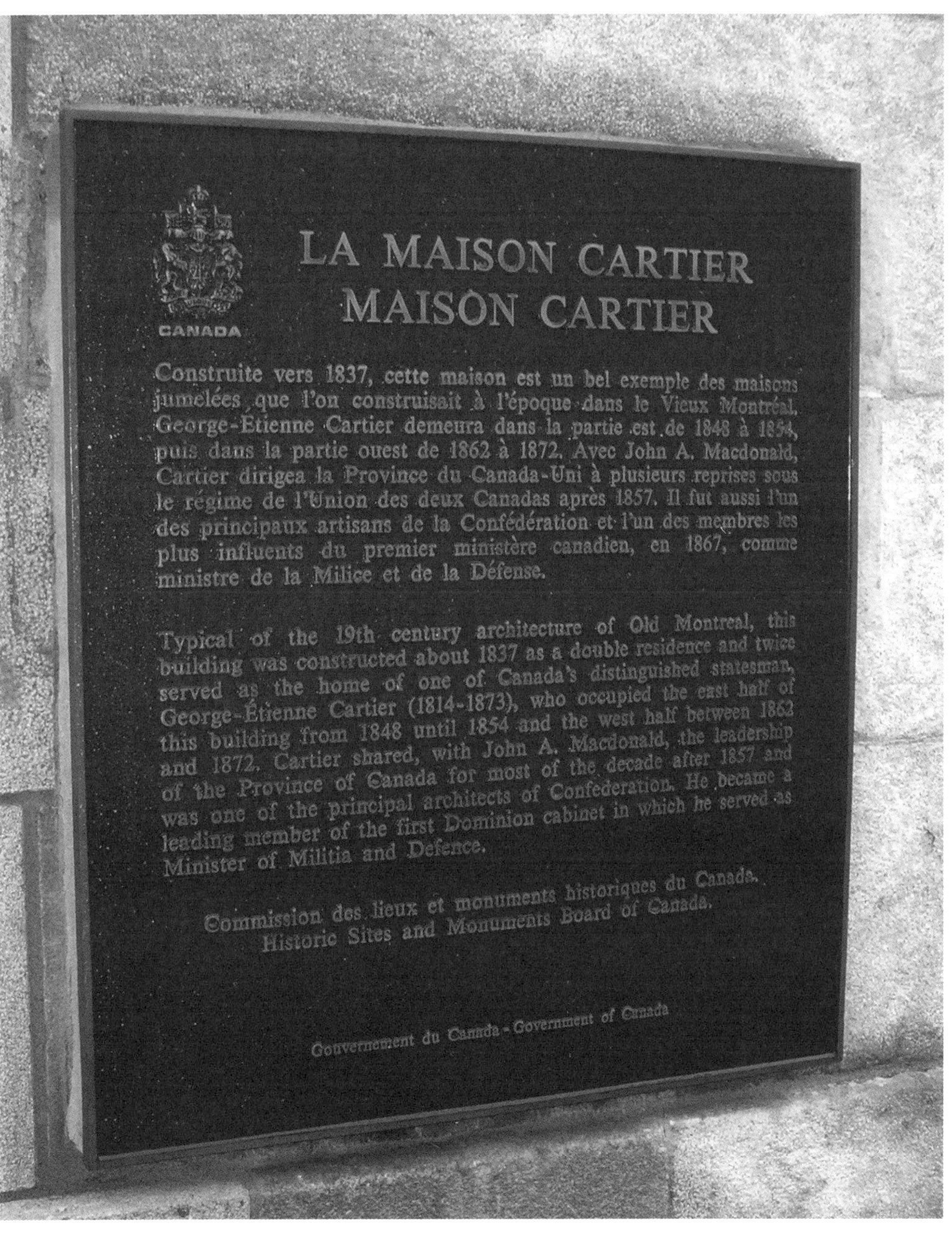

4.1 Historic Sites and Monuments Board, La Maison Cartier/Maison Cartier Plaque, circa 2005.

Moreover, neither text is a direct translation of the other, although both French and English texts articulate the pertinent dates and factual information in their respective languages, thereby upholding the principle of linguistic equality embedded in the Official Languages in Act (1969). Both function as Canada's "official languages," an epithet that is synonymous with legal endorsement and used in federal ministries, departments, programs, and, in this case, commemorations.[67]

Along with the distinctive maroon and gold coloured bronze design, the bilingual yet independently written texts deliberately mark the plaque – and by extension the museum – as being produced and managed by a federal agency. Both texts characterize the architectural structure as "un bel example des maisons jumelées … dans le Vieux Montréal" or "typical." Both paragraphs proceed to cite the dates of Cartier's occupation in each home and finally, his most prominent or well-known political positions: sharing leadership of the Province of Canada with John A. MacDonald in the late 1850s, one of the "principaux artisans de la Confédération/principle architects of Confederation," and his position as the Minister of Militia and Defense. In 2006, the bronze plaque – along with seven other HSMBC plaques from Old Montreal – was stolen and, four years later, replaced by a temporary aluminum one (marked as such) and notably redesigned so that the French and English paragraphs sit alongside each other.

By April 2006, the Montreal police recorded 25 of 85 historical markers in Old Montreal had gone missing, two dozen of which installed by both the municipal and provincial governments. According to Giles Morel, director of the local heritage group Bureau de promotion et de mise en valeur du Vieux Montréal, the thieves were well organized in their planned attacks, given the measures in place to anchor the plaques.[68] Other HSMBC monuments stolen include those identifying the Church of St Leon de Westmount in Westmount, one honouring one of Montreal's founders Jeanne Mance, and another commemorating René-Robert Cavalier, the seventeenth-century French explorer. While Morel refused to "speculate" as to what motivated the thefts, unnamed sources in the newspaper coverage suggested that the brass plaques might have been taken given their worth as "scrap metal." Others suggested "it might be the work of an anarchist doing it for kicks, or the doings of a deranged collector."[69] Despite any conclusive findings to date, the thefts underscore the contentious nature of heritage in Montreal, be it undertaken by the city, province, or state. Moreover, Parks Canada's 2006 declaration to replace this plaque has yet to

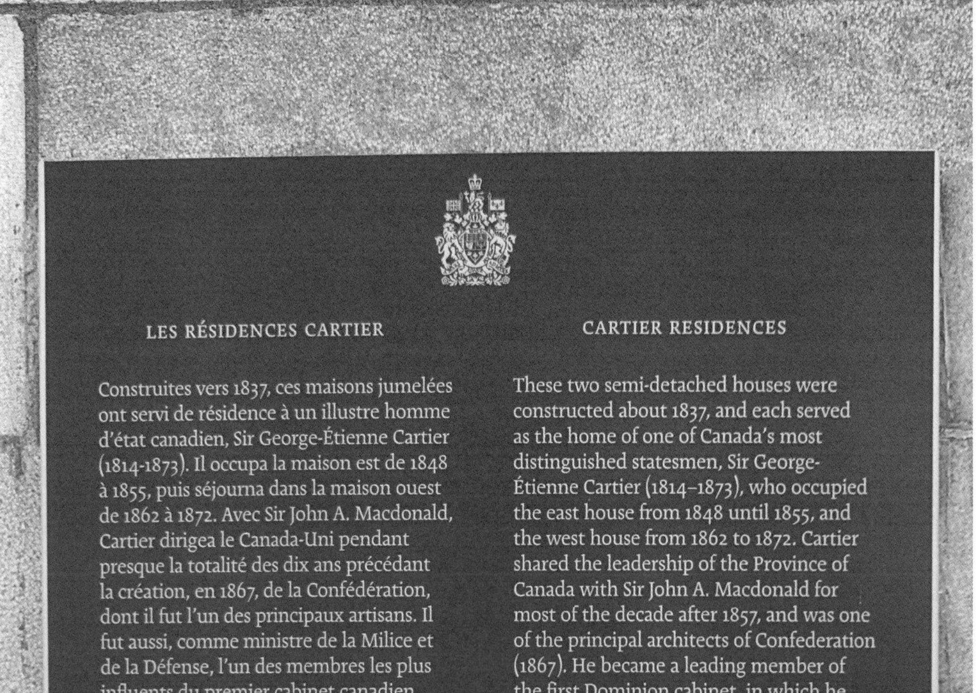

4.2 Historic Sites and Monuments Board. La Maison Cartier/Maison Cartier Plaque, 2014.

be realized as of 2014. Finally, no HSMBC plaque has, as yet, been installed at the site – nor anywhere else – commemorating Cartier as a "National Historic Person," despite the Board's identification of him as such in 1985.[70] Seemingly, identifying him as the homes' original owner proved sufficient in this museological context. Alternatively, it stands to reason, as Ian McKay states, that "the medium of commemorative plaques itself has come to a point of exhaustion, for it assumes too many common memories, too much of a unifying narrative ... too coherent an historical identity."[71]

As far as the homes go, upon opening in 1985, Parks Canada had turned the east house into an interpretation centre with permanent exhibitions installed on both the ground and first floors representing for visitors "Cartier's life and career, as seen through a contemporary ideological and socioeconomic prism."[72] In contrast, the west house contains restored period rooms that act as a "historical setting" within which interpreters, posing as household servants or members of the nineteenth-century bourgeoisie, conduct guided tours.[73] Parks Canada thus arranged the east house so that the exhibitions acknowledge Cartier's life and political achievements while the west house allows visitors to "live history." Significantly, the agency deemed it "essential" that it offer "new exhibits and activities" to "ensure constant local visitation."[74] Because the exhibitions in the east house were designed to be permanent fixtures in the museum's representation of the past, site workers began developing programs that dealt with particular themes to be performed in the west house so that visitors might "live history."

In 2013–14, various Parks Canada historic sites, including the Cartier House, began exploring alternative exhibitionary strategies to offset operational costs while, at the same time, working to increase visitation rates. In 2012, the federal government, under Prime Minister Stephen Harper, introduced cuts to Parks Canada's budget that definitively affected the management and operations of the agency's 167 national historic sites, 44 national parks, and four marine conservation areas. The loss of $29.2 million over three years resulted in job cuts – 617 anticipated or actual departures as of May 2013, approximately 13 per cent of its entire work force[75] – but encouraged site managers to explore "non-personal interpretation" methods,[76] such as the July 2014 launch of Parks Canada's "official" Explora guided tour application (free for download through the App Store or at Google Play) for select sites, including the Cartier House. The application – deployed on people's smart devices – leads visitors through a digital guided tour conducted at their own pace.[77] Visitors follow the prescribed path laid out by the site's arrangement, proceeding through the east house's interpretation centres and then onto the restored period interior located in the west house. In the east house's permanent exhibition spaces – the content of which will be analyzed in the following chapter – visitors peruse the various displays replete with illustrated text panels and have the option of completing a series of quizzes on the app, possibly done in the hopes of encouraging factual retention. In the west house's period rooms, visitors enter the number assigned to the room on the application's keypad to bring up images and textual information so they can read about the interpretive socio-political relevance of the artifactual arrangement. Certain texts also call attention to particular artifacts of note in the space. Additionally, the app features maps and photographs to ensure that visitors will have "a memorable, informative and fun visit."[78]

Even with the launch of the Explora app, however, the Cartier House continues to host "personal" guided tours for "special events" geared to target audiences,[79] such as elementary school groups, language classes, and families, all notably drawn from the site's surrounding metropolitan area. "The Etiquette Game" program targets Grades five and six class trip groups. According to the program description, students assume the role of "some of the Cartier family's favourite guests" and so interpreters introduce nineteenth-century social conventions, manners, and etiquette to the students. The "game" functions to familiarize students with the socio-economic realities of nineteenth-century Montreal, the operations of democracy past and present, as well as the history of Quebec and Canada. Another educational program has been developed specifically for English or French language learning groups, particularly those organized by provincial agencies that work with "newcomers," such as the Ministère de l'Immigration et des Communautés culturelle (Immigration-Québec). The tour is called "Bienvenue chez les Cartier! et Bienvenue au Canada!/Welcome at the Cartier's! and Welcome to Canada!" and it offers pupils of "all levels of learning" an interactive tour of the restored period interior, where students might not only "discover the lifestyle of wealthy Montrealers" but also listen observe, read, and converse with interpreters "learning one of Canada's official languages," with the aim of "deepening the vocabulary associated with the house."[80] Finally, the Noël victorien/Victorian Christmas program aims to attract family groups from the region.

While all three programs indicate how Canadian house museums act as pedagogical instruments, with the first two pointedly offering "dynamic lesson[s] of the History of Canada in the 19th century,"[81] the Christmas program aims to draw in the most "diverse" and ostensibly largest number of visitors with its thematic "living history" program – in place since the museum opened in 1985. Interpreters reanimate the west house in the guise of a seasonal celebration to augment exhibitions of Cartier's political accomplishments, which are located in the east house, by focusing on the family life during the festivities in the restored period interior. This program, as will be further detailed in the next chapter, is the result of site workers' efforts to produce a performative program that is seemingly devoid of overt political associations in order to render the site more "attractive" to visitors. As conservator Diane Bélanger explains, "L'événement 'Noël victorien' permet au site un accroissement et une diversification de la clientèle, un accroissement des revenues, une diversification des activités qui utilise les éléments de l'exposition permanente et enfin, une augmentation de la visibilité et du pouvoir d'attraction du site."[82] Thus the so-called "value" of the program and, by extension, the institution is not as much ideologically determined as it is market-driven, despite the fact that, as I argue, these two aspects are inextricably linked.[83]

CHAPTER FIVE

The Political Dimensions of Personal Memories

The Sir George-Étienne Cartier National Historic Site of Canada has been designed so that the east house acts as an interpretation centre exhibiting Cartier's "life's journey," while the west house's period rooms showcase the lifestyle of the mid-nineteenth century Montreal bourgeoisie.[1] In my consideration of Parks Canada's management of the museum, I explore how the federal agency has arranged the site so that it not only venerates a French-Canadian historical figure but also performs to draw in people living in Quebec, a particularly complex endeavour. As Richard Handler points out, "What to federalists may seem a legitimate aspiration to include all Canadian 'subcultures' as full-fledged constituents of a greater Canadian whole is to nationalists in Quebec nothing more than cultural imperialism."[2] I consider how the site's arrangement allows for part of it to be reanimated in the context of its Victorian Christmas program in order to entice Montrealers, using the 2008 season as my case study.

I hope to more fully convey how site workers use a particular theme to interpret the period rooms so that the living history portion not only projects but also privileges a specific way of life.[3] Subsequent to this, I interrogate the ways in which the site's performance encourages visitors to achieve a "contextual departure" from the present so that they might remember history as a personal – rather than political – experience.[4] The

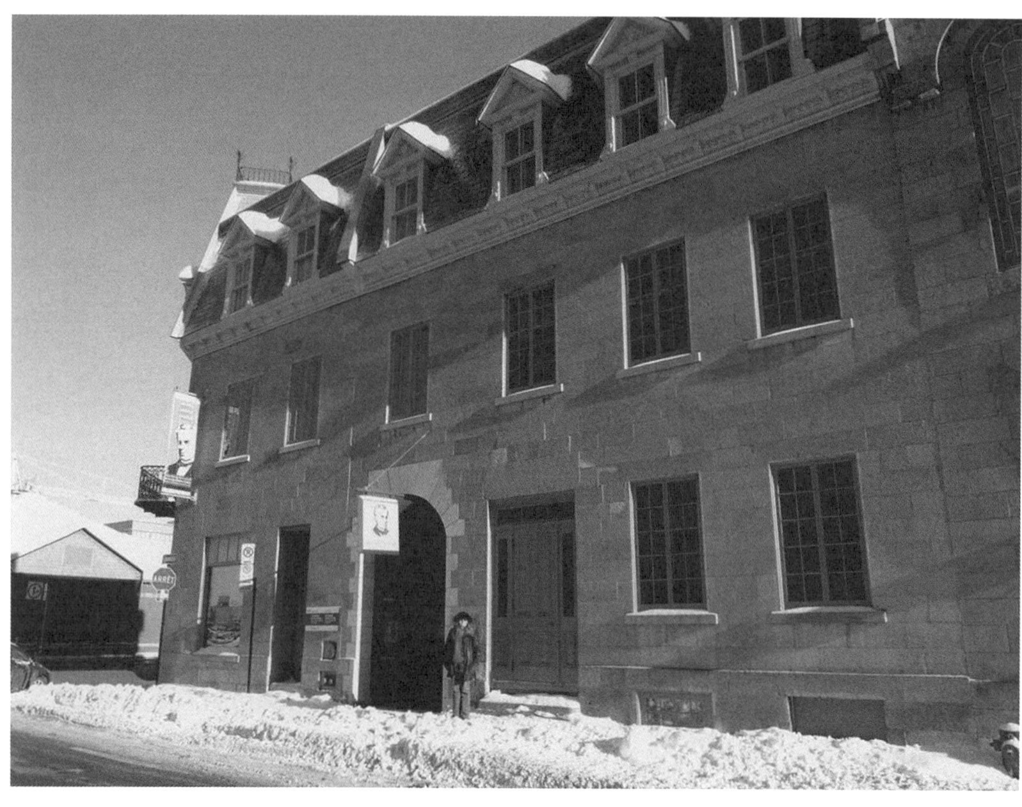

5.1 Front façade of Sir George-Étienne Cartier National Historic Site of Canada with author in foreground, Montreal, Quebec, 2008.

east house functions as a visitors' centre with object-based exhibitions portraying Cartier's life, and the west functions as a living history museum with fully furnished rooms to reflect the lifestyle of both the original owner and his peer group. This house therefore operates as an "immersive environment," one that visitors experience and thus find, according to Parks Canada, more "memorable" than the object-based exhibitions.[5] Since the east house's exhibitions are permanent fixtures, site workers devise thematic programs solely for the west house, programs that the agency itself characterizes as "highlights of Greater Montreal's museum tradition."[6] Parks Canada explains further, stating that while the east house's exhibits "ensure[ ] proper communication of the site's commemorative intent," it is the "dynamic interpretation activities" that "capture[ ] the richness of Canadian identity and offer[ ] visitors an opportunity to better understand the history of both Quebec and Canada."[7]

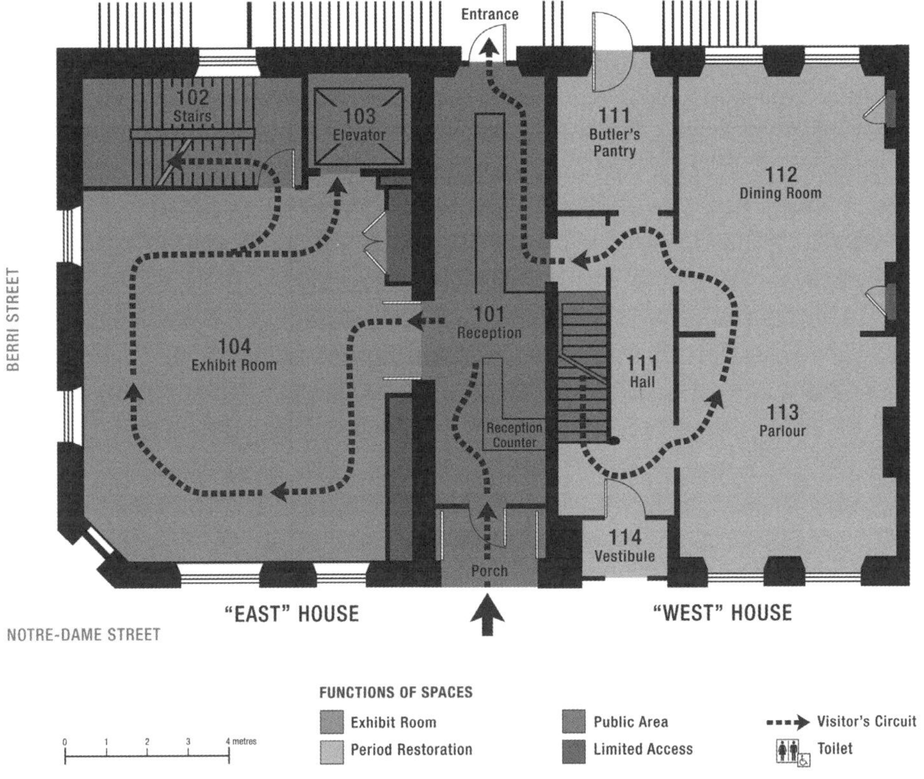

5.2 Ground level – arrangement of the interior spaces, Sir George-Étienne Cartier National Historic Site of Canada.

These programs aim to offer "a memorable and exceptional heritage experience" in order to "generate[ ] pride among the old town's population and among Canadians of all origins."[8] Therefore, the museum's living history programs, such as the Victorian Christmas tour, reanimate the west house so that part of the site locates visitors within an experiential atmosphere, one that works to generate among Montrealers a sense of pride in Canada's past.

In the late 1980s, site workers designed programming for the west house that took into account the original utilitarian function of the structure along with the identity (and cultural predilections) of the houses' original owner. Prior to the opening of the site, Parks Canada workers, such as conservator Georges-Pierre Léonidoff, pointed out that Montreal's historic sites typically garnered the lowest attendance rates in the month of December.[9] Accordingly, in 1988, the Sir George-Étienne Cartier National Historic Site

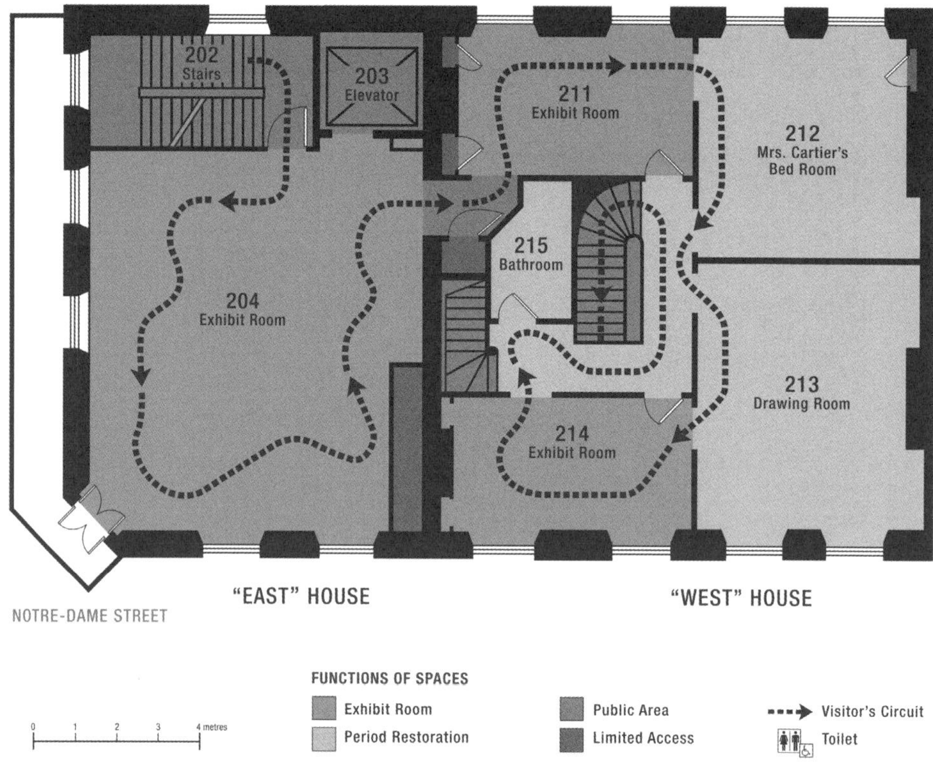

5.3 First floor – arrangement of the interior spaces, Sir George-Étienne Cartier National Historic Site of Canada.

of Canada mounted its first Noël victorien/Victorian Christmas program. Taking into account Cartier's cultural preferences, or more specifically as Young puts it, Cartier's "persistent anglophilism," site workers decorated the furnished rooms with decorations from the Victorian time period.[10] The program continued to be offered every year thereafter and has since been expanded to include an artifactual exhibition within the confines of the west house that showcases period gifts, games, and decorations and includes a seasonal soundtrack piped into the period rooms and guided tours offered by costumed interpreters.

The enduring popularity of this program indicates the extent to which site workers work to develop particular historical narratives in the west house so that the site's reanimation eclipses or obfuscates political connotations. For example, in 1998, the site received over 3,000 visitors during the 25 days during which the program was run.[11] Three years later, Parks

Canada decided to close the site in January and February. Accordingly, the shorter operating period meant average attendance leveled off, with only 15,700 visitors in 2003 after having received approximately 30,000 visitors annually between 1985 and 1995. Notably, the Christmas tour continued to be one of the most popular programs, generating 18 per cent of annual attendance in 2004 in the four-to-five-week period that defines the Christmas season.[12]

While the site's commemorative designation requires that it monumentalize the identity of its original owner, the reanimation, most particularly in the context of the Christmas program, concentrates on specific aspects of the historic festivities to encourage site visitation. According to one interpreter, the Christmas program is "really a history of Christmas time. [It is] a Victorian Christmas exhibition using the house of the Cartiers, but we're not using the history of the Cartiers." She goes on to explain that,

> Actually, we don't have much information about the private life about the Cartiers. It's the national historic site about the life and work of the man, Sir George-Étienne Cartier. And in this national historic site, there is the reconstructed house – the family home in which his wife and daughters lived mostly in the 1860s and included in it for six weeks, there's the Victorian Christmas. So it leads us to give interpretation about the festival and festivities around that period and their evolution. And we can actually go and be quite precise on how Christmas changed in the mid-19th century ... [and on] what happened at Christmas time amongst the upper-class.

Based on this characterization, one might suggest that the restored period setting in the west house allows the representation of an upper-class familial celebration to take precedence over the identity (and accomplishments) of the original owner. And so I consider how the site, upon reanimation during the Christmas season, encourages visitors to "live history" so as to cultivate among the local constituency a communal sense of cultural history.[13] Taking into account the fact that the east house contains exhibitions that acknowledge Cartier's life and political achievements, I explore how this composition allows the west house to host a markedly domestic and, by extension, depoliticized performance of the past.[14]

The site's arrangement requires visitors to first go through the east house and then proceed to the west one so that, as one interpreter explains, visitors "will make good use of the rooms where we [give] information about the man." Upon entering the museum, visitors must progress through the exhibition on the ground floor of the east house and up to the first floor, moving through that exhibit space to get to the west house's period rooms. This layout necessitates visitors travel through exhibitions designed to convey, as mentioned above, the museum's "commemorative intent" as the private residences of "one of Canada's most distinguished politicians."[15] The ground floor exhibition represents for visitors "the effervescence of a fast-growing metropolis."[16]

The permanent exhibition on the ground floor – its entrance directly across from the reception desk – functions as a staging area replete with a broad assortment of nineteenth-century artifacts, theatrical props, as well as illustrated text panels. The cumulative purpose of the space seemingly operates so as to prepare viewers for the multitude of exhibitionary designs they will encounter over the course of their site visit. Given the diversity of exhibitions deployed in this first area, this room functions in a manner similar to that of a "cabinet of curiosities," a term coined in sixteenth-century Europe describing one of the precursors of the modern museum. As Edward Alexander explains, a cabinet of curiosities, also popularly known by its German name *Wunderkammer,* is defined as a "square-shaped room filled with stuffed animals, botanical rarities, small works of art such as medallions or statuettes, artifacts, and curios."[17] The eclectic combination of curios dominating a small space typically aimed to convey the owner's cultural affluence. In the case of the Cartier houses, the combination of historical, modern, and contemporary "curios" signals the diverse wealth of information and perspectives one can expect to glean upon completion of the museum visit.

Divided roughly by strategic arrangement of text panels and curios, the room – on the whole – represents for visitors the sweeping economic, political, and social changes that took place in Montreal during Cartier's lifetime. In portraying Victorian Montreal as a place that witnessed profound changes in all areas of life, the exhibition sets the time frame represented in the houses as marked by progress that ultimately paved the way for the city, province, and state visitors know today. For example, visitors enter the room on the left side and proceed through the exhibition space, moving to the right side and then traversing up the staircase to the first floor of the east house. The first section, marked by a text panel entitled "A Changing Economy" and surrounded by various plaqued period broadsheets and advertisements, showcases the wealth of technological innovations brought about by the advent of industrialization. The text panel encapsulates the purpose of the assemblage, stating, "Canal and railway construction and the advent of industrialization stimulated progress."

A life-size mannequin dressed in full-period suited garb, complete with a visible watch chain hanging from his breast pocket, stands to the right of the economical display. With one hand perched on his hip and the other resting on a chair beside him, visitors identify him as Cartier, given the cartoon bubble plaque situated above his head meant to signal the figure's proclamation of the text contained therein, "Je suis une espèce d'homme de loi qui s'occupe de politique et de commerce," with the citation below crediting Cartier with this quote, dated 23 décembre 1869.[18] Behind the mannequin runs a model train track with a large text panel hanging above, stating that the railways, industrialization, and political upheaval shaped nineteenth-century Montreal society. The railway's location calls visitors' visual attention to Cartier's link and involvement with the railway system, which they will read more about in the upstairs exhibition. The figure stands as both a visual and conceptual divider, as well as a transitional link between the "Economics" and the "Politics" sections of curios, positioned to the mannequin's left and right side.

To the left of the Cartier mannequin (on Cartier's right) sit a quartet of stuffed puppet-like dolls, an array of illustrated text panels, and a grandfather clock in the background, with the largest of the text panels labelled "The Politics of Progress." The overall arrangement seeks to locate Cartier's political activities as those undertaken within a broader movement that paved the way to Confederation and, by extension, the founding of the Canadian state. Three puppets in full period suits sit with a blanket emblazoned with a map of the Canada East and Canada West territories draped across their laps while the fourth sits in front, clearly demarcated as separate from the trio, holding a handkerchief to dab at non-existent tears. All four wear nametags on their suit lapels identifying them by their last names; from left to right, Macdonald, Cartier, and Brown sit under the quilted map, while Dorien resides on the precipice of the display. To the right of Dorien stands a medium-height illustrated text panel with a portrait of Antoine-Aimé Dorien (1818–1891) at the top and text below charting Dorien's political affiliation and leadership of the *Rouge* party. The fact that this party denounced ties with Britain and opposed Confederation explains the dejected facial expression and staging of his puppet effigy. The other three figures are located next to the text panels of Cartier (1814–1873) (notably the tallest of the three panels), John A. Macdonald (1815–1891), and George Brown (1818–1880). Each text panel is topped with a portrait photograph followed by a description of the political affiliations of each man, all notably identified as contributors to the realization of Confederation.

Located along the short wall at the end of the room resides the final section, titled, according to the largest text panel, "A Society on the Move," which is designed to make the connection between all three sections for visitors. The final staging is replete with historical artifacts such as rifles, a drum, and headless mannequins adorned with period costumes such as a military jacket and a woman's dress. According to the text panel, "Economic progress and political reforms created profound social changes. People had to learn to adapt." The exhibition in its entirety thus characterizes Cartier's lifetime as a time of profound change, expedited through industrialization, political reform, and ultimately the development of urban metropolis life. Seemingly, the prioritization of progress seeks to celebrate "modernity," which, according to French poet, essayist, and art critic Charles Baudelaire (1821–1867), offered opportunities to decisively improve people's material existence.[19]

East House/Maison Est – first floor/le premier étage

The exhibition on the first floor, in turn, consists of two separate assemblages that document Cartier's life span and political career, locating him within the teleological narrative of socio-political progress established on the ground floor. The first assemblage includes a series of lecterns – text panels containing copies of both historical photographs and graphic illustrations mounted on stands – that line the perimeter of the room. Of the twenty-one lecterns, some document major events during Cartier's life, such as his birth and education within a bourgeois family that "made its fortune in the grain trade," his appointment as the Grand Trunk Railway's primary solicitor, his investiture as a baronet by Queen Victoria in 1868, and his death, the result of kidney disease known as Bright's disease. The texts seem to lay the facts bare ostensibly so as to suppress the complexities of an individual's decision-making processes. For example, in the third lectern, the text states

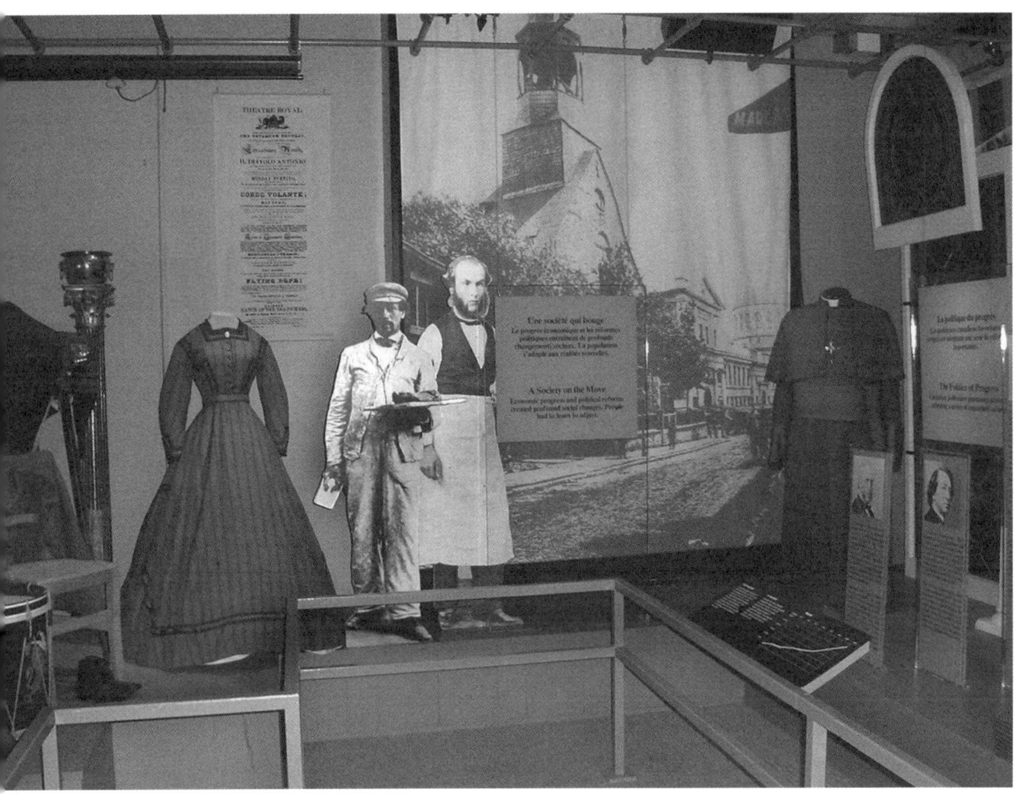

5.4 Ground floor Exhibition detail, east house, 2008.

that Cartier had met and worked with the leaders of the Patriot movement, such as Louis-Joseph Papineau (1786–1871), Louis Hippolyte Lafontaine (1807–1864), and Édouard-Raymond Fabre (1799–1854), his future father-in-law. It goes on to state that, "like many other young members of the bourgeoisie embittered by the English-Canadian domination of politics and commerce, Cartier participated in the Rebellion of 1837. He refused, however, to take part in the insurrections of 1838. In a letter dated September 1838, addressed to Lord Durham's secretary, Cartier proclaimed his loyalty to the British Crown and its institutions." The blow-by-blow account here seemingly functions so as to gloss over factors that informed Cartier's conduct. Moreover, the lectern itself is arranged so it sits as part of a trio – as are the other twenty lecterns – in the centre of which resides a small white text panel that provides an abridged version of the three combined. In this instance, the abbreviation describes Cartier's procurement of an "education typical of the French-Canadian elite of the time," his family background and schooling allowing him to access "the bourgeois circles of Montreal society." Accordingly, any discussion or analysis of Cartier's different affiliations over the course of the Lower Canadian rebellion and its aftermath is neatly side-stepped.

Other lecterns highlight various reforms within which Cartier participated – labelled with titles such as "Education Reform," "Abolition of the Seigniorial System," "Codification of Civil Law," "Militia Act" – all of which operate to signal "the modernization of society." In the case of educational reform, the text here iterates that given the lack of teacher training and, subsequent to that, "proper schooling," Cartier "intervened" in 1856 as the then-Attorney General of Lower Canada and named Pierre-Joseph-Olivier Chauveau superintendent of public schools. Chauveau in turn established three teachers' colleges to produce "competent teachers" and also formed the Council of Public Instruction (1856), funded by government grants allocated by Cartier. Notably, the Council was composed of fifteen members, ten Catholics, four Protestants, and a superintendent. The Catholic members supervised the French-speaking system while the Protestants oversaw the English language curriculum,[20] and so, as the text panel rather loosely puts it, "a school system headed by the clergy was established." While the description of the nineteenth-century educational reform, in which Cartier seemingly played a pivotal role, implies a trajectory bent on progression, contemporary perceptions regarding the educational system's modernization beg to differ. As The Pasts Collective explains in their findings based on interviews conducted with Francophones in Quebec in 2006 regarding their perceptions of the past, in "the current narrative of franco-Québécois collective remembering, the family and the Roman Catholic Church are associated with conservatism, oppression, and backwardness. Modernization advanced dramatically during the Quiet Revolution of the 1960s, when the church gave way to the state in the management of schools and social services."[21] The cumulative effect of the Quiet Revolution on contemporary reminiscences will be considered in greater detail below. Parks Canada's temporal location of society's modernization, effected through this educational reform, indicates the extent to which conceptualizations of modernity differ. Moreover, the fact that Parks Canada has not given voice to these facts, as is the case in the homes' "living history" portion, suggests that site organizers prefer to allow visitors to consider this interpretation on their own terms.

The second assemblage includes a round table that sits in the middle of the room with eight white mannequins positioned around it, seven of whom sit while one stands. On the table in front of the standing figure is a stack of six books, signaling to visitors that this figure represents Cartier. The titles on the books' spines refer to political reforms that Cartier helped develop, including Confederation and the 1852 parliamentary bill that resulted in the creation of the Grand Trunk Railway Company. By arranging Cartier as one man among others, the museum workers aim to convey to visitors "l'esprit de collaboration associé aux réformes," valued arguably both in the past and present.[22]

In contrast, the west house's restored period rooms showcase particular aspects of Victorian Montreal's bourgeoisie domestic culture. In the context of the Victorian Christmas tour, this house's reanimation allows interpreters to explore "what happened at Christmas time amongst the upper-class." In order to authorize the way in which they choose to represent the past for visitors, site workers look to documented evidence of Cartier's cultural tastes. While there is no primary evidence that sets out how or if the Cartier family celebrated Christmas, what information survives indicates that it is, as one interpreter puts it, "believable that the Cartiers did put up a Christmas tree." They cite, for example, a list of the contents of Cartier's library, auctioned off two years after his death in 1873, which included numerous back copies of the *Illustrated London News*; although it is unknown whether he owned a copy, the front page of the December 1848 issue shows the British Royal family – Queen Victoria, Prince Albert, and their children – standing around a decorated tree.[23] (The caption underneath the print reads, "Christmas Tree at Windsor Castle."[24]) In light of this image, and the suggestion that Cartier may have seen it, interpreters posit that he was aware of the "popularity of having a Christmas tree just like the Christmas tree set up in the Windsor Castle." Accordingly, museum staff construct speculative object-based representations of what might have been in place during the Cartier family Christmas celebration.

Situating the Cartiers' lives and lifestyle within a general "history of Christmas time," interpreters use the artifactual arrangements to portray and discuss the type of celebration that might have been mounted by the "10 to 15 per cent of the population that were spending life like the Cartiers." More specifically, they discuss how certain festive traditions and activities, which originated in antiquity and evolved most particularly during the mid-nineteenth century, were performed by members of Montreal's upper-class. According to one interpreter, the tour's thematic focus and interpretive content are deliberately designed to draw in visitors because, as she puts it, "with politics, it's not something that will attract the mass of people."

In contrast to Dundurn Castle, as discussed in the previous section, costumed interpreters at the Cartier House routinely assume character roles, performing what is known as "first-person interpretation," even as they act as guides to provide visitors – anglophones and francophones alike – with an informed experience. In the west house, visitors meet different types of interpreters on each floor, each type posing as a member of a different class. On the first floor, interpreters pose as servants, while those on the ground floor present themselves as upper-class individuals; in these roles, interpreters work both to portray the "interdependence between these two social classes" and to "create an experience with visitors."[25] Interpreters deliver information in both French and English, depending on the language preferred or used by visitors, although interpreters are quick to point out that the type of information they relay depends on where visitors are from, rather than what language they speak. According to one interpreter, "If [visitors] are from Montreal, they have something in common, even if they're different language speakers. But if the English language speakers are from the United States, well, then, the information can be totally different." Another interpreter states that being able to give both anglophone and francophone Montrealers the "same basic information" so that they might have the "same experience" signals "the importance of being professional and doing your best" for visitors. My examination of the Cartier House's Victorian Christmas tour considers the type of information interpreters discuss with visitors – what sort of traditions and activities are discussed at length – to interrogate what types of messages the site conveys through its reanimation. As I show in the following analysis, interpreters encourage visitors to experience "what it felt like to live back then" so as to "depoliticize" the past.[26] Ultimately, I argue that the site performs in order to evoke among people living in Quebec a communal sense of cultural history and, in doing so, portray the past so that the present appears as the natural outcome – a highly politicized undertaking.

West House/Maison Ouest – first floor/le premier étage

While the exhibitions in the east house represent developments in nineteenth-century Montreal society and significant events in Cartier's life and political career, characterizing Cartier and the time period as inherently progressive on multiple fronts, the west house provides a "historical setting" within which interpreters conduct guided tours, discussing with visitors celebratory activities typically performed by Cartier's peers, the Montreal bourgeoisie.[27] In other words, the east house uses exhibitions to introduce visitors to the history of both the site and the region, as well as the forward-looking nature of the time, while the west house has been reanimated so that it allows visitors to "live history." In the period rooms, interpreters typically point out decorations and artifactual arrangements, describing for visitors how the upper-classes might have used particular objects in the context of the historical celebration; subsequent to that, they discuss the lineage of these traditions, explaining how certain activities developed out of both religious and "pagan customs." Interpreters therefore use the artifactual arrangements as catalysts to describe for visitors how Christmas traditions and festivities evolved over time. After visitors have passed through the east house, they enter the west house, coming first into the room that has been restored as the master bedroom, where interpreters, dressed as servants, greet them for the first of the guided tours.

Interpreters use the artifacts in the master bedroom, such as the series of cards sitting on the dresser and a crèche located on the table positioned at the foot of the bed, to discuss nineteenth-century Christian customs as well as what are referred to on the tours as "pagan" rituals. They routinely begin by calling attention to the cards, explaining that, in the nineteenth-century, people began purchasing greeting cards, which upper-class wives and ladies would send out to friends and family over the course of the Christmas season. Interpreters state that cards illustrating the spring season were typically imported to Canada while others, such as the one depicting a family sliding down the Mont-Royal Hill in winter, were Canadian cards.[28] While consideration of the cards allows interpreters to describe particular nineteenth-century customs, they use the crèche to introduce the celebration's religious aspects.

The location of the crèche permits interpreters not only to address the Nativity theme but to describe connections between Christian traditions and pagan ones or, more specifically, practices developed in classical antiquity. Interpreters therefore use particular artifacts to trace for visitors the larger history of the Christmas celebration. Pointing to the artifact, interpreters explain that Ursuline nuns in Quebec created crèches with wax figures rendered to represent the infant Jesus in order to both "prepare and thank Jesus."[29] Interpreters therefore use this particular object to recall for visitors the religious aspect of the Christmas season and then go on to

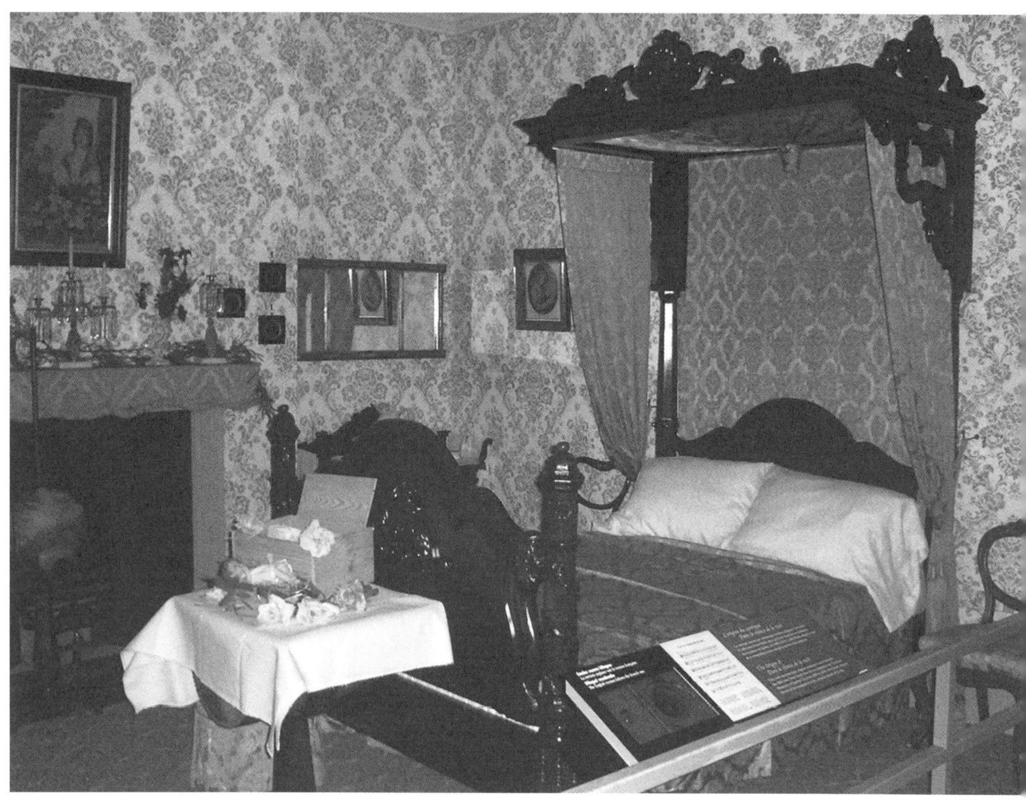

5.5 Master bedroom, west house, 2008.

describe the connection between the Nativity celebration and festivities performed in ancient times. For example, the crèche, according to one interpreter, is "there just to remind us of the birth of Jesus. It's a symbol of the Nativity. The birth of Jesus on 25 December was a chosen date. You see, it wasn't his real birthday."[30] Interpreters routinely stipulate that, in 354 AD, the Roman emperor Constantine and Pope Liberius chose to commemorate Christ's birth on 25 December, notably a time of year during which many other "pagan customs" and festivities took place, including winter solstice and Saturnalia – a week-long festival celebrated between 17 and 24 December that concluded with a "big party" and gift exchange on 25 December.[31] In the case of the winter solstice celebrations, interpreters explain that, during classical antiquity, people generally believed that the sun disappeared on 21 December and 25 December marked the sun's return, which they celebrated by putting on various festive events. The emperor and pope therefore chose to venerate Christ's birth in and around the winter solstice celebration to establish a connection between popular customs and Christianity and also encourage people to convert to the Christian faith. As one interpreter puts it:

> So in the winter solstice, you know that is the shortest day in the year – December 21st ... [people] thought that the sun was disappearing. They thought ... it would be the end of time and for them. But then – surprise – around December 25th, something will happen – a miracle – light. The sun will come back brighter than ever. And then they thought that they should do something every year in order for the sun to come back because they weren't sure if the sun will come back. So they made a big, big fire just to celebrate the sun and also that's related to fire light and Jesus – light of the world. So you see why [Emperor Constantine and Pope Liberius] chose December 25th? Because they wanted people that were celebrating all the pagan customs to come and embrace the new religion and bring them to light. You see? That's the reason why they chose December 25th.[32]

Using the interpretation of the crèche to advance a discussion of connections between nineteenth-century Christmas traditions and classical antiquity or, more broadly, establishing the so-called "timelessness" of the Roman Catholic religion by linking it to events in ancient Rome, interpreters set the connection up as a "natural symbolic union."[33] In so doing, they encourage visitors to take into account the larger and longer history of the festive celebration and assert a longer, Catholic narrative, one that distinguishes the Cartier family celebration from those put on by people like, for instance, the MacNab family in Hamilton, Ontario.

In the adjacent drawing room, the artifactual arrangement allows interpreters to discuss ways in which Cartier's peer group might have entertained guests in their homes. Interpreters begin by introducing the drawing room to visitors, describing it as a space in which people would retire after dinner. Calling attention to the piano located alongside the side wall and the tea service laid out on a table in the back of the room, interpreters explain that people oftentimes would listen to musical performances and have tea in this particular space.

Sitting on the table in the middle of the room is a lantern used to put on shows, a form of entertainment that was, as one interpreter puts it, "very popular" in the nineteenth-century. She goes on to explain that because

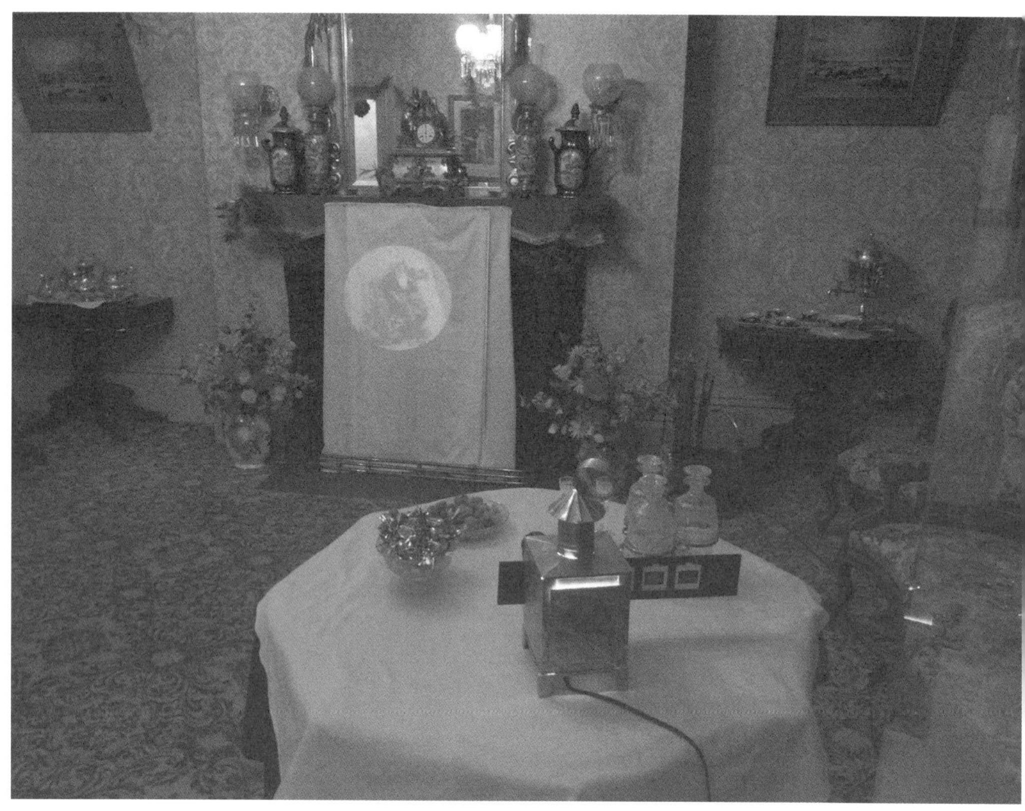

5.6 Drawing room, west house, 2008.

the lantern uses light to project images onto walls, people of the time often thought that the device had "some magical powers" and often called it a "magic lantern." Using the lantern, interpreters project images of different "gift giving characters" that appeared in various print media throughout the nineteenth-century, including St Nicholas, Jesus portrayed as a young boy on a greeting card, and three different versions of Santa Claus.[34]

The magic lantern functions as an interpretive tool in that interpreters explain how particular aspects of each image reflect specific socio-economic developments in nineteenth-century Canadian society. For example, one interpreter points out that the 1875 character of Santa Claus has a faded outfit and his facial expression suggests that he seems "unhappy with something." She goes on to explain that "he is unhappy because, in 1875, it was the year of an economic crisis here in Canada. So the illustrator, Henri Julien, he wanted to show people that you could share, Christmas is a time to share with others. That's the symbolism related to the image – share." The 1884 image of Santa Claus, on the other hand, reflects how things had changed. The interpreter characterizes this particular Santa as one that is "fat but ... happy. But there is more to it, there is drink and you could have a happy life, happy festivities. So the images, they ... tell you that you could celebrate as you wish. But as you know, an image sends us information – it shows what happens by eating too much."[35] Following the show's conclusion, interpreters instruct visitors to proceed downstairs where they meet with another interpreter.

West House/Maison Ouest – Ground floor/ le rez-de-chaussée

Entering the parlour on the ground floor, visitors are greeted by a second interpreter, one posing as an upper-class woman. The interpreter explains that she is there to "[help] Mme Cartier ... decorate the house." Because she is, as she puts it, "knowledgeable about the latest fashions and [knows] how to decorate the house," she proceeds to give visitors some "hints" so that they might decorate their houses "in the latest fashion."[36] For instance, she recommends draping evergreens over cornices, mantelpieces, and doorways because the greenery conveys "the hope that nature will live again." Turning her attention to the decorated tabletop Christmas tree, the interpreter explains that the tree is "dressed in the German fashion."

In contrast to the introduction of the Christmas tree offered in Dundurn Castle where its Anglo-Saxon lineage is stressed, significantly, interpreters here introduce the tree as a German tradition imported to both Britain and France by German immigrants in the eighteenth-century, although, as one interpreter explains, "what really helped spread the fashion [in Canada] is ... the Royal Family."[37]

While the interpretation acknowledges different factors that contributed to the popularity of the decorated Christmas tree, overall, interpreters emphasize the idea that the Montreal bourgeoisie put up trees in order to follow the British Royal tradition. According to one interpreter, "Queen Victoria married Prince Albert of Saxe-Cobourg. He was from Germany, and he took that fashion into the Windsor Court. An important illustration of the Royal Family around the Christmas tree will be drawn and published in the very first illustrated paper, which is the *Illustrated London News* in 1848. We can say from that moment the fashion started to spread amongst the wealthy ... approximately 10 per cent of the population [who] could afford to have a Christmas tree."[38] In referencing this sort of historical

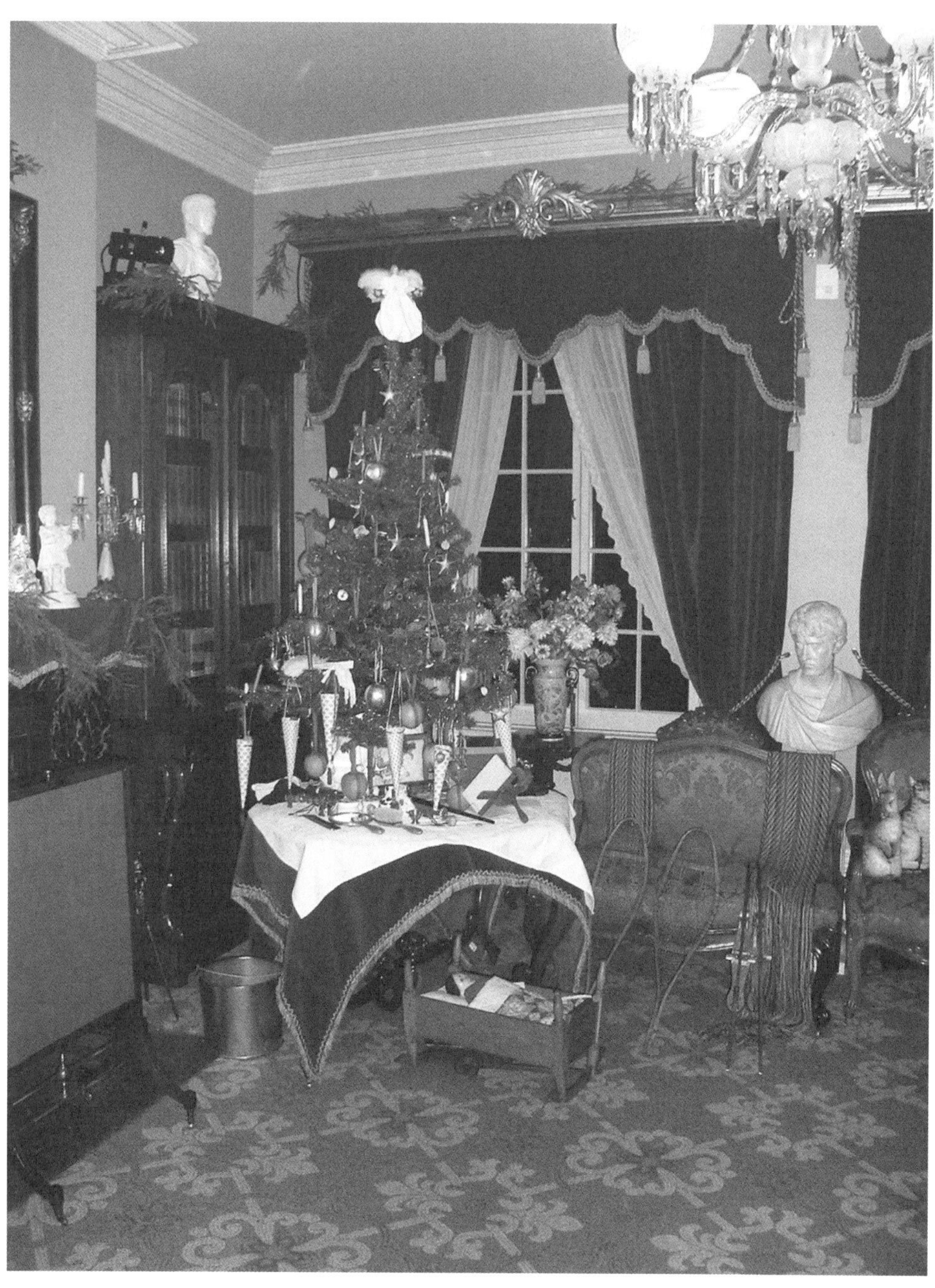

5.7 Parlour, west house, 2008.

evidence, the interpreter characterizes the celebration that might have been performed by wealthy Montrealers as one that looked to standards set by the Victorian British monarchy and aristocracy. Seemingly in an effort to offset this ethnicized conceptualization, interpreters point out that some of the tree's decorations were also used in festivities put on in ancient times.

In discussing how particular decorative elements of the nineteenth-century Christmas celebration relate to classical antiquity, interpreters expand the site's frame of reference to acquaint visitors with a more extensive history of Christmas. For instance, interpreters call attention to the candles perched on the tree's branches, referring to them as "the oldest decoration [we have] in our home."[39] They use the candles to discuss the connection between the Victorian celebration and festivities in ancient times. Christmas, they explain, commemorates the birth of Jesus Christ as "the light of the world/la lumière du monde," and the candles symbolize Jesus Christ. Candles were also used in the Festival of the Light, a ritualistic celebration dating back to antiquity and performed in order to commemorate the passing of the shortest day of the year.[40] Interpreters state that the oranges hanging from the tree's boughs also symbolize "light of the sun, in terms of the shape, the sphere." They go on to explain that oranges were typically given as presents "since antiquity to important people, people from the aristocracy." Moreover, because, during the nineteenth-century, oranges had to be imported to people living in Canada, giving an orange was "really a present because it's a sign of luxury as well."[41] In this instance, interpreters forge connections between religious particulars and pagan customs, thereby attenuating the conceptualization of Christmas as a religious holiday to appeal to a diverse clientele.

Following discussion of the tree's decorative elements, however, interpreters explain how, in nineteenth-century Montreal, people's religious beliefs and practices generally determined when they put up their Christmas trees. French-speaking Montrealers of the Catholic faith, they declare, often set up their Christmas trees after midnight mass. As one interpreter points out, the tree in the parlour is "a fresh Christmas tree. It arrived only on the night of the celebration. But those of the French origin that adopted the Christmas tree, they will find a Christmas tree in their house after midnight mass [on Christmas Eve night], which is an important moment. They go to the midnight mass and when they come back home after [midnight], that's when they would find the Christmas tree with the presents."[42] Interpreters therefore recall for visitors the fact that the parlour portrays the type of celebration that might have been put on by a French-Canadian family.

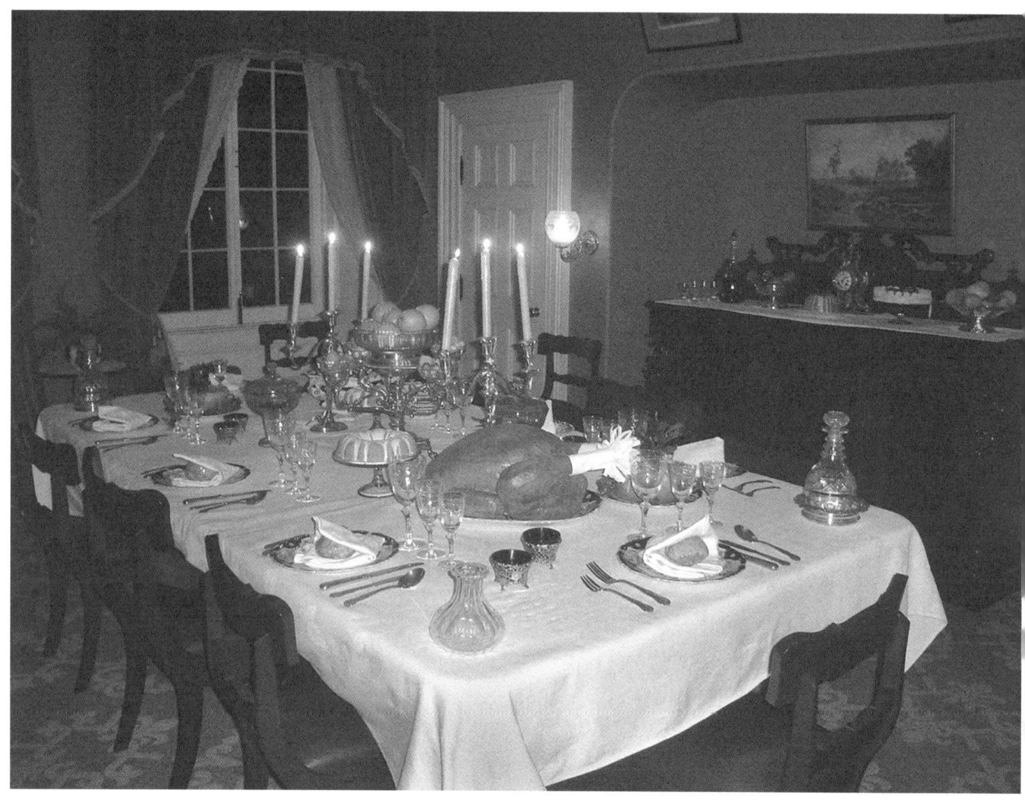

5.8 Dining room, west house, 2008.

Likewise, in the adjacent dining room, the table arrangement allows interpreters to discuss particular aspects of the festive dinner that might have been put on by nineteenth-century French-speaking Catholics in Montreal. Interpreters characterize the elaborately decorated table as one that represents the traditional celebratory feast known as *le réveillon.*

According to one interpreter, "In the French tradition, we will have, after the midnight mass [on Christmas Eve], a big dinner party in the middle of the night, which we call le réveillon. Réveillon. Réveillon comes from the verb réveiller, to awake. And to awake your senses, they were having light, people, and lovely fruit as well. So le réveillon, that's a typical French tradition." This same interpreter goes on to explain that this activity "is not shared with those of British origin [for whom] Christmas starts on the 25th of December."[43] Subsequent to that, interpreters point out the various dishes laid out on the table, including the turkey, cranberries, and tourtières. Notably, they refer to the turkey, located near the head of the table or, more specifically, in "the place of honour at the table," explaining that it was served "especially amongst French Canadians for the Christmas dinner."[44] In contrast, "British tables" typically featured goose as the main dish and Americans generally served turkey with cranberries, following the example put forward by Amelia Simmons in her 1796 cookery book. Charting the ethnic origins of particular dishes located on the table (and ones not represented) serves to underscore the fact that the arrangement portrays that which might have been put out by an upper-class Québécois family. One might suggest that the interpretation in the dining room operates so as to counterbalance or offset the prominence of "British" traditions, such as the decorated Christmas tree in the adjoining parlour.

Overall, the tour content and interpretation examines the type of Christmas celebration that might have been put on by upper-class families living in Montreal during the mid-nineteenth century. Site workers reanimate the west house so as to showcase, not so much the life of the original owner (which is represented in the east house) or a wider spectrum of Québécois culture, but rather the Montreal bourgeois lifestyle and domestic culture, thereby demonstrating how the character of the historic structure informs the representation. Furthermore, they use the guise of a particular theme to augment discussions of nineteenth-century social conventions, routines, and conduct. Guiding visitors through the period rooms in order to "reveal[ ] the tastes and customs of privileged society," interpreters also connect particular aspects of the nineteenth-century celebration with festivities and events dating back to ancient times.[45] One might suggest that interpreters explore these connections so that they might encourage visitors to not only experience what it "felt like to live back then" but also appreciate the larger and longer "history of Christmas time."[46] To push the point, I would argue that the interpretive trajectory diffuses the classification of Christmas as a religious holiday in order to entice a broader clientele and bolster visitation rates.

For these reasons, it could be argued that, while the east house represents both major events in Cartier's life and his political accomplishments, the museum staff interpret the west house's decorated period rooms so that the living history format appears to depoliticize the past.[47] Given that the site is located in a major urban centre with a large souverainiste constituency, I suggest that Parks Canada staff work to reanimate the site so that the performance projects a selective version of the past to draw in local visitors and, at the same time, celebrate the history of the nation in the present. As Kammen explains, heritage administrators work to "depoliticize the past" in order to "minimize memories (and causes) of conflict." State-sanctioned historic sites portray culturally constructed representations of the past, designed to "render them acceptable to as many people as possible." More specifically, these institutions work to promote among visitors a communal understanding or appreciation of the nation's past in the present in order to "heal[ ] wounds of sectional animosity."[48] Because these types of institutions endeavour to not only construct but also provide an experience of past that connects or unites citizenry who visit the site, "the appearance of depoliticization," as museologist Erna Macleod puts it, might be "more accurately described as an intensely political act."[49] Similarly, Alan Gordon points out that historic sites typically operate in order to assemble and also maintain certain identities so that they "repackage the past as a period removed from the present yet at the same time linked to the present by a continuity of social and political values."[50] Therefore, in the following section, I explore how Parks Canada's management of the Cartier House allows for the interpretation and reanimation of a particular version of the past, one that not only celebrates but also venerates the legitimacy of Canadian – rather than Québécois – nationalism.

The Cartier House's arrangement is such that the east house contains exhibitions that acknowledge the life and times of Sir George-Étienne Cartier while the west house's restored period rooms, upon reanimation, portray the lifestyle of Cartier's peer group. Because the east house's object-based exhibitions chart the development of Cartier's political career, interpreters take visitors through the west house and explore topics that might be of interest to the local populace, such as the evolution and development of Christmas festivities in the Victorian time period. Such efforts demonstrate ways in which site workers strive to depoliticize the past for visitors; they encourage visitors to "step out of time" so that visitors might gain a greater understanding and appreciation of the socio-cultural history of Montreal in particular and Canada at large. Given Parks Canada's determination that the site's living history programs be "aimed particularly at the Montreal public, considered to be the park's special target group," I argue that the site, most particularly when it is reanimated in the guise of a Victorian Christmas celebration, functions as a hegemonic cultural tool, one strategically designed to both commemorate and reinvigorate the legitimacy of Canada's "founding nations" mythologies and, by extension, Canadian nationalism.[51] In other words, I propose that the site's reanimation appears to depoliticize the past so that the performance might foster among local visitors a collective sense of cultural history and, subsequent to that, cause them to feel linked to the current, larger (political) community that is the Canadian nation.[52]

Because the reanimation of the Cartier Houses portrays a fictionalized account of the past deliberately designed to draw in visitors, the west house represents a state-sanctioned "storied space," to use Donald Preziosi's conceptualization. Preziosi explains that artifactual arrangements located in museums are typically designed and thus manufactured to portray the past as the prologue to the present, thereby reaffirming the authority of present-day circumstances.[53] The institutionalized depiction therefore represents a "particular mode of fiction," one that "has become an indispensable component of statehood and of national ... identity and heritage in every corner of the world."[54] He explains further, writing, "This museological 'past' is thus an *instrument* for the imaginative production and sustenance of the present."[55] Drawing on Preziosi, I would suggest that, because the Cartier House's reanimation avoids extensive consideration of nineteenth-century politics (presumably because this topic is represented in the east house's exhibitions), this evasion represents a tactical strategy; site workers take into account present-day circumstances and depoliticize the site's performance of the past, working to portray the present as a "logical" outcome of the nation's past.[56] In other words, cultural administrators develop the Victorian Christmas tour theme and interpretive content so the site's reanimation might render both the site and the version of the past it portrays pleasing to the populis in Quebec, the site's target demographic.[57] Rather than focusing strictly on French-Canadian heritage and traditions, site workers, in the context of the tour, discuss activities performed by members of a particular socio-economic class, the Montreal bourgeoisie. They even chart the evolution of the celebration from ancient times to its incarnation in the nineteenth-century. In so doing, interpreters characterize particular events, such as putting up and decorating the Christmas tree and the Réveillon celebration, as emblematic of a particular "Canadian" lifestyle, a way of life supposedly defined by both English-Canadian and French-Canadian practices, customs, and ideologies. This conceptualization of the past makes evident the extent to which federal heritage workers, more specifically those employed at Parks Canada, take into account perceptions regarding French-Canadian nationalism in Quebec.

In the 1960s, the Québécois began to re-examine their status within the Canadian federation and, by extension, their past. As mentioned previously, the Quiet Revolution inspired the installation of Quebec's Ministry of Education and the Ministère des Affaires culturelle. According to Raymond Breton, however, the "substitution of *Québécois* for 'French-Canadian' as the acceptable self-denotation" represented the "most significant" change, in that they came to regard themselves not as a cultural minority within the Canadian federation but rather as a territorial majority.[58] During the time of Confederation, Breton states that francophones initially viewed what later became the province of Quebec as the "homeland of the French in North America," but as time went on, they became increasingly aware of what they perceived to be the growing dominance of English Canadian nationalism.[59] For example, throughout the course of the twentieth-century, immigrants coming to Canada largely adopted English as their primary language of communication, a development that, for Francophones, represented the domination of anglo-conformity.[60] As a result, they sought to defend the legitimacy of the French language and their culture, adopting "an ideology of *survivance*/survival."[61] The defensive, survivalist mentality of French-Canadian nationalism, however, caused francophones to focus on how they had been victimized in the past.[62] As Jocelyn Létourneau explains, French-Canadian nationalism conceptualizes the past as "a breeding ground of painful, depressing memories rather than pretext for positive remembering."[63] In the 1960s, francophones in Quebec shed the defensive, survivalist character of French-Canadian nationalism and adopted a more assertive, forward-looking Québécois nationalist ideology, one that inspired them to take control of governmental structures and processes that defined their "political, economic and cultural well-being."[64] One might ask then what role might the material culture of Quebec's nineteenth-century past hold in a society that dedicates itself to looking to the future?

As a Quebec historian, Létourneau suggests that "the stakes and challenges of the present" should inform francophones' approach to or understanding of their past.[65] He explains further, "The stakes of today should determine the uses of the old ... With no past, the present risks falling into 'absence.' But if the past outweighs the present, it can lead to a vicious circle of repetition."[66] He thus recommends that francophones interrogate their past, acknowledge it, recognize it, and distance themselves emotionally from it so that they might learn from it. The past, he suggests, can be liberating for the Québécois if they reflect upon it critically; critical reflection allows a society to create "the conditions for transcending itself and advancing through future human action, and ... it is able to give rise to new events that mark its evolution in time ... Society emancipates itself from a memory that would otherwise crush it."[67] In other words, he advocates that they both acknowledge and evaluate the past, using their present-day understanding to learn from it and move "beyond the old torments rather than constantly coming back to them" so that they might in turn work to "build an open future."[68]

The past represented by the Cartier House during the Christmas season, however, deliberately plays upon the emotive qualities of the holiday, operating so that it evokes among visitors a nostalgia for that which is ideologically charged and politically motivated. As Susan Stewart explains, nostalgia "is always ideological; the past it seeks has never existed except as narrative, and hence, always absent, that past continually threatens to reproduce itself as a felt lack."[69] While Parks Canada strove to take the Quebec public's present-day evaluations of the past into account, they did so after conducting a public consultation program in the mid-1980s, during the formulation of the site's design and arrangement. Ten years after the Cartier House's opened to the public, the 1995 Quebec Referendum took place. The motion for Quebec to secede from the rest of Canada was defeated by a slim margin, signaling, as Ian McKay points out, that the citizens of Canada already resided in a "post-Canadian terrain." The national narratives that once offered Canadians reassurance that they belonged to a unified nation had been called into question and found lacking.[70] The case of the Cartier House's performance in the twenty-first century, I suggest, demonstrates Parks Canada's perpetual efforts to wrestle with this dearth – to shore up the relevance of the past in order to consolidate (rather than open up) the nation's socio-political future. More precisely, the agency has taken into account perceptions of both the past and present within the province and arranged the site so that, upon reanimation, it functions as a hegemonic cultural tool that performs and thus projects the primacy of Canadian nationalism to those living in Quebec. In so doing, it seeks to collapse the critical distance between the past and the present, a distance called for by individuals like Létourneau.

Because Parks Canada has arranged the site so that permanent exhibitions acknowledge Cartier's political career and achievements while the living history component puts on special events programs, such as the Victorian Christmas tour, the site's arrangement separates politics from the performance. Accordingly, I suggest that this separation is politically motivated in that the reanimation encourages visitors – Montrealers in particular – to not only "live history" but to "re-experience a kind of personal identification with the [Canadian] nation."[71] The artifactual arrangements and interpretive content illustrate activities routinely performed by people of a particular socio-economic class, anglophones and francophones alike. Further, interpreters locate these events within a larger framework in that they refer to factors and festivities from Antiquity that shaped nineteenth-century attitudes and perceptions. In their presentation of Christmas festivities as a broad and all-encompassing cultural construction, interpreters situate discussions of nineteenth-century culture within a larger context. Such a portrayal suggests the degree to which federal heritage practitioners work to construct within the site a vision of "colonial utopianism" so that the museum might portray a "harmonious past that never existed and a unified nation that can only be imagined."[72] The federal agency itself characterizes the site as one that "captures the richness of Canadian identity."[73] In other words, by seeking to evoke a communal sense of cultural history among people living in Quebec so that the present appears as the natural outcome of the past, this performance actually becomes a highly politicized enterprise. As a result, the restoration, commemoration, and reanimation of the Cartier House work to portray and project a depoliticized version of the nation's past so that the museum might, in turn, distinguish Canada as a unified socio-political entity. Ironically, it is this impetus that demonstrates the inescapable political dimension of the endeavour to depoliticize heritage, "living history," and memory.

PART THREE

Heritage-as-Resource in the Global Marketplace: Mackenzie House, Toronto, ON

CHAPTER SIX

Toronto's Branded Histories: Sustaining Nationalist Agendas in a Global City

The late twentieth-century witnessed a shift in the marketplace from being largely sustained by nation-states to being defined by advancements in communicative technologies, transport, and global competition. This configuration has had a decisive effect on cultural assets, including but not limited to art galleries, museums, and historic sites. Take, for example, the Art Gallery of Ontario and the Royal Ontario Museum in Toronto, ON, designed by Frank Gehry and Daniel Libeskind respectively. These sites have been reconstructed by architects with international reputations in order to distinguish the Toronto region as a formidable player in the global cultural economy.[1] In this chapter, I interrogate the socio-political roots of globalizing processes informing heritage resource management through the lens provided by the William Lyon Mackenzie House, the retirement home of Toronto's first mayor and 1837 Upper Canada Rebellion leader. Taking into account the Toronto municipal government's 2003 efforts to bolster Toronto's reputation as a global city by mandating local sites showcase the city's culturally diverse population, I explore how heritage practitioners work to imbue Mackenzie House with a sense of cultural diversity, most particularly in its "Victorian Christmas" program.[2] My consideration of Mackenzie House's institutional history explores how twentieth-century nation-building frameworks fostered the home's institutionalization as a living history museum, thereby paving the way for contemporary cultural policies (and politics) that require both the site and the region in which it is located be branded as culturally diverse, a policy emerging out of what Wimal Dissanayake calls the "matrix of the nation."[3] Ultimately, this section contends that we must bear in mind the legacy of nation-building frameworks and historical and contextual aspects to apprehend factors that inform connections between house museums, their respective constituencies, and the global marketplace.

Because nationalist agendas arguably motivated the museumification of Mackenzie House, I suggest that they also provided the foundation for current "branding" strategies.[4] In the early 1930s, with the centennial of the 1837 Rebellion fast approaching, local citizens sought to venerate the memory of Mackenzie, a man whom many believed ushered in "the appearance of responsible government" and, by extension, provided the framework for pre-Confederation politics. With this in mind, a group of like-minded individuals purchased and developed Mackenzie's former Toronto residence as a historic house museum and, in so doing, worked to connect the historical figure with Canada's national narrative, one that, particularly in the 1930s, revered those perceived to be "pioneers of political freedom."[5] In the 1970s, the federal government's adoption of a multiculturalism policy, representing a change in nation-building strategy, encouraged Toronto heritage administrators in turn to consider how the city's material past and present population might be more coherently unified.[6] As then-Toronto Historical Board chairman Andrew Gregorovich put it in 1982, "We can no longer consider the City's history as the preserve of an elite group of British origin. Our history belongs to all Torontonians of all ethnic origins."[7] In 2003, city officials mandated that Toronto's heritage sites be "branded" as "culturally diverse" to "address gaps in the history it presents ... [and] tell the stories of the First Nations communities and of the diverse groups who arrived in Toronto during the 20th century."[8] City officials therefore sought to re-deploy heritage sites in such a way as to enhance Toronto's position as a global city. This longstanding interest in representing Toronto's ethnically diverse population by Toronto's cultural administrators indicates the degree to which heritage workers merge past and present-day circumstances to honour the city's populations.

The next two chapters in Part Three of this book attend to the politics of place and interrogate not only the factors that contributed to the site's adaptation and to the choice of what historical narratives to project, but also the factors that informed cultural administrators' most recent determination to use its heritage resources, particularly historic residences, to distinguish the region as a global city. Because I explore how Canadian homes have been reconstructed as evidentiary – as *artifacts* for use as civic instruments in the practice *and* performance of history – this section connects Mackenzie House as an artifact to its performance of history. This chapter therefore focuses on Mackenzie House's institutional history while the next explores how heritage workers develop programs, particularly during the winter months, so that the museumified nineteenth-century residence might monumentalize both Toronto's past and present.[9] Because city officials mandated that the region's heritage sites be seen as culturally diverse, in 2004, Mackenzie House staff, along with various local ethnic communities, compiled a series of banners for the Christmas program that hang in the visitors' gallery, a modern exhibition space appended to the house in the 1960s.[10] The banners, which contain both written text and photographs, describe various cultural celebrations that take place in and around the winter months, such as Kwanzaa, Chanukah, winter solstice, and Chinese New Year. These banners, however, are not historical artifacts and notably reside outside of the confines of the "house proper."[11] Furthermore, because they ostensibly function in order to fill in "gaps in the history" that Mackenzie House represents, I explore what types of messages are conveyed through both the presence and absence of artifactual objects and compare inferences of "soft" temporary displays – dedicated to the representation of ethnic diversity – verses "hard" object-based displays installed in the house's period rooms.

Given my study's critical concentration on the types of narratives deployed in historic homes that have been reincarnated as living history museums, this particular case study offers the opportunity to explore those that incorporate notions of cultural diversity. It suggests the degree to which heritage professionals endeavour to redeploy historic museums as socio-economic resources, cultural assets that aid in branding Toronto as a multicultural global city and subsequently foster economic expansion.[12] Attempts to "open up," expand, and reconfigure dominant historical narratives, however, have "largely missed the point." As Christopher Steiner explains, what must be considered is the socio-political structures that mandate such inclusions.[13] Accordingly, I consider how multiculturalism discourse has become a reference point for both policies and practices developed at Mackenzie House and what the implications of such references are, particularly in the contemporary global era.

Exploring how Toronto heritage administrators currently manage its resources to consolidate Toronto's position as a global city requires sensitivity to the history of nationalist ideologies. The discussion that follows examines how twentieth-century nation-building frameworks informed the museumification of Mackenzie House. I focus on four particular stages of the site's institutional history, considering aspects of each stage that helped determine the present-day prescribed function to represent and reflect Toronto's ethnically diverse population. Mackenzie House has been a private residence and a historic house museum and, following its reincarnation as a living history museum, has been managed by two different governmental bodies – the Toronto Historical Board and Toronto Culture. In Part I of my examination of the house as William Lyon Mackenzie's retirement residence, I consider why his supporters, in recognition of his lifelong public service and persistent financial hardships, bought him the Toronto residence and what, by extension, this particular site suggests about the owner's life. In Part II, I explore how, in the 1930s, the house came to be reconceptualized as a historic house museum. Inspired by nation-building frameworks prevalent at the time, the institutionalization of the house signals efforts made, as historian Dennis Duffy puts it, to "rehabilitate" the mythical personae of Mackenzie, re-establishing him as the primary historical figure who fought (and sacrificed) for responsible government.[14] And in Part III, in the context of the Toronto Historical Board's management of the house as a living history museum, I examine how cultural administrators, particularly in the 1970s and 80s following the federal government's adoption of a multiculturalism policy, worked to reflect the diversity of the city's population with (but not within) the site. Finally, in Part IV, I look into how, in the twenty-first century, Toronto Culture endeavoured to deploy Mackenzie House as a living history museum offering "special event" programs to showcase the city's ethnic diversity and, ultimately, to bolster the city's reputation as a global city.

I

As a private residence, Mackenzie's house supplied a space for both the man and his family to withdraw from public life. While William Lyon Mackenzie's extensive political career made him a well-known public figure, it provided little in the way of financial security and so, upon the occasion of his retirement from politics in the late 1850s, his Toronto-based supporters purchased the house for him and his family.[15] The fact that some of the most defining moments in Mackenzie's career occurred within the Toronto area seems to have inspired the community's munificence. After all, the Scottish-born newspaper editor had been the first mayor of the newly incorporated city of Toronto. What is more, his dedication to governmental reform became so pronounced that he went on to lead a group of like-minded radical reformers – all dedicated to the principle of responsible government – to take up arms against the Family Compact, a conflict that took place on Toronto soil and became known as the 1837 Upper Canada Rebellion.[16] Following the rebels' defeat by government military forces, Mackenzie fled to the United States. Lord Durham, then-governor general of British North America, sought to defuse tensions brought about by the Upper Canada Rebellion led by Mackenzie *and* the Lower Canada Rebellion led by Louis-Joseph Papineau (also mounted in 1837). Accordingly, he recommended, among other things, that the two Canadas be united, which, through the Union Act, resulted in the creation of the Province of Canada in 1841. He also advocated that the unified constituency be granted "responsible government" or, more precisely, be given the right and ability to maintain an elective legislative council.[17] In 1850, following the Province's 1848 implementation of responsible government, Mackenzie returned to Toronto but found himself in dire financial straits.[18] In 1856, his political colleagues, publishing affiliates, and friends in the Toronto area organized the William Lyon Mackenzie Homestead fundraising campaign "as a Token of gratitude by the People of Canada, for [Mackenzie's] unswerving integrity and consistency during a long period of useful Public Life."[19] By 1859, the Homestead Committee had raised enough money and purchased a Greek revival brick row house for the Mackenzie family, located on the west side of Bond Street, just south of present-day Dundas Street.[20]

While the house had been given to Mackenzie in recognition of his public service, the architectural structure – a conventional mid-nineteenth century row house – reflected the socio-economic standing of the resident family. In other words, while the bequest of the house sought to offer "some degree of ease in [Mackenzie's] worldly circumstances," Mackenzie's son-in-law and biographer Charles Lindsay explains, "the truth was that ... the product was very little."[21] In this particular period, builders conventionally erected rows of houses joined on the sides by common walls. Because the floor plans for

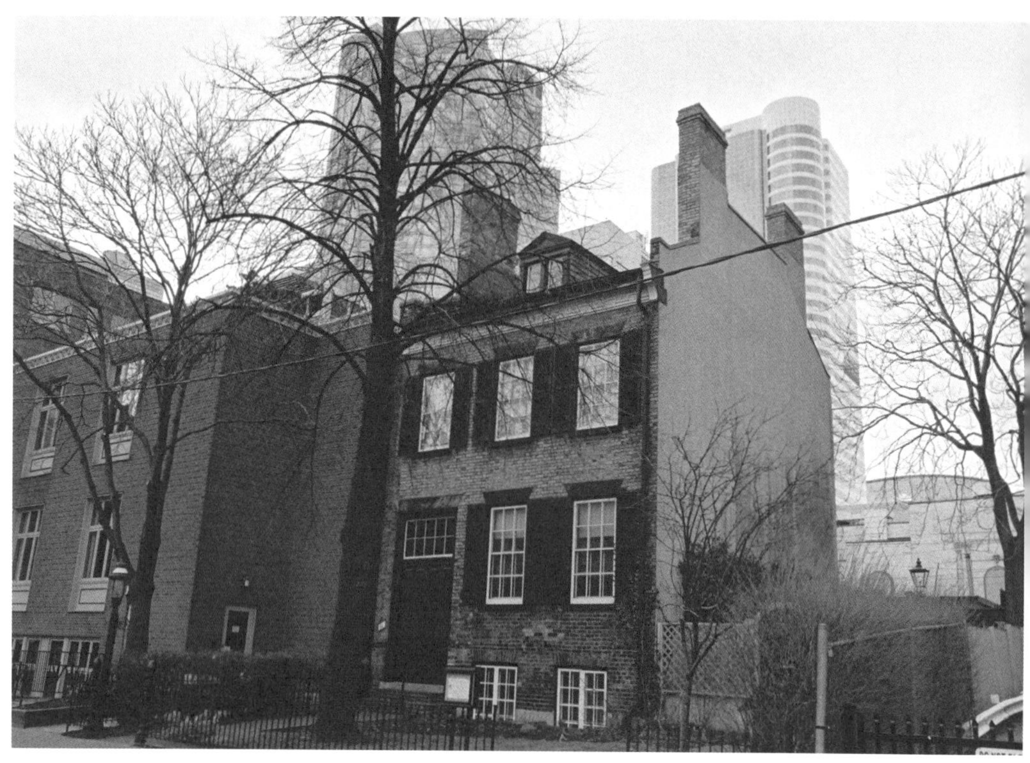

6.1 Front façade, Mackenzie House, Toronto, Ontario, 2006.

each house in the row were typically based on a standardized plan, builders commonly found these types of residences more economical to construct.[22] Accordingly, selling prices for row houses often proved more modest than the purchase of a completely detached residence.[23] Standardized floor plans for row houses typically include, as is the case in Mackenzie's house, a main floor with a parlour and dining room, a second floor housing bedrooms, as well as an attic and basement.[24] The Mackenzie family moved into the house in August 1859 and, following Mackenzie's death on 28 August 1861 from what was referred to as "brain-softening," continued to live there for another decade until eventually it was sold and turned into a boarding house.[25]

II

By the early 1930s, nation-building designs had fostered public desire to commemorate the upcoming centennial of the 1837 Upper Canadian Rebellion, which, in turn, generated a heightened interest in historic sites associated with Mackenzie. This interest gave rise to a second stage in the development of Mackenzie's house, in which the residence took on the trappings of a historic house museum.[26] As Duffy points out, nationalist ideologies prevalent in the late-nineteenth and early-twentieth centuries inspired historians to characterize particular historical events as pivotal moments in Canada's formation. Popular history texts published in and around this time, for example, portrayed Mackenzie and his fellow rebels as central figures in the "master narrative of Upper Canadian history's climax: the appearance of responsible government." This particular narrative logic thus re-positioned the installation of responsible government as that which paved the way for pre-Confederation politics.[27] Consequently, by the beginning of World War One, according to Duffy, a "pro-Mackenzie stream of opinion had made its way into respectability," an opinion that venerated Mackenzie within the realm of "founding nations" mythologies.[28] Moreover, in the 1930s, a host of interested parties, including Mackenzie's grandson, then-Prime Minister William Lyon Mackenzie King, erected and restored an assortment of commemorative monuments to venerate not only the centennial of the rebellion but also, more particularly, Mackenzie's accomplishments.[29] Impending threats to demolish Mackenzie's Toronto residence also seemed to inspire decisive action.[30] In 1936, printing press proprietor T. Wilbur Best, aware of the house's provenance, bought the site to save it from imminent destruction. He went on to form the William Lyon Mackenzie Foundation, the administrative body that turned the site into a museum.[31]

When Mackenzie House opened to the public on 9 May 1950 as a restored historic house museum, government officials described Mackenzie as a historical figure who fought for and ultimately ushered in a political landscape that made Confederation possible.[32] Then-Ontario premier Leslie Frost's opening address at the site articulated the connection between the 1837 Rebellion and Confederation, seemingly in order to (re)assert the prescribed status of the house's owner:

> It matters not now who was right or who was wrong in the controversies of [the 1830s] ... What matters is what they achieved. From it all came responsible government. From it came a working partnership between the French and English Communities ... On the foundations laid by the men of the 1830s – Mackenzie, the Governor [Louis-Hippolyte] LaFontaine, [Francis] Hinks ... and the rest – Macdonald and his great lieutenant, Cartier, and those

other Fathers of Confederation through the ensuing years, were in 1867, able to build the Dominion of Canada, which became a pattern for the British Commonwealth of Nations and, indeed, we believe, a pattern for world government in the tomorrow.[33]

In positioning Mackenzie as a forefather of the "Fathers of Confederation," Frost suggests that the museumification of Mackenzie's house memorializes not only the accomplishments of the original owner but also the nation at large. One year later, the Historic Sites and Monuments Board mounted a plaque in the home's garden, thereby publicly announcing the 1949 designation of Mackenzie as a National Historic Person. Parks Canada replaced this marker, installing a new plaque in 1984. Like Frost's articulation, the Parks Canada plaque text describes for visitors Mackenzie's struggle for "Canadian self-government," thereby making evident ways in which politicians and governmental heritage organizations collectively sought to (re)position Mackenzie as a vital contributor to Canada's narrative of nation-building. In its entirety, it reads:

WILLIAM LYON MACKENZIE
1795–1861
Born in Scotland, Mackenzie came to Upper Canada in 1820. He became a prominent radical journalist and was first elected to the assembly in 1828, building up a strong popular following. He was the first mayor of the city of Toronto in 1834. Frustrated by political setbacks, Mackenzie led an abortive rebellion in 1837, and fled to the United States. From there he watched the achievement of Canadian self-government, which he had sought ardently but without success. Returning under amnesty in 1850, he sat in Parliament again until 1858.

Né en Écosse, Mackenzie émigra au Canada en 1820. Il y eut une carrière influente et tumultueuse comme journaliste radical, membre de l'Assemblée, où it fut élu en 1828, et premier maire de Toronto en 1834. Déçu par des échecs politiques, il prit la tête d'une rébellion en 1837. Vaincu, il dut s'exiler aux États-Unis. C'est de là qu'il suivit la conquête du gouvernement responsable, pour lequel il avait combattu avec tant d'ardeur mais sans succès.

Amnistié, it revient au Canada en 1850 et siégea de nouveau au Parlement jusqu'a 1858.[34]

Parks Canada's text identifies Mackenzie as being born in Scotland and coming to Upper Canada in 1820 and cites his most prominent political roles, such as his being Toronto City's first mayor (1834) and his occupation of a Parliamentarian seat until 1858, following his 1850 return from the United States "under amnesty." Notably, the text takes into account both Mackenzie's political career trajectory and his personality, referring to him as "a prominent radical journalist" frequently "frustrated by political setbacks," what with his leading of the "abortive rebellion in 1837." In so doing, the text characterizes Mackenzie as one who "ardently" fought for the "achievement of Canadian self-government," despite the fact that he himself never saw it come to pass.

III

Toward the end of the 1950s, public concern regarding the state of Toronto's architectural heritage became more pronounced, which instigated a third stage in Mackenzie House's development – its incarnation as a living history museum managed by the Toronto Historical Board.[35] The eradication of various historic structures to make way for newer "modern" buildings, factories, and urban planning strategies in and around the Toronto area generated a heightened interest in and concern for the city's remaining historic structures.[36] Accordingly, on 1 July 1960, Toronto City Council established the Toronto Historical Board, an administrative body charged with managing the city's heritage sites.[37] Moreover, because the William Lyon Mackenzie Homestead Foundation had been, as Nancy Luno puts it, "waiting for just such an organization," on 12 October 1960, the Foundation presented Mackenzie House to the city so that it might be run by the Board.[38] Notably, Mackenzie House was the first historic house museum acquired by the Toronto Historical Board.[39] The Board closed the house and restored it so that it might "be more truly representative of the period ... [and] the story of Mackenzie's life may be clearly depicted," and on 31 July 1962, they reopened the site as a living history museum offering guided tours.[40] Site workers also developed special event programs, such as the Victorian Christmas program, to boost the site's popularity and its role as a living history museum.[41]

Significantly, Board members determined that, for the house to effectively showcase the life and times of Mackenzie "with a particular emphasis placed on his publishing and political life," additions to the historic structure should be made. Because the house had been restored as a domestic dwelling reflecting what might have been in place during the Mackenzie family's occupancy, Board members decided to add an area onto the house "for objects, which could not otherwise be suitably displayed in the house proper."[42] Once the Board acquired adequate funding for the project, it commissioned construction of the gallery that is now appended to the site, which houses an exhibition space, replica print shop, public washrooms, kitchen, and storage.[43] According to the Board's 1967 operations report, the exhibition gallery provided room to exhibit a "variety of displays relating to the life and pursuits of Mackenzie."[44] Moreover, because this space exists outside of the confines of the "house proper," it allowed site workers to explore and display material culture pertaining to broader-based themes, such as the history and expansion of the city at large. Representing Toronto's development and evolution, in fact, soon became a priority for heritage administrators.

In the mid-1970s, following the federal government's 1971 adoption of a multiculturalism policy, the Toronto Historical Board re-evaluated the function of city-owned and operated heritage sites. In 1978, then-managing Board director J.A. McGinnis expressed the Board's intention to develop programs that would both recognize and represent those aspects of Canada's national identity endorsed by the state – in short, those that cultivated nationalism based on the concept of "unity-in-diversity." According to McGinnis, "One of the most important aspects to be recognized is that the various sites operated by the Board represent specific periods of life styles in our history and, therefore, must be subjective. Even though our history may be recent in relation to that of countries whose citizens have now become Canadians ... we are endeavouring to establish a closer relationship and greater understanding among us all."[45] In a sign of support for the Board, Toronto City Council took the "unprecedented step" of tripling the Board's 1979 budget.[46] The Board channeled the surplus finances into the development of a travelling exhibition program, "The Torontonians," which focused on "the multi-cultural history of Toronto."[47] Twenty-four double-sided panels that "describe[d]" fourteen ethnic groups were erected and dismantled at thirteen different locations in the Toronto region, one location being the garden area of the Mackenzie House property, described as outside the "house proper."[48] Travelling throughout the geographical domain of the Board's jurisdiction, the exhibition showcased the "contribution of many immigrant groups to the growth and development of Toronto."[49] It is significant that, despite the Board's intentions to celebrate Toronto's ethnic diversity, the exhibition was a travelling one with no permanent residence; even when it was located on the Mackenzie House property, it remained clearly outside of and thus distinctly separate from the historical structure.

While, over the course of the 1980s, the Toronto Historical Board continued to develop temporary travelling programs that celebrated the region's cultural diversity, it refused to erect permanent markers of the city's "multicultural nature."[50] As a result, the Board honoured the city's present and past in different ways in that it mounted transient exhibitions that recognized Toronto's diversity while working to restore stable, concrete examples of the region's perceived past. Because the Board regarded "The Torontonians" as one of its "most effective existing tools" in the promotion of the Board's public profile, organizers expanded both the touring schedule and content of the exhibition.[51] In 1984, for instance, the exhibition travelled to nineteen different locations – the most ever in the program's history – and, two years later, organizers included six more ethnic groups not identified or represented in the previous tours.[52] In the wake of such moves, different ethnic groups petitioned the Board, asking that memorials be erected to recognize their achievements. The Board, however, citing anticipated incurrence of maintenance and repair costs as an "aspect of concern," deemed it "*inappropriate* for these commemorative pieces to be erected in the City of Toronto."[53] Budgetary concerns subsequently became a dominant source of concern for the Board, and City Council cutbacks to the Board's operating budget forced the Board to discontinue "The Torontonians."[54] Both the cutbacks and the city's 1998 amalgamation of various municipalities into what currently exists as the Greater Toronto Area necessitated extensive administrative reorganization. The Toronto Historical Board, consequently, was restructured and named Toronto Culture.[55] While Toronto Culture remained dedicated to representing and celebrating the region's ethnic diversity, this administrative body, guided by particularly strategic economic rationales, sought to do so *within* the heritage sites it administered.

IV

In contrast to the Historical Board's focus on the city of Toronto, Toronto Culture mandated that the sites be managed in such a way as to improve the socio-economic standing of the Toronto region. As a result, in the case of Mackenzie House, site workers re-deployed the living history museum as one that would – in and through such programs as its Victorian Christmas tour – showcase the region's ethnic diversity to augment Toronto's reputation as a global city. In 2000, Toronto Culture considered how it might utilize the city's historic museums to "reinvent ... the old industrial Toronto ... as a global, Creative City, a leading international cultural capital."[56] Because cultural administrators characterized Torontonians as "the most diverse population of any city in the world," Toronto Culture proposed to "engage Torontonians" in what it described as "the *retelling* of our various pasts."[57] This particular proposal makes evident, as Yasmeen Abu-Laban and Christina Gabriel explain, how heritage practitioners have worked to "sell diversity" in an effort to enhance Toronto's stature in the global marketplace. In other words, Toronto Culture recommended redevelopment of historic institutions under its administration in such a way as to market and thus commodify the ethnic backgrounds of people in the area.[58] Toronto Culture thus sought to turn the region's heritage sites into cultural resources that would validate Toronto's efforts to brand itself as a multicultural global city and foster economic expansion; in short, potential for economic gains took precedence in the minds and actions of policy makers and cultural administrators.[59]

Toronto Culture determined ways in which to manage its heritage sites to improve the city's financial outlook.[60] In April 2003, Toronto City Council formally adopted a ten-year cultural action plan that had been developed by Toronto Culture. The plan mandated, among other things, that Toronto's historic museums be "branded" as "culturally diverse." Again, the idea was to use the region's heritage sites to single the city out in the current globalized world in a bid to consolidate its "economic future."[61] The plan required that the sites "tell Toronto's stories in all their complexity." "The city has done a good job presenting the Toronto of the 19th century," the plan states, "[but] many new communities arrived in the 20th. These communities are rightly determined to see their journeys and contributions reflected in Toronto's museum exhibits and programs."[62] As a result, it called for Toronto Culture to develop "initiatives to address the gaps in the history it presents," focusing specifically on the histories of ethnic groups that settled in Toronto.[63] This stratagem thus sought to integrate particular accounts of Toronto's development in order to construct and, by extension, promote diversity as the primary characteristic defining the region. While some scholars, Barbara Jenkins and Richard Florida among them, suggest that such policies reflect contemporary determinations of the role of culture in the global era, I argue that these mandates have a more extensive lineage.[64] Based on my analysis of the institutionalization and management of Mackenzie House, it is my contention that nationalist agendas – especially those prominent in the 1930s and late 1960s – provided the foundation for current branding strategies. Because, as I have demonstrated above, nationalist agendas inspired the preservation and reincarnation of Toronto's historic sites, such as Mackenzie House, the same ideologies provided physical examples of the city's past to be branded. While Toronto explicitly touts itself as being a multicultural city – evidenced in the City of Toronto's official motto "Diversity Our Strength" – for such an assertion to be credible, it must be, as Patricia Wood and Liette Gilbert explain, "grounded in concrete spaces."[65] Mackenzie House thus exists as a tangible cultural resource that not only reanimates the past but also, based on current city-wide mandates for Toronto's historic sites, ostensibly represents the cultural diversity of the present.

CHAPTER SEVEN

Soft Selling Diversity in a Hard Realm

In accordance with the City of Toronto's branding initiative, Mackenzie House workers developed the living history museum as well as its programs – among them the Victorian Christmas tour, the museum's longest running special event program – so that the house might commemorate both the city's past and present. In order to mark Mackenzie House as culturally diverse, site administrator Janet Schwartz and programs officer Kelly Nesbitt developed a series of banners in 2004 that hang in the visitor's gallery during the Christmas program. Developed in partnership with various Toronto-based ethnic communities, the banners use both written texts and photographs to describe how people celebrate Kwanzaa, Chanukah, winter solstice, and the Chinese New Year, celebrations that all conventionally take place in and around the winter months. Prior to the commencement of the one-hour tour that is now offered as part of the program, visitors are free to peruse the banners at their leisure. Interpreters begin the tours in the gallery space, where they introduce themselves and the site to visitors. Visitors then experience the period rooms decorated in the style of a Victorian Christmas, eat festive treats, and hear about activities associated with the celebration, as well as the daily life and routines of the Mackenzie family. In so doing, site workers seek to reanimate the house in the guise of a seasonal celebration to augment discussions of Mackenzie's political accomplishments and family life. Moreover, because the house reflects what might be afforded a family of limited financial means – in other words, a lower-middle class family living in Toronto during the mid-nineteenth century – interpreters typically characterize the representation as one that depicts the "genteel poverty of the middle class." In the context of this chapter, I investigate inferences of "soft" temporary displays – dedicated to the representation of ethnic diversity – verses "hard" object-based displays installed in the house's period rooms. Specifically, I assess the implications of multicultural references developed at this historic site. This case study analysis summons up one of my study's primary purposes – to explore the implications of narratives deployed in nineteenth-century Canadian historic homes that have been reconfigured as living history museums, in this instance focusing on those that aim to deliberately and explicitly incorporate notions of cultural diversity.

Given that Mackenzie's house frames the way in which the past is reanimated, in the following section, I first consider how the perceived present – the cultural diversity of Toronto – is portrayed in this particular exhibitionary context and then explore the implications of marking the site as representational of the region's cultural diversity through the use of banners. As objects produced in the present, they provide a distinct contrast to the historical artifactual displays installed in the house's period rooms. The addition of these banners reveals the efforts made to celebrate the present, even though, as David Bennett explains, such additive models typically wind up reproducing both representational and social inequalities by treating particular ethnic celebrations as "other," as add-ons to Toronto's socio-historical spectrum.[1] Therefore, this chapter interrogates issues inherent in this particular institution's dealings with or negotiation of past and present-day circumstances. Taking into account the fact that the site uses historical, artifactual objects to reanimate the past and, by way of contrast, mounts temporary displays to represent the present, I explore the types of narratives deployed in accordance with administrative guidelines in the context of its Victorian Christmas program, using the 2006 season as my case study.

As a fully functioning, state-sanctioned living history museum, Mackenzie House offers programs designed to convey to visitors the experience of "what it felt like to live back then" while simultaneously working to advance present-day values in Canada's culturally diverse present.[2] It is the Christmas program in particular that enables Mackenzie House interpreters to use the architectural structure, the artifactual arrangements, and historical research to make the past "come alive" for visitors, even as they deal with a living history format that has incorporated alternative celebrations during the season in the form of banners intended to disrupt an authoritative experience of the Victorian past. For these reasons, this chapter also considers facts, objects, events, and activities interpreters routinely discuss over the course of Mackenzie House's 2006 Victorian Christmas tour. In doing so, I hope to more fully convey how site workers use artifactual objects and live interpretation to reanimate the site's portrayal of the seasonal celebration of the lower-middle class in mid-nineteenth century Toronto. Subsequent to that, I explore what such strategies suggest in relation to the banner displays that exist outside the confines of the historic architectural structure – displays that ultimately aim to portray both the house museum and the region in which it is located as culturally diverse.

Because Mackenzie House was restored as a Greek Revival row house, the architectural context of the site provides the ideal stage on which to portray speculative accounts of how a lower-middle class family living in mid-nineteenth century Toronto might have celebrated the Christmas season. While the Victorian Christmas tour is the site's longest running special event program – first mounted when the house re-opened as a living history museum in 1962 and offered every year thereafter – research has revealed that Mackenzie, as a Scottish Presbyterian, considered Christmas to be, in the words of one historian, "just another working day."[3] Site workers thus rely on the architectural structure of the historic house – as an artifactual object – to authorize the execution of the Christmas tour. Taking into account the fact that the house represents that which people of limited financial means could afford, Programs Officer Rita Russell sets up artifactual arrangements in the period rooms so that interpreters might present to visitors a type of celebration that is both "authentic in terms of the time period and a general middle-class Christmas."[4] In so doing, Russell explains, site workers "have found a compromise in the middle of the road," in that they represent "things that are appropriate for the time but [they] are not reflecting a true Mackenzie Christmas."

In other words, the existence of the site itself allows interpreters to naturalize, as Donald Preziosi puts it, "the truth of what is intended."[5] In order to legitimize the fact that the restored period rooms portray how "a good number of people would have celebrated Christmas in Toronto during the mid-Victorian era but ... [not] specifically ... the Mackenzies" (to use Russell's conceptualization), interpreters guide visitors through the historic house, referring to particular objects, facts, and events.[6] This targeted attention on general historical details reflects the degree to which interpreters conduct research so as to lend a sense of historical accuracy to a speculative performance. Both Russell and other museum workers make a concerted effort to "go straight to primary sources," which they see in such publications as the Toronto *Globe and Mail*, nineteenth-century British settler Susanna Moodie's memoir *Roughing It in the Bush* (1852), and the literary works of Charles Dickens. Based on such research, site workers decide what objects to place in the period rooms and, importantly, what objects to leave out.[7] Accordingly, site workers discuss artifactual arrangements in the house's period rooms to convey to visitors how those less than wealthy, yet still genteel, might have celebrated the Christmas season.[8] Notably, representations of the region's culturally diverse, contemporary population reside outside the confines of the "house proper."[9]

Given that contemporary cultural policies require that Toronto's heritage sites include evidence of the region's cultural diversity, Mackenzie House staff work to make local ethnic groups "partners in [the site's] interpretation."[10] As mentioned above, site workers have cooperated with community-based organizations to produce banners describing cultural festivities that, like Christmas, take place during the winter season. Mackenzie House site administrator Fiona Lucas states that this collaborative process seeks to give Toronto's communities an opportunity not only to express but also to represent themselves: "To do it on our own," she declares, "would be, I think, presumptuous ... So it's their words, their point-of-view, their expressiveness that needs to go into what we do. So we provide the venue, the marketing, and some of the finances, but they provide all of their expertise ... It all blends together in these programs."[11] While the banners' production signals the move by museum workers to align the present and the past, the design and location of the banners in the visitor's gallery sets them apart from the site's decisively domesticated period portrayal. Presumably, it is because the banners are not historical artifacts but explanatory placards that merits their display in the gallery space appended to the house in the 1960s.[12] In historic house museums, however, the architecture, decorated period rooms, and live interpretation ultimately define the visitor's experience. My analysis of Mackenzie House's Victorian Christmas tour content therefore considers both how and why this particular house has been reincarnated as a living history museum that gives a performative voice to certain objects while letting others "speak for themselves." In so doing, I interrogate what types of messages the site conveys as it reanimates the past while, conversely, exhibiting the present.

Visitors enter the Mackenzie House through the front garden walkway. As they proceed, they pass not only the Parks Canada plaque (installed in 1985 – commemorating William Lyon Mackenzie as a person of "national significance") but also one installed by the municipality. Unlike the characteristically distinct maroon and yellow brass plaque set up by the federal agency, the city's plaque contains both text, historical photographs of the house as it originally stood as the middle residence in a series of conjoined row houses in the early twentieth-century, black-and-white photographic copies of different portraits of Mackenzie found within the home, as well as floor plans for all three levels of the home, including the main floor, the upper floor, and the basement.

While the Parks Canada plaque charts the life, political accomplishments, and aspirations of Mackenzie, the illustrated panel produced by the city focuses on the house itself through both text and pictures. Titled "Mackenzie House," the plaque reveals that the house is the "last home" of Toronto's first mayor, "outspoken newspaper editor," and leader of the 1837 Upper Canada Rebellion. When Mackenzie retired from politics, the text explains, his friends and supporters bought this house for him and he lived there up until his death in 1861. It goes on to identify the fact that the house first opened as a house museum in 1950 and, in 1967, a new addition was built "to re-create a 19th-century printing shop." Accordingly, the ground floor plan, pictured to the right of the text, shows visitors that they must enter the house through a "public entrance," proceed past the re-created print shop and through the "exhibit gallery" before reaching the "house proper."

The rather compact, modular design of the nineteenth-century structure, depicted in the floor plans, reflects the standardized nature of row house floor plans, which – as mentioned in Chapter 6 – typically include a main floor, with a parlour and dining room, and a second floor for bedrooms, as well as an attic and basement.[13]

Main Floor

The Christmas tour begins in the visitors' gallery. While visitors wait for interpreters to formally welcome them, museum staff routinely invite them to peruse the exhibition mounted in the gallery. The exhibition includes a

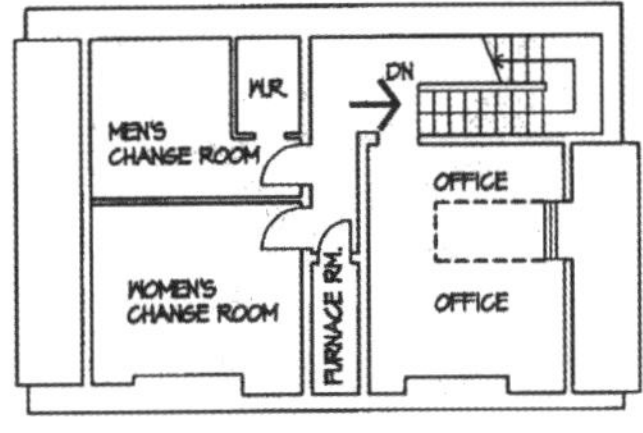

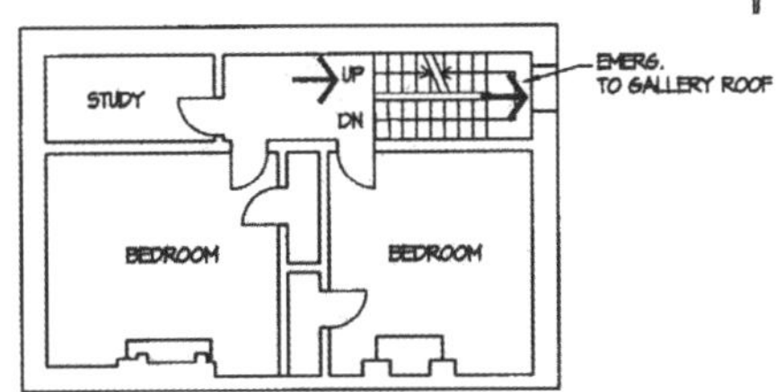

THIRD FLOOR PLAN   SECOND FLOOR PLAN

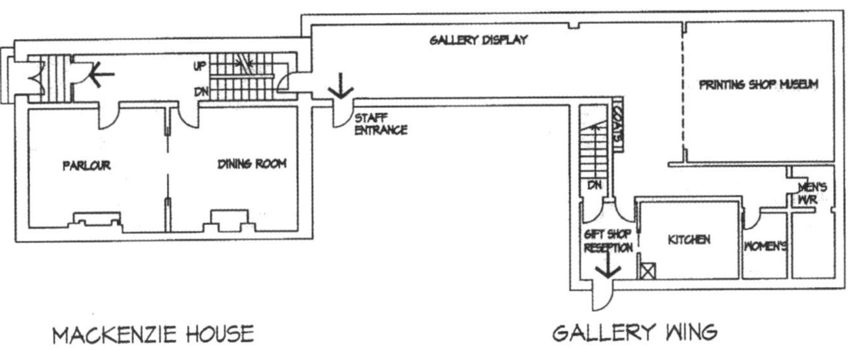

MACKENZIE HOUSE   GALLERY WING

FIRST FLOOR PLAN

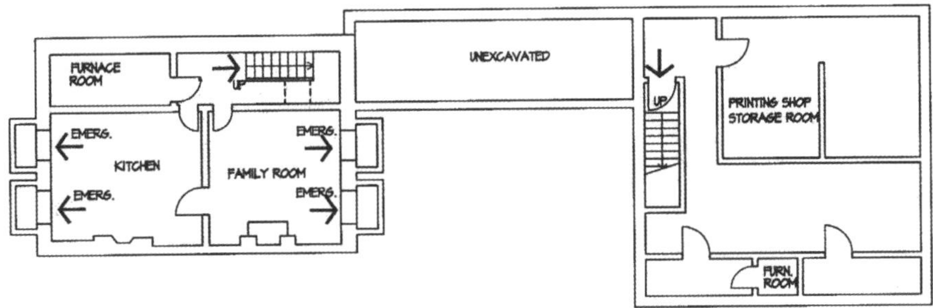

MACKENZIE HOUSE   GALLERY WING

BASEMENT FLOOR PLAN

7.1 Mackenzie House floor plans

series of banners hanging along the gallery's south-facing wall. As mentioned above, some describe Kwanzaa, Chanukah, winter solstice, and Chinese New Year, while others – nine in total – portray activities that people in mid-nineteenth Canada commonly engaged in during the Christmas season, including ice skating, carol singing, and card and gift exchange.[14] The four celebrations described on the banners all begin by identifying the respective group – the African-Canadian Community, the Jewish Community, the First Nations Community, and the Chinese Community. Labelling each as a specific "community" in the banner title, the text proceeds to outline the respective community's arrival in the Toronto area and, moreover, the fact that each was "established" there by the late nineteenth-century. In the case of the First Nations Community, the text pointedly states, "First Nations people are the original inhabitants of Old Toronto." In each case, the banner text goes on to describe the respective cultural traditions or festivities observed by each community, all of which demonstrate the parties' dedication to communal gathering, sharing foods or feasts, and celebration. Significantly, the 1984 Torontonians travelling exhibition featured placards representing twenty different communities. Similarly, the Toronto Transit Commission offers multilingual services, articulating transit information in – as of March 2014 – eighty different languages to accommodate those living in the region. And so this banner exhibition makes evident the fact that Toronto Culture staff clearly chose to collaborate with organizations and represent those that had a "well established" presence in the region dating back to the mid-nineteenth century.

On the opposite wall hangs a framed portrait of William Lyon Mackenzie painted around 1906 by Canadian artist John Wycliffe Lowes Forster (1850–1938). Unlike the banners, the painting resides on a wall by itself, devoid of explanatory text. Accordingly, interpreters use the painting – a historic artifact – to introduce both the identity of the home's original owner and the history of the site. Upon greeting visitors, interpreters first call attention to the painting and explain that this work was produced after Mackenzie's death; his youngest daughter, Isabel Grace, who "resembled him very much," sat in his place. The result, according to one interpreter, is a "pretty accurate depiction of what he looked like when he was living in this home here."[15] Interpreters proceed to describe Mackenzie as a man who was staunchly dedicated to governmental reform, a dedication that not only inhibited his income but also prevented him from purchasing a house for himself and his family. Upon the occasion of Mackenzie's retirement from public life, interpreters explain, his supporters bought the house for him.[16] One interpreter, for example, states:

> Mr Mackenzie, from the start of his life in Canada ... always rented homes ... Then, after the [1837] Rebellion, he and other rebels had to flee to the United States. He spent twelve years living in exile, and he never owned a house till this one, and this one was bought for him in appreciation of the work that he did. And funds were raised by friends and citizens of Toronto who wanted to thank him and see him retire. He never would have been able to afford this home himself. His political choices, living by his principles rather than sound business practices, basically led him to the point where he needed that kind of help.[17]

Interpreters thus characterize Mackenzie as a historical figure who sacrificed domestic security for his political ideals and, subsequent to that, portray the house as emblematic of the community's esteem. They also call attention to the formulaic layout of the Greek revival row house, explaining that both the architectural style of the house and, by extension, the type of Christmas celebration portrayed within it reflect the class standing of the Mackenzie family; more specifically, they state that the house's "simple design" reflects "the genteel poverty of the middle class."[18]

Following the introduction delivered in the visitors' gallery, interpreters stipulate that entering the confines of the historic house signals visitors' "official" entry into Mackenzie's house. In making such a clear and definitive distinction for visitors between the exhibition gallery as a contemporary space and the "original" historic architecture, interpreters usher visitors into the realm in which they will be "living history." Over the course of the tour, the house's three floors, which include the main floor, upper floor, and basement, are distinguished as three separate areas where different types of activities took place. The main floor, which includes the entrance hallway, parlour, and dining room, is positioned as the place where Christmas festivities would have taken place. The upper floor and basement, on the other hand, represent utilitarian spaces in that the artifactual arrangements in rooms on these floors reflect household members' daily routines, customs, and chores.

In order to demonstrate for visitors that the house reflects the type of celebration commonly mounted by members of a particular class, interpreters

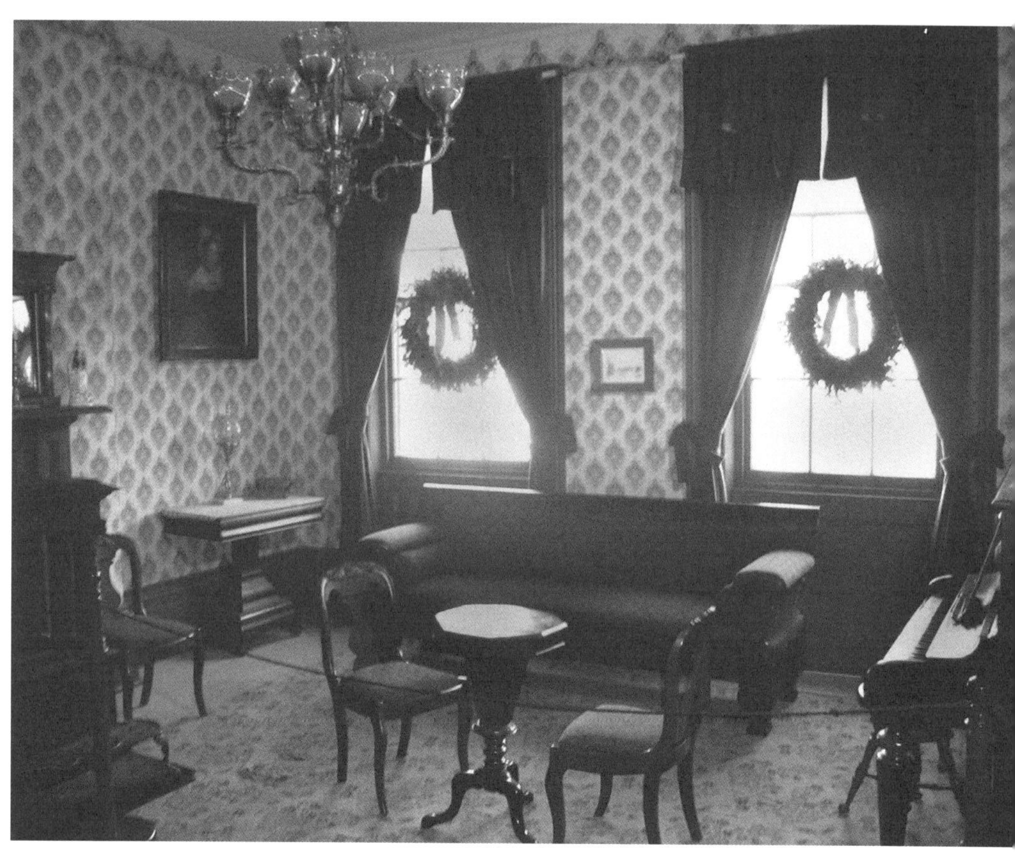

7.2 Parlour, Mackenzie House, 2006.

typically refer to both the parlour and dining room – the two areas that are most prominently decorated in the guise of a Victorian Christmas – as "showpiece" rooms. In the case of the parlour, wreaths hang on the inside of the parlour windows because, as the interpreters explain, a wreath hung on the outside signaled that there had been a death in the house.

Garlands made of greenery, popcorn, and cranberries array the pocket doorway that separates the parlour from the adjacent dining room. Christmas gifts for children, including an etiquette book, skates, a doll, and a stereoscope lie on a table in the corner of the parlour. One interpreter explains that the room, upon decoration, would have been used primarily for "special occasions." The interpreter then states, "it was pretty common for middle-class homes to have a showpiece room that you didn't use every day but would have all your nicest things in it. So this room they would have used during the holidays if they had visitors over or for other special holidays."[19]

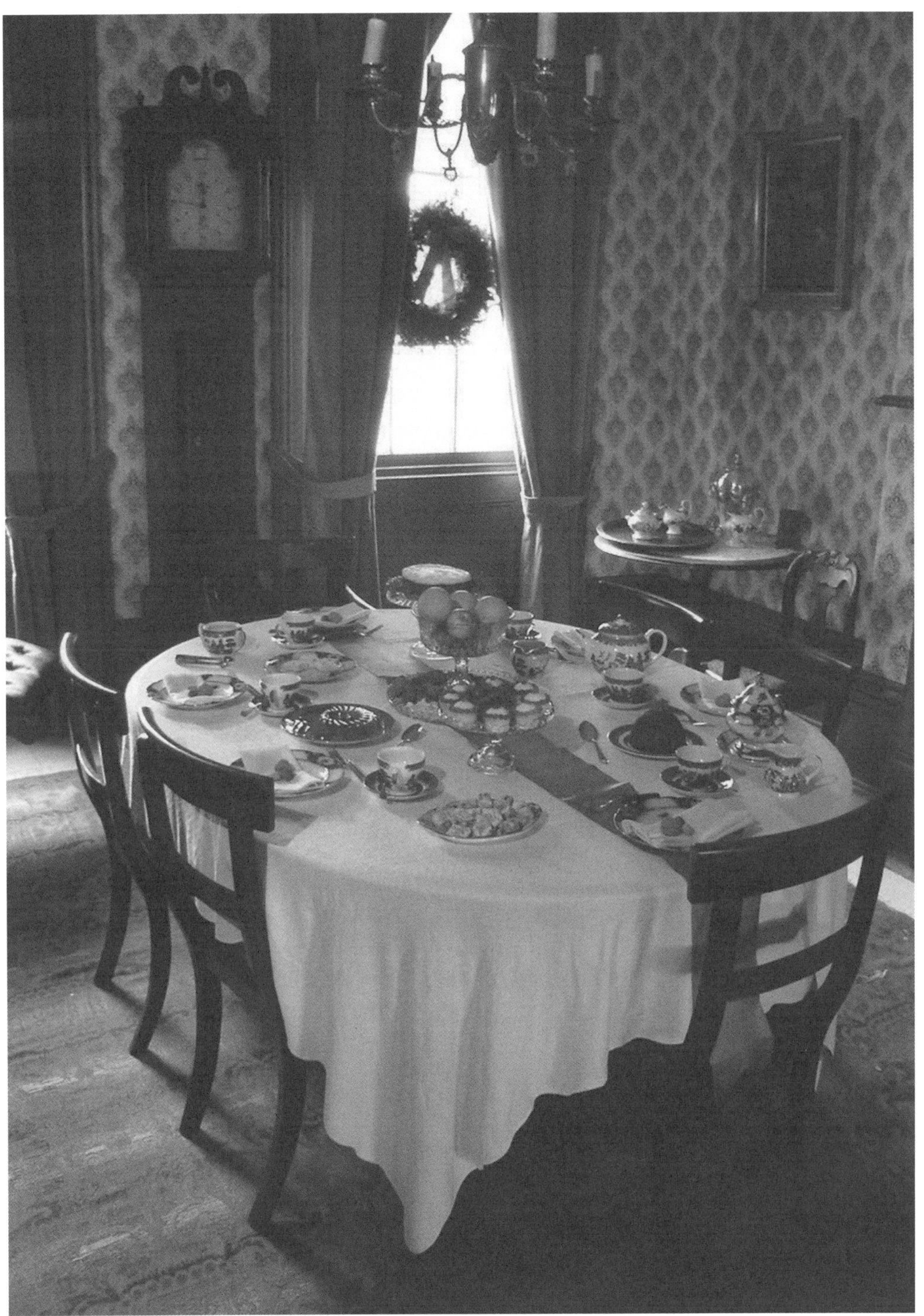

7.3 Dining room, Mackenzie House, 2006.

While interpreters call visitors' attention to the various decorations and gifts located in the parlour, they also routinely point out the absence of a Christmas tree. In so doing, interpreters customarily acknowledge that, during the late 1850s and early 1860s – the period that the house represents – upper-class mid-Victorian society had adopted Christmas tree decorating following the activity's launch in Britain by Queen Victoria's consort, Prince Albert, but, in the words of one interpreter, "it was a long time before middle-class families would have had a Christmas tree."[20] Interpreters also typically cite Mackenzie's religious affiliation, thereby using documentary evidence to legitimize the tree's absence. As they explain it, those of the Catholic faith put up Christmas trees, while members of Toronto's Protestant denomination, such as Mackenzie and his family, often did not.[21]

Likewise, in the adjacent dining room, the table arrangement allows interpreters to discuss the types of culinary delicacies that might have been put out by a lower-middle class family. Set up for Christmas dessert, the dining room table is arrayed with treats, such as Turkish delight, Christmas pudding, Christmas cake, and shortbread along with a mounded bowl of apples and oranges as the centerpiece. While interpreters characterize apples as "common" fruits consumed year-round by people of mid-nineteenth century Canada, they describe oranges, conversely, as treats that were customarily offered "only ... at Christmas time, because they had to be imported from countries such as Spain and Portugal."[22] Interpreters go on to inform visitors that, given the costly nature and consequent scarcity of this particular fruit, people of the time often used the entire orange. As one interpreter explains, "Once you received an orange ... you wouldn't want to waste anything. And what I have here [she motions to an item on the table] is candied orange peel, and it goes to show the extent to which they would want to ... prolong the pleasure of the orange."[23] Interpreters also routinely draw visitors' attention to the Flow Blue earthenware set, stipulating that these objects also reflect the family's class-standing. They explain that European manufacturers produced this particular line of tableware in the early nineteenth-century in an attempt to replicate the appearance of Chinese cobalt blue and white porcelain.[24] The manufacturers' experimental techniques proved unsuccessful in that the blue paint bled into the white ceramic; accordingly, because both manufacturers and potential European consumers considered the results to be "substandard," Flow Blue china was shipped to North America and oftentimes sold at reduced rates to lower-middle class families.[25]

Upper Floor

In contrast, the interpretation offered on the upper floor focuses on more "private" aspects of the Mackenzie family's lifestyle. In other words, the upper floor, which contains family members' bedrooms and a reconstructed office space, reflects most particularly the sleeping arrangements and grooming routines of a known family circle. This floor is thus positioned as a predominantly utilitarian space, one in which members of the household slept, dressed themselves, and performed their daily ablutions.

In the master bedroom, interpreters habitually identify objects that were once owned by the Mackenzies, using the provenance of these artifacts to recall for visitors the identity of the home's original owner. While discussing bathing, grooming, and dressing customs, interpreters point out two pieces – the Empire style, burled walnut dresser and a sampler hanging on the room's north-facing wall – as "original [Mackenzie] family artifacts."[26] Moreover, interpreters typically refer to the sampler, produced by Isabel Baxter Mackenzie in 1815 when she was thirteen years old, as the museum's "oldest artifact."[27] Interpreters explain that Mackenzie's wife brought the sampler with her when she left Scotland and travelled to Canada. Additionally, they use this artifact as a platform to launch into a discussion of household practices, explaining how, in the mid-nineteenth century, young girls would produce these types of samplers so that they might improve their embroidery and cross-stitching skills.[28]

Interpreters not only identify "original" Mackenzie artifacts, they also refer to historical documentation that describes Mackenzie's final days in this particular room to validate the artifactual arrangement. Because Mackenzie's failing health forced him to spend his final days in bed until his death on 27 August 1861, interpreters explain that the room has been arranged "much like it would have appeared when Mackenzie was alive." More specifically, they state that documented medical advice issued to the family in the wake of Mackenzie's physical decline has determined the type of bed that is located in this space and its current position in front of one of the two windows in the room. According to one interpreter, "We actually have a doctor's note from the period, recommending that he rest in a sleigh bed, a bed of this design, with a high headboard towards the window to protect him from the draft. His health was deteriorating, and it was felt that he needed that extra bit of protection. So it's an odd position, but it's exactly what the doctor recommended."[29] Interpreters thus base the

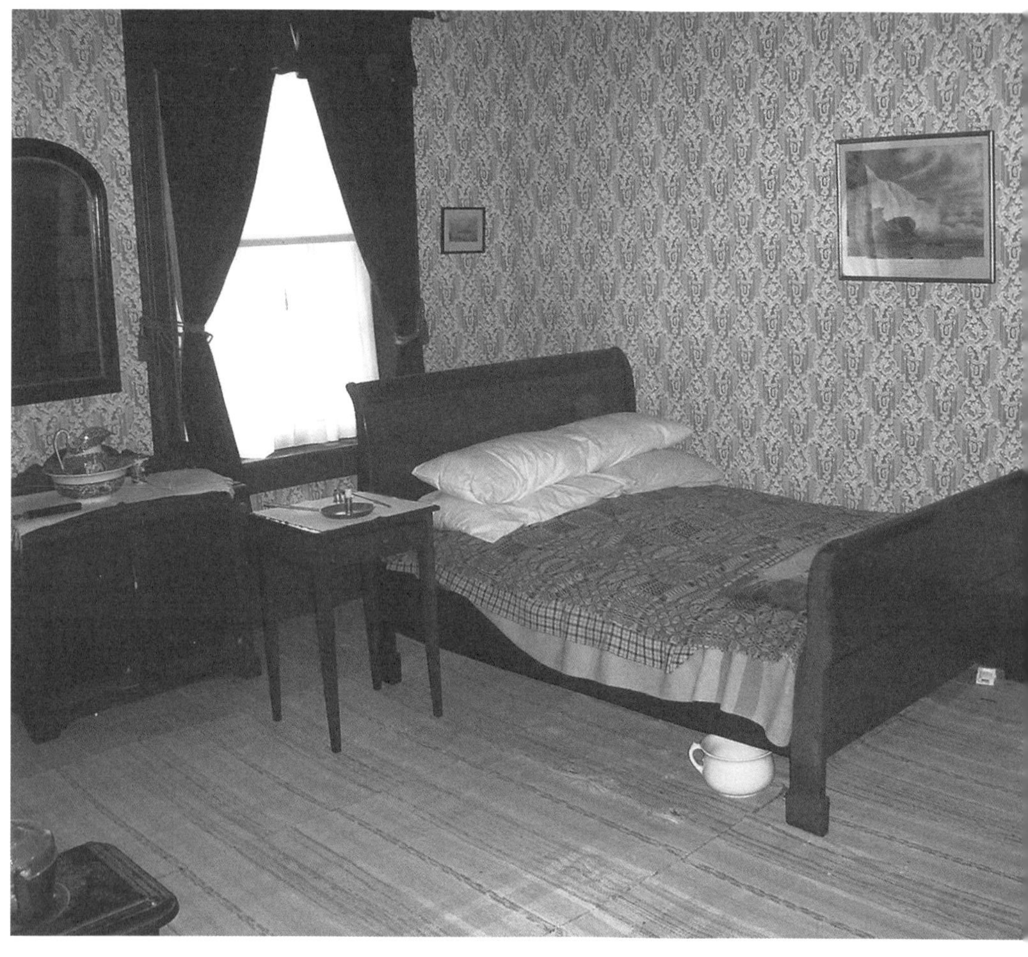

7.4 Master bedroom, Mackenzie House, 2006.

arrangement of the room on documentation to authenticate the portrayal.[30] One might suggest that this approach works to validate discussion of a family member's illness and ultimate demise in the context of a tour that, on the first floor in any case, showcases a celebratory festive season.[31]

Consideration of the artifactual arrangement and interpretation of the reconstructed office space makes evident how history is simultaneously petitioned and transcended in order to concretize and, by extension, recall for visitors some of Mackenzie's accomplishments. While interpreters acknowledge that this room may have originally been used as a storage space or spare bedroom, they explain that site workers chose to turn it into an office because, when Mackenzie lived in the house, he published newspapers and therefore "could [have] work[ed] in there."[32]

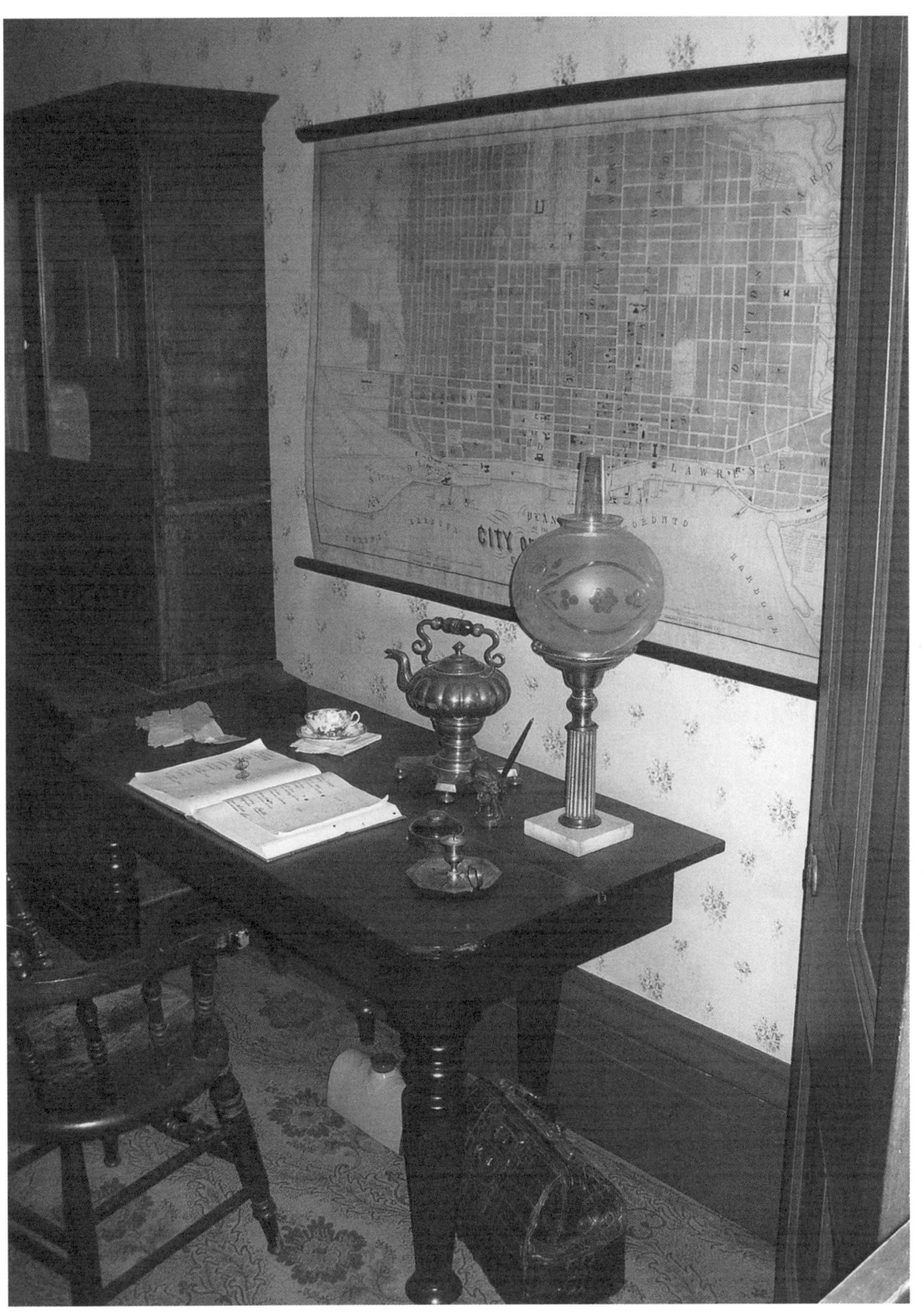

7.5 Office, Mackenzie House, 2006.

In so doing, interpreters reference historical facts to encourage visitors to "suspend disbelief."[33] They call attention to historical artifacts to not only legitimize the representation but also to reiterate some of Mackenzie's most prominent contributions to nation-building designs. For example, interpreters habitually direct visitors' attention to a framed proclamation hanging on the wall, which one interpreter characterizes as a "wanted poster" for Mackenzie, issued in 1837.[34] Interpreters explain that, following the government's suppression of Mackenzie's forces in the 1837 Upper Canadian Rebellion, Mackenzie fled to the United States, and the colonial government issued a warrant for his arrest, charging him with treason and offering a £1,000 reward for his capture. Upon Mackenzie's formal pardon and return to Canada in 1850, he acquired a proclamation. As one interpreter puts it to visitors, Mackenzie "had it framed and always displayed it proudly in the most public part of the home, which would be the hall, the main hall. And that is the copy that he had taken down and had framed. That's the original copy. So that's an interesting story. It really reflects the type of character he had, where he thought he had done the right thing, and he was quite proud."[35] While historical evidence, acknowledged here by the interpreter, indicates the placement of the proclamation here is "inaccurate," the artifact's placement within a reconstructed office space allows interpreters to incorporate discussion of Mackenzie's political ventures and achievements, which appears to take precedence over the staging of historical accuracy. In other words, the artifact's provenance and location affords interpreters the opportunity to recall for visitors key reasons for the site's existence. The performance thus reinforces the commemorative aims of the site.[36]

Basement

The basement offers visitors an impression of the day-to-day lives of the Mackenzie family. Having conceptualized the basement as "the heart of the house" (in the words of one interpreter), interpreters take visitors through the day room and kitchen, describing certain aspects of the Mackenzie family's daily routine.[37] The family's socio-economic status, they claim, dictated this arrangement. As one interpreter puts it, "Because the family wasn't really that well off ... they wouldn't want to use all of their nice stuff every day, so things were a lot more casual down here."[38]

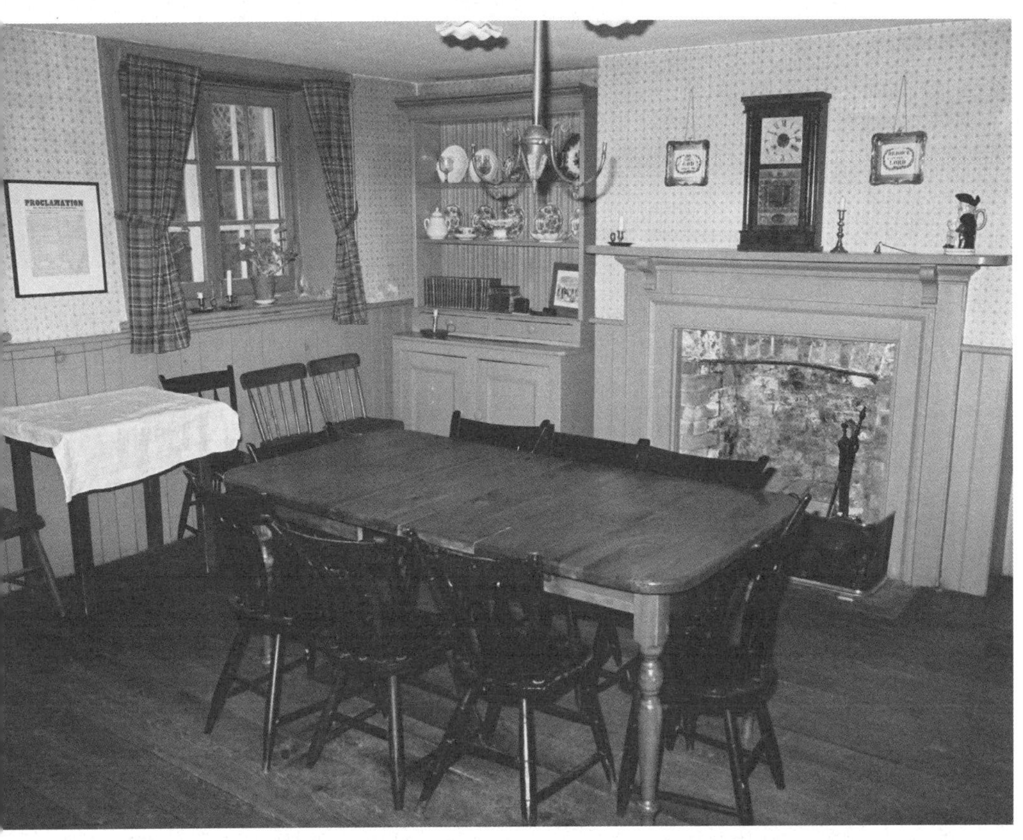

7.6 Day room, Mackenzie House, 2006.

The day room situated next to the kitchen would have been the warmest room in the house, interpreters state, and so it was the space where "the family would spend their day."[39] In the day room, which contains a day bed, a dining table with eight chairs surrounding it, and a small table with knitting accoutrements on its lower shelf, interpreters describe various activities that the Mackenzie family members might have done, such as knitting, sewing, writing, reading, and eating.[40]

In the kitchen, on the other hand, they routinely explain how people of Mackenzie's day would have used both the built-in cooking stove and particular culinary artifacts, including a coffee roaster, apple peeler, gelatin moulds, and baking pans, as well as measuring cups, to prepare drinks and food for meals.[41] They also discuss how, in the mid-nineteenth century, people laundered and ironed their clothes and bathed themselves in the kitchen.

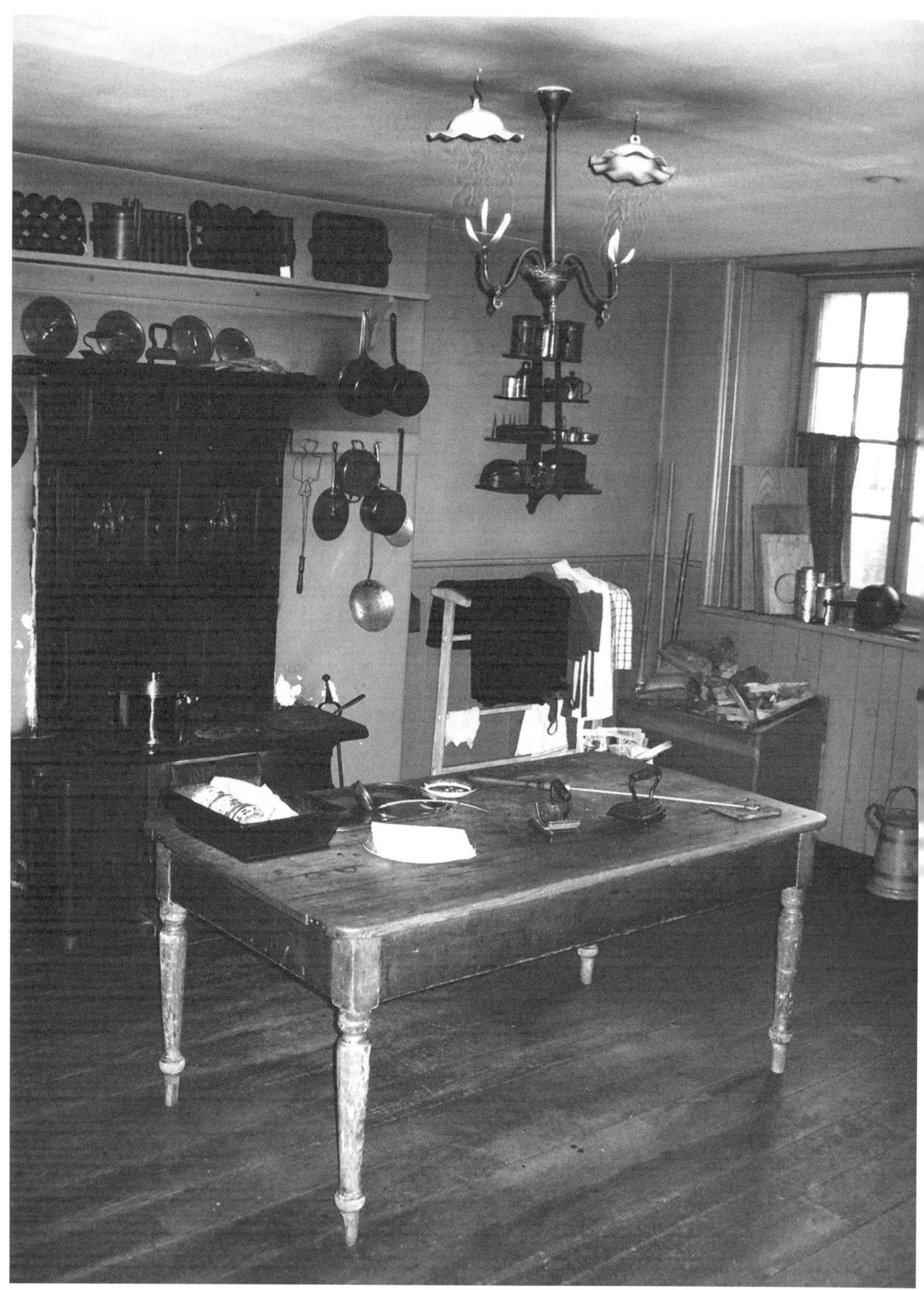

7.7 Kitchen, Mackenzie House, 2006.

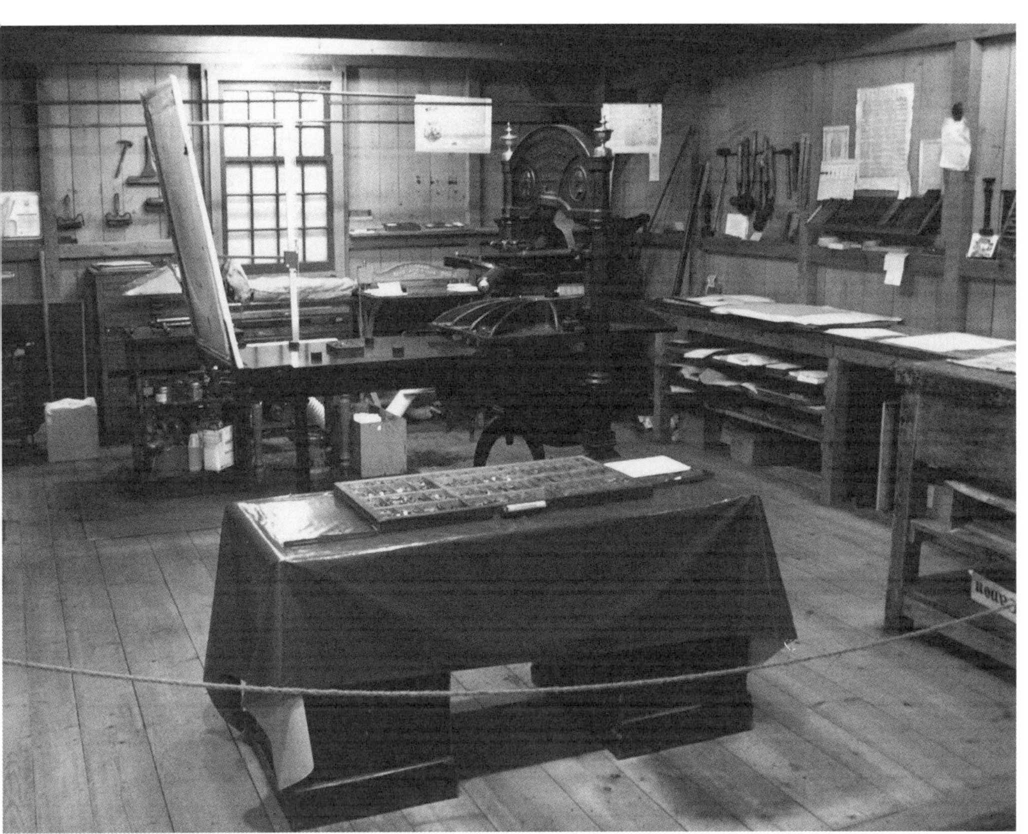

7.8 Print shop, Mackenzie House, 2006.

Main Floor – Print Shop

Tours conclude in the reconstructed print shop, located at the west end of the visitors' gallery, opposite the entranceway to the historic house; this particular space affords the site – in its entirety – the opportunity to showcase Mackenzie's personal and political interests as well as his entrepreneurial pursuits.[42] Acknowledging the fictionalized nature of the print shop space, interpreters call visitors' attention to the fact that this "reproduction" exists outside the parameters of the historic house.[43] In order to account for the purpose of the reconstruction, they call to mind Mackenzie's publishing exploits referencing particular historical facts; they begin by reminding visitors that, during his lifetime, Mackenzie published fourteen different newspapers but, during his residency in the house, his newspaper offices were not located in the house but on nearby King Street.[44] They explain that

Mackenzie, acting oftentimes as both proprietor and editor, wrote articles to acquaint the public with his views regarding, for instance, the benefits of responsible government and the necessity of governmental reform. Subsequent to that, interpreters, attempting to authorize the apparent historical accuracy of the reconstructed space, frequently point out that most of the artifacts in this space, including most particularly the 1845 Washington Flatbed Press, are "original to [Mackenzie's] time."

While there, interpreters encourage visitors to not only bear witness to the space but also to participate in activities within it, thus allowing visitors to "live history." So that they might gain a first-hand appreciation of the physicality of the printing process, for example, visitors are invited, with assistance from interpreters, to print their own Christmas cards, an activity that aims to reinstate the thematic premise of the Victorian Christmas tour program. Interpreters explain that, during the mid-nineteenth century Christmas season, publishers would have printed manuscripts, books, newspaper serials – such as Charles Dickens's *A Christmas Carol* – and Christmas cards, but that the actual printing of materials would have been executed by professional printers and not the office proprietor. Interpreters then take visitors through the printing process, getting them to arrange type-set letters on a Christmas card galley (or frame), ink the galley, and print the cards by running the galley through the historic press, which visitors then take as tour souvenirs. Overall, the tour content and interpretation showcases not so much the Christmas celebration as the lifestyle of a middle-class family living in Toronto during the mid-nineteenth century. In other words, the house itself, even in the context of the Victorian Christmas tour, has been animated in such a way so that it reflects a particular standard of living; in view of this, the Christmas decorations are noticeably confined to rooms on the main floor. Interpreters refer to "original" objects owned by the Mackenzie family to endorse the apparent historical accuracy of the representation and, subsequent to that, recall for visitors the fact that the house reflects a particular class-based way of life. In short, the decorated atmosphere, artifactual arrangements, interpretation, and associated participatory activities encourage visitors to experience what it "felt like to live back then" so that they might achieve a "contextual departure" from the present.[45]

For this reason, it could be argued that, while the banner-based exhibition aims to expand the site's content and brand Mackenzie House as a culturally diverse heritage institution, the inclusion of the banners, in reality, helps shore up the dominance of Anglo-Canadian culture.[46] The banners represent Toronto's cultural diversity by referencing different ethnicities within the museum's representation but, because they do not do so inside the historic house, the site reproduces existing social hierarchies. Banners hanging in the visitors' gallery present ethnic celebrations other than that represented in the house, and visitors peruse the display at their leisure. In contrast, interpreters lend voice to historical artifacts so that the living history format might transport visitors back in time. Its performance seemingly operates to evoke a sense of nostalgia in visitors – a yearning for a time (and place) that can never actually be known or recreated and so the reanimation of the Mackenzie family's festivities and lifestyle comes to function as a gauge by which to measure or classify ethnicities exhibited in the gallery space.

Mackenzie House's Victorian Christmas program utilizes different strategies to expose visitors to various cultural celebrations, with a banner-based exhibition outlining the particulars of Kwanzaa, Chanukah, winter solstice, and Chinese New Year festivities, while providing guided tours through the historic house so that visitors might "live history." In compiling banner displays that recall the region's ethnic make-up, heritage practitioners endeavor to portray Mackenzie House as representational of the population's diversity, thereby marking Toronto as a global city. Such efforts demonstrate ways in which site workers aim to expand the program's narrative content to include previously marginalized groups but do not, as I have suggested, solve issues pertaining to social, cultural, or political inequity. In order to apprehend both the shortcomings and ramifications of this approach, one must consider the political structures that call for such additions. Because the branding mandate assigned to Toronto's historic sites responds to ideas of diversity embedded in Canada's multiculturalism policy, the very nature of the policy authorizes ways in which Mackenzie House represents cultural diversity. Exploring how the site's inclusion of various ethnic groups compares with the reanimation of the house demonstrates the museum's advancement of the dominance of what Eva Mackey refers to as the unmarked whiteness of a core Canadianism, an ideological construction defined by those who determine who is (not) authentic or "real" Canadians.[47]

It has been argued that the inclusion of previously marginalized peoples in museums does not challenge but rather reinforces the authority of the hierarchical structures within which groups (or objects) are classified and ranked within the museum system.[48] As David Bennett explains, "additive model[s] of representation" conventionally treat minorities as "add-ons" to membership in public institutions.[49] For example, museums that advance themselves as culturally inclusive conventionally identify particular ethnic identities and represent them using objects and information believed to reflect their respective cultural traditions and practices. Accordingly, these "dumb" objects, as Lynda Jessup puts it, "*stand for* specific social groups, subordinate or dominate."[50] In the case of Mackenzie House, I argue that site workers use the banners to stand for ethnic groups other than the one represented in the House proper, thus allowing the animation of the House to reinforce a specific type of cultural dominance; in other words, explanatory banners that represent cultures other than the one displayed in the historic house set up a binary dynamic between a historicized core Canadianism and a more recent and distinctly localized reality. Moreover, the representation of cultural diversity within Mackenzie House is based on the concept of tolerance, a concept put forth most prominently in Canada's multiculturalism policy.

Expanding on my discussion in the first section of this study, particularly in Chapter 3, which examines how Canada's multiculturalism policy came into being and the type of national identity it promotes, I would argue, as do other scholars, that the policy recognizes ethnic groups so as to act as a "doctrine of tolerance."[51] In turn, the concept of tolerance advanced by the policy not only effects but also mobilizes Mackenzie House's representation of cultural diversity. Canada's multiculturalism policy, understood on a popular level as "unity-in-diversity," has fostered the idea among Canadians that ethnic diversity is a national virtue.[52] It suggests that all citizens have equal access to legal, political, and socioeconomic rights, regardless of their country of origin or distinguishing ethnic traits. Despite such accessions, the policy is essentially hierarchical. While state-sanctioned multiculturalism is predicated on the principles of recognition and equality, it is ultimately defined by, as David Bennett writes, the "liberal imperative to 'tolerate' cultural difference ... for in what sense can a minoritised culture be asked to 'tolerate' the majority or 'national' culture that assigns it the marginal status *of* a minority?"[53] The policy implicitly credits those in power with the ability to recognize and, further, to tolerate ethnic diversity in order to validate Canada's identity as a self-proclaimed multinational state.[54] In other words, it acts as a "*structuring* structure," one that reproduces power relations.[55]

As Ghassan Hage terms it, "multicultural tolerance" seeks to advance egalitarianism, thereby obscuring its dominating tendencies. This determination emanates from a standpoint of power. Tolerance, Hage argues, "always presupposes control over what is tolerated. That is, tolerance presupposes that the object of tolerance is just that: an object of the will of the tolerator ... To tolerate is not to just accept, it is to accept and position the other within specific limits and boundaries."[56]

Because Canada's multiculturalism policy positions ethnic groups within a particular nationalistic framework, the policy has been designed to reinforce Western cultural hegemony.[57] While the primary mandate of the Canadian Multiculturalism Act (1988) is to help preserve and enhance different ethnicities, the Act does not identify any specific group of Canadians as ethnic and so constructs ethnicity as a condition of commonality.[58] Multiculturalism discourse therefore seeks to convey to the world the belief that, in Canada, ethnic communities can practice and thus maintain the cultural traditions and activities performed in their countries of origin.[59] In granting ethnic groups the right to both preserve and enhance their cultural traditions while living in Canada, the Act imposes upon the ethnic subject "a stability that belies the incommensurability of identity." Smaro Kamboureli explains further, writing, "[The Act's] insistence on 'preservation' affirms the history of ethnic subjectivity as a differential sign, but it does so by appropriating that difference. While no subject can exist outside the history that has produced her, history is imaged [in the Act] as a finished product – for how else could it be 'preserved?'"[60] Similarly, Neil Bissoondath explains that official multiculturalism demands that people position themselves as unchanged despite migration, an experience that effects its own change; such demands in fact strip people of their uniqueness, equating them not as an individual but rather as part of their cultural collectivity within the Canadian state.[61] In other words, the multiculturalism policy recognizes and upholds the concept of diversity to construct a particular national image, one that is, as Bannerji writes, "predicated upon the existence of a homogeneous national, that is, a Canadian cultural self with its multiple and different others."[62] The policy thus affords "real" or "true" Canadians the ability and right to tolerate the existence (and practices) of ethnic communities within the Canadian state.[63]

More specifically, multiculturalism constructs the unmarked whiteness of the core culture as the standard by which to identify or measure citizens of other ethnic backgrounds. The fact that this core culture is unmarked suggests the degree to which the policy constructs it as being normative. "[To] call white Canadianness an ethnicity does not capture its specificity," Eva Mackey explains. "The point about these categories of identity – could we think of them as 'dominant and unmarked ethnicities'? – is that people do not think about themselves as 'ethnic,' but rather, see their customs, beliefs, practices, morals and values as normative and universal."[64] Accordingly, because Canada's multiculturalism policy positions ethnic communities outside of the "normative nation," the policy constructs, projects, and promotes the concept of Anglo-conformativity, thereby demonstrating the degree to which, as Yúdice puts it, "whiteness is valued."[65]

In working to advance present-day values in contemporary Canada, incorporation of cultural diversity at Mackenzie House indicates the extent to which inclusive strategies wind up replicating political and social hierarchies. As Irit Rogoff explains, "Museums' encounters with cultural difference are in a sense an opportunity to contract rather than to expand, to contract the staunch belief system that organizes, classifies, locates, and judges everything from the prevailing perspective of the West."[66] Expanding on the above discussion, I argue that, in the case of the Mackenzie House Victorian Christmas program, the site's banner display outlines for visitors different ethnic celebrations, while the reanimation of the museumified dwelling operates so as to naturalize and, by extension, normalize the original residents' lifestyle as typical of a middle-class nineteenth-century family who presumably drew on British values, customs, and activities. In other words, the museum includes representations of seemingly contemporary, ethnic festivities to showcase Toronto's culturally diverse population, but such inclusions provide a contrast that propels the dominance of the representation of the past performed within the house. As a result, the site's negotiation of both past and present-day circumstances reproduces British-based cultural hegemony. Despite the banners' inclusion – intended to destabilize the visitor's experience of the Victorian past – the living history performance executed within the House proper works to concretize, project, and naturalize a given hegemonic "social," thus ultimately advancing values associated with a core Canadianism and re-presenting their dominance.[67]

Conclusion

In an effort to explore the institutional relationship between heritage, living history, and memory in Canadian house museums, this study looks at the museumification of Dundurn Castle, Mackenzie House, and the Cartier House and their distinctive performances of the past. By connecting the artifact – that is, the historical building – with the Victorian Christmas program performed within it, I interrogate how these three different state-sanctioned living history museums play out a particular type of mythologized history that monumentalizes "founding nations" mythologies. In this ideological construction, Confederation represents a crucial moment in Canada's development as a federal state, one that stands for the unification of anglophones and francophones as the nation's "two founding cultures" and bolsters Canada's formation as a binational achievement.[1] The formation of these three house museums, their current operations, and their respective portrayals of anglophone and francophone cultures collectively demonstrate how representations of the past at heritage sites depend upon "artifactual accuracy" as well as the flexibility of historical narratives, making these homes rich sites for art historical investigation.

Dundurn Castle, Mackenzie House, and the Cartier House represent the past to attract and subsequently unify the citizenry. Each endeavours to concretize, privilege, and project particular concepts, such as the primacy of the family unit and the significance of community. Accordingly, these institutions have been developed in such as way – as evidentiary artifacts that perform – so that they might not only address but also manage issues associated with past and present-day concerns such as ethnicity and diversity, memory, veneration, and identity. Significantly, the manner in which "founding nations" mythologies are redeployed depends not only on the existence of the historical building but also on its location and size and the character of the site's local constituency. Furthermore, while historic venues provide visitors with experiential moments of a different time and place, such moments are increasingly being unsettled through contemporary art installations and interventions. Given that such additions conventionally seek to disrupt authoritative experiences of the past to cultivate a unified global citizenry, a brief analysis of both the products and the processes underscores the advantages of approaching heritage sites from an art historical perspective.

Notably, restorations of the selected homes were contingent upon the perceived historical importance of the original owners. Each represents the life and times of a major political figure identified within the Confederation period in British North America, including Sir Allan MacNab, Prime Minister of the United Canadas (1854–56) and Family Compact leader; Sir George-Étienne Cartier, who as John A. Macdonald's "Quebec lieutenant" is credited with having brought that province into Confederation; and William Lyon Mackenzie, first mayor of Toronto (1834) and leader of the 1837 Rebellion in Upper Canada. The monumentalization of these homes signals the socio-political importance assigned in and around the mid-twentieth century to Confederation and particular regions by historians, heritage workers and, by extension, the public, a venture that persists to this day with the sustained operation of each of the three sites.

In the mid-nineteenth century, those dedicated to governmental reform lived and worked primarily in what is now south central Canada. For example, in 1848 Montreal, Cartier purchased the first of the two homes that, together, have since been restored as the national historic site I consider here. His purchase was sensible, in view of the relocation of Canada's capital in 1844 from Kingston to Montreal. He would not have known that, by 1849, government officials would decide to institute a "perambulating system" in which the seat of government rotated every four years between Toronto and Quebec City. It was only in 1857 that governmental officials requested that Queen Victoria exercise what was called "Royal Prerogative" to select a permanent seat of government. (In the end, she selected Ottawa.[2]) As such, in the mid-nineteenth century, many politically-minded individuals lived within the vicinity of the rotating capital, which allowed them to travel frequently to the political hotbed of the time while still maintaining private, professional, or business interests as well as permanent residences.

It is not my intention to suggest that all nation-building endeavours or events in the mid-nineteenth century took place solely within this region. Nor do I wish to argue that this region is the only one that holds monuments devoted to such efforts. It was in Charlottetown, Prince Edward Island, for instance, that colonial politicians met in 1864 to discuss the possibility of a British North American federation incorporating the Maritime Colonies, and the site of the conference, known at the time as the new Colonial Building, is now largely restored with period rooms and artifacts to represent the year 1864.[3] Atlantic Canada was, in fact, the primary destination for those making "cultural/heritage visits" in the late 1990s.[4] In today's environment of rapidly shifting political, economic, and social climates, however, such visitorship is rarely consistent. As of 2006, for instance, the *Survey of Service Industries: Heritage Institutions* notes that the three most densely populated provinces – Ontario, Quebec, and British Columbia – garnered 80 per cent of the heritage industry's revenues.[5]

It is also noteworthy that Dundurn, Mackenzie House, and the Cartier House reside in large urban centres, with constituencies large enough to allow them to offer programs in the winter months. Their locations make evident why I did not include, for example, Bellevue House in Kingston, Ontario – the house museum representing the life and times of Sir John A. Macdonald, Canada's first post-Confederation prime minister and perhaps most widely recognized "Father of Confederation."[6]

Like the other sites discussed in this book, Bellevue was cultivated as a performative house museum during the nation-building years of the 1960s. Those vested in restoring the Tuscan-style villa determined that Macdonald's political accomplishments called for the site's monumentalization, even though Macdonald rented the property for only one year.[7] As Kingston's Member of Parliament E.J. Benson put it to members of the House of Commons in 1964, "Sir John A. Macdonald is looked upon as Kingston's most famous son, and the fact that he was the first prime minister of Canada and did so much for both the city of Kingston and for our country as a whole makes him obviously worthy of commemoration."[8] Later that year, the federal government purchased Bellevue and had it restored so that the

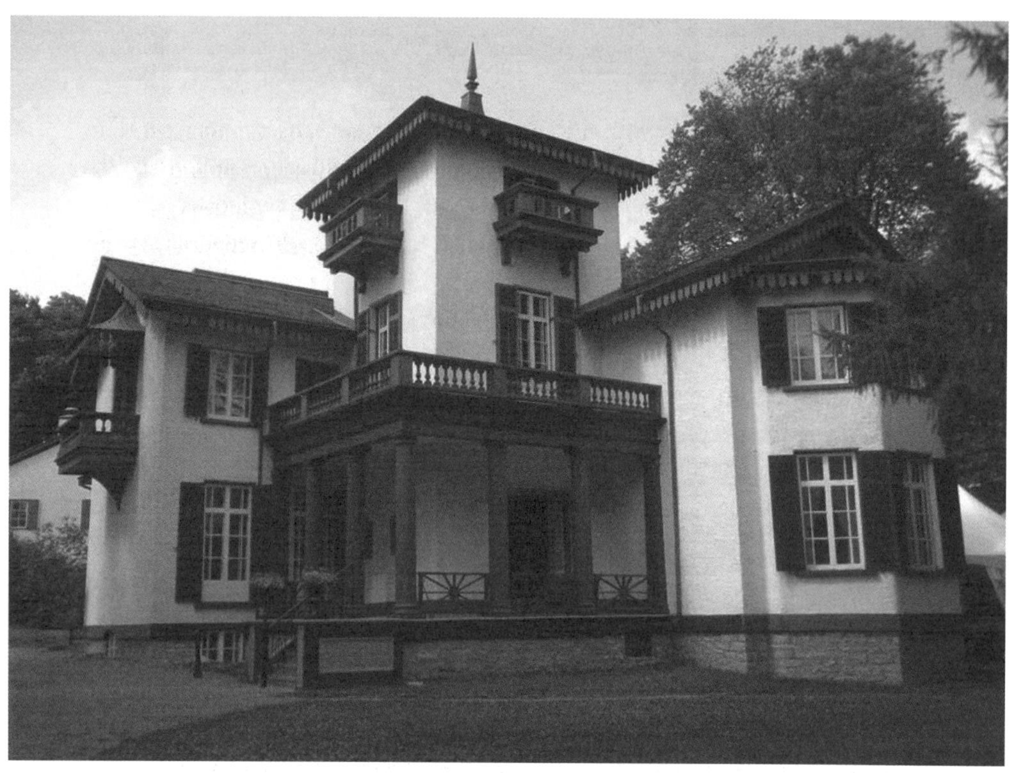

8.1 Bellevue House National Historic Site of Canada, Kingston, Ontario, 2010.

site officially opened to the public in 1967, the year of Canada's Centennial celebrations, as a "living history" museum. Today the site only offers tours from April until October, suggesting that Kingston cannot support a winter tourism market to the same extent as Hamilton, Montreal, and Toronto. In other words, while a building's perceived historic value might determine its function, the structure's location determines the nature of its operation and the degree of its participation in advancing "founding nations" mythologies.

The reanimation of Dundurn, Mackenzie House, and the Cartier House functions so as to communicate to visitors the site's symbolic purpose. Each site's operation, as a result, is based on how historians, curators, and tour guides interpret not only the historical building but also the historical figure represented by it. While Dundurn exists as a Picturesque Regency-style villa, and thus a notable architectural monument as well as a living history museum, Mackenzie's row house and Cartier's London-style townhouse are less architecturally pretentious – originally designed as utilitarian residential structures that would blend into the surrounding urban landscape.[9] As living history museums, however, the buildings and artifacts in the period rooms act, in the context of guided tours, as objects that, by virtue of their existence, historical documentation, and institutionalization, privilege particular aspects of Canada's national narrative.

Present-day circumstances often require reinventing perceptions of the past and so heritage initiatives manage collective remembrances as well as amnesia.[10] Nationalist ideologies often compel the creation of monuments so as to situate them, in seemingly "national" terms, as part of Canada's past, a location from which they act in turn as foundational of national identity.[11] In the case of Dundurn Castle, cultural workers strove to reconfigure public perceptions of Sir Allan MacNab so that the restoration of his home might set the site up as an emblem of the nation's past. In the late 1820s, Hamilton-based lawyer MacNab cultivated connections with the Family Compact, a political faction comprised of wealthy individuals who maintained the Loyalist tradition of social hierarchy and opposed republican institutions. As the faction's head in 1837, MacNab aided in the military suppression of rebel forces led by William Lyon Mackenzie, who desired an Upper Canadian frontier agrarian democracy, during what is now known as the Upper Canadian Rebellion and, for his part, was later knighted by Queen Victoria. His political career climaxed when, in 1854, he was elected prime minister of the United Canadas (1854–56).

The restoration of Dundurn Castle therefore entailed reinventing both the site and MacNab as a historical figure, particularly in light of the negative associations of the Family Compact commonly espoused in historical studies.[12] In 1961, for example, Scott Symons, then curator of Canadian art at the Royal Ontario Museum, argued that "Old Sir Allan MacNab represented all that was good and walrus-hopeless in the Family Compact. He has been maligned; and I feel is due for a 'restoration.' Whatever the compacters may or may not have done, they did establish here in Canada a cultivated, dignified rich life. *Their homes* show it."[13] Accordingly, those involved in the restoration project fostered a narrative that emphasized how MacNab not only cultivated elite British culture in the Canadian colony but also brought a physical example of that culture into being through the construction of his house.

In the case of the Sir George-Étienne Cartier National Historic Site of Canada, the owner's connection to nation-building endeavours is immediate and obvious. As Attorney General of Lower Canada (1858–62), lawyer, and politician, Cartier shared leadership of the United Canadas with John A. Macdonald; he also attended and participated in the Charlottetown,

Quebec, and London Conferences. Accordingly, in the mid-twentieth century, Cartier was included in the Historic Sites and Monuments Board's official list of the "Fathers of Confederation," compiled in 1959 to be held in trust by the Public Archives of Canada (now Library and Archives Canada). Board members then turned their attention to his former Montreal residences.[14] As part of a developing initiative to mount a program to honour the Fathers of Confederation, the Board approved a motion in October 1964 to designate Cartier's two semi-detached houses a site of "national historical importance."[15] In 1973, the government purchased both houses and turned them into a national historic site, which opened to the public in 1985.

In order to set Mackenzie up as a "great man" who helped establish the nation, parties vested in the restoration of his Toronto residence chose to portray him as the primary figure who fought (and sacrificed) for responsible government, which, in turn, provided the framework necessary for pre-Confederation politics. For example, when the Mackenzie House, furnished as a mid-nineteenth-century-period historical museum and library, opened to the public on 9 May 1950, Ontario premier Leslie Frost's opening remarks focused on Mackenzie's contributions to the Canadian nation:

> It matters not now who was right or who was wrong in the controversies of [the 1830s] ... What matters is what they achieved. From it all came responsible government ... On the foundations laid by the men of the 1830s – Mackenzie ... and the rest – Macdonald and his great lieutenant, Cartier, and those other Fathers of Confederation through the ensuing years, were in 1867, able to build the Dominion of Canada ... [I] dedicate the house and its historic contents as a memorial to the men and women of long ago, all of whom had their part in laying the foundations of our country, and upon whose courage, toleration, vision and experience the Canada of today has been built.[16]

In characterizing Mackenzie as a forefather of the "Fathers of Confederation," Frost positions the museum as that which memorializes not only the accomplishments of its original owner but also the nation at large. A decade later, the municipal government acquired the house and closed it, taking two years to restore it so that it might be "more truly representative of the period ... [and] the story of Mackenzie's life may be clearly depicted." On 31 July 1962, it reopened as a living history museum offering guided tours.[17]

In mounting Victorian Christmas programs, all three house museums portray a particular type of historic celebration, one that might have been performed by the original owner's family in residence. The reconceptualization of each site as an institutionalized domestic and festive space, however, showcases a certain type of lifestyle so as to convey to visitors the importance of the familial and, by extension, national community.[18] In this context, they emphasize family values, such as kinship, loyalty, and generosity, projecting representations of the family that work to elicit emotional responses from visitors and subsequently to unify the citizenry. In other words, they encourage visitors to identify strongly with that which is represented – the life and lifestyle of the family within the "home" – to generate feelings of loyalty not only to the nation's past but also its present.[19] In exploring how these performances function as hegemonic cultural tools to celebrate and promote the validity of the nation's past, my study demonstrates ways in which Canada's national narrative is adapted to address the politics of the place.[20]

⁂

To push the point, one might consider the example of Riel House National Historic Site of Canada in the St Vital area of Winnipeg, Manitoba. Although it does not offer Victorian Christmas tours (at least, not yet), Riel House currently provides a means through which to advance the contributions of Aboriginal peoples to Canada's "founding nations" mythologies. At Riel House, interpreters conduct tours so that the site, upon reanimation, portrays the Métis leader Louis Riel as a "nationally significant" historical figure.[21] Purchased by the federal agency Parks Canada in 1970, the Red River frame building opened to the public ten years later as a fully-functioning living history museum offering guided tours.[22] Significantly, in 1992, the federal government cited Riel's contribution to the development of the Manitoba Act (1870), which brought that province into Confederation, and designated him the founder of Manitoba.[23] And in 2000, Parks Canada developed the Riel House's management plan, determining that the site's primary mandate is to commemorate Riel as a "person of national historical significance."[24]

While site workers use information pertaining to Riel's death to develop representations within the house that advance the man as a heroic (national) symbol of martyrdom, it was Riel's mother, Julie Lagimodière-Riel, who

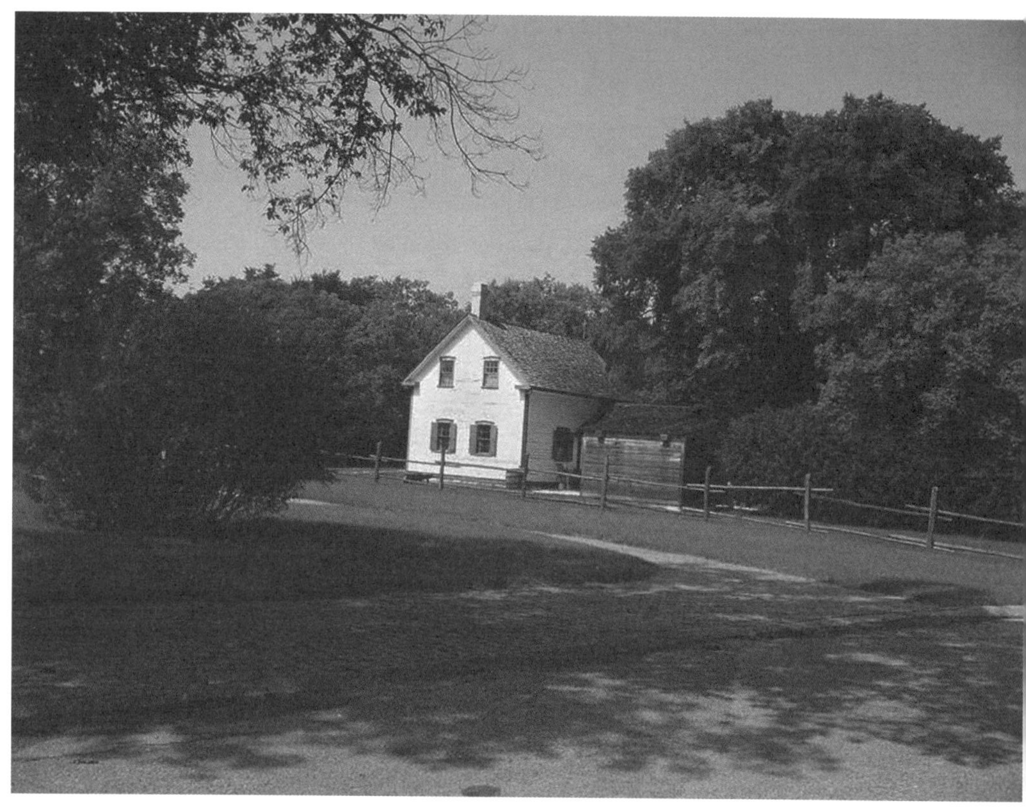

8.2 Riel House National Historic Site of Canada, St Vital, Winnipeg, Manitoba, 2009.

originally owned the residence.[25] Riel, having led the Métis uprisings of 1869 and 1885 to defend Métis land rights from usurpation by the Canadian government, was ultimately prosecuted for treason by the state and hanged in December 1885. Significantly, his body lay in state in his mother's house for two days prior to burial. As such, the Riel House's living room is (re)arranged so that artifactual arrangement reflects what might have been in place during the family's period of mourning.[26] Grounding the representation in such "historical fact" allows the museum to identify itself with a symbolic conception of Riel and, in doing so, authorize itself as a national historic site.

Because house museums showcase the past in the present-day, they reflect, upon reanimation, contemporary interests and priorities. In their formation, however, as evidenced in this study, nationalistic frameworks oftentimes spur the restoration of historic sites and, in turn, their reincarnation as living history museums. More broadly, as Pierre Nora explains, nation-building interests represent the "push and pull" that produces "sites

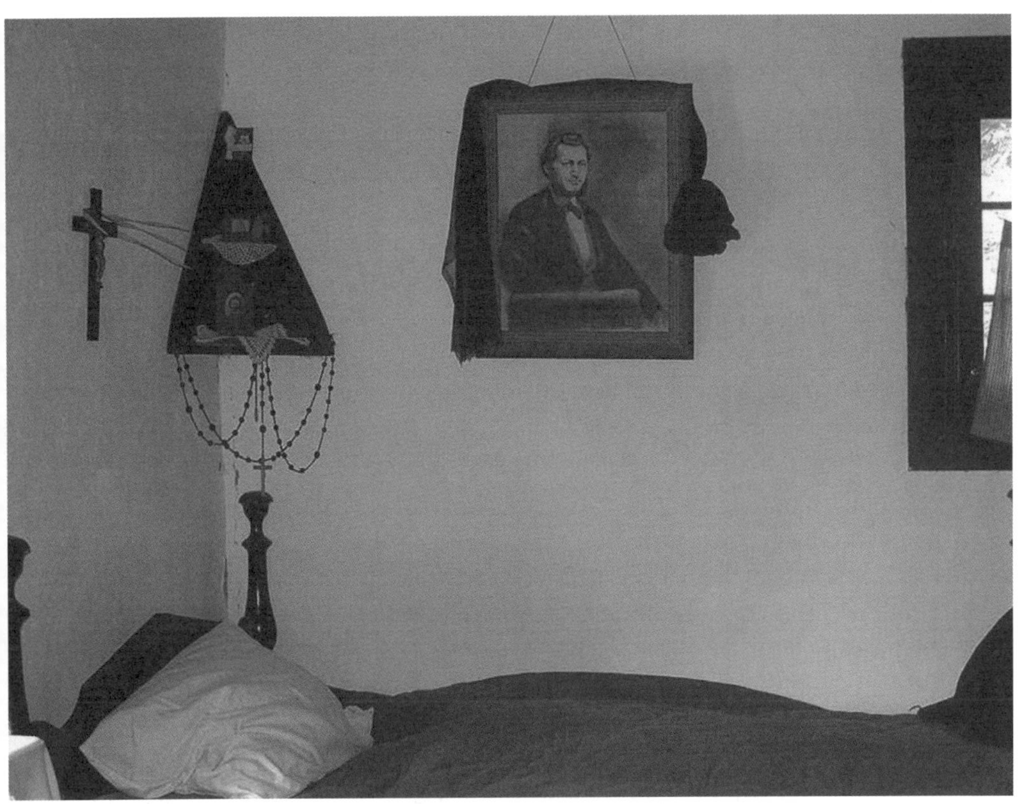

8.3 Living room, Riel House, 2009.

of memory" or lieux de mémoire.[27] As "sites of memory," living history museums are "material, symbolic and functional." These aspects "always" coexist, Nora argues, because such sites are "created by a play of memory and history."[28] In the case of Dundurn Castle, Mackenzie House, and the Cartier House, the respective architectural contexts and artifactual arrangements represent the material aspect while the live interpretation reinforces the house's symbolic function – its veneration of a major political figure identified with the Confederation period. Accordingly, I make the case that the house museum's credibility and attractiveness relies – as does disciplinary art history – on its calculated deployment of objects to naturalize its interpretation of the past, representing it so that the present appears as the natural outcome. In other words, my identification of these institutions as large artifacts makes evident the possibility of evaluating these objects and their restored period rooms within the artifactual domain of disciplinary art history.[29] There is, however, also their practical function to consider – their operation as tourist destinations. As such, their purpose depends upon their ability to generate sufficient visitation to validate their sustained operations. With the advent of Web 2.0 and social media, the need to reinvigorate historic sites has intensified, as evidenced by Parks Canada 2012 budget cuts and subsequent development of guided tour applications discussed in Chapter 4. Such needs also take into account the expectations of citizens, particularly those attached to their "smart" devices, mesmerized by cyber games and dependent on social media for interaction. In the twenty-first century, curator Lowry Stokes Sims explains, historic museums are expected "to address an appetite for unique experiences, novel experiences, and authentic experiences."[30] Therefore, heritage practitioners, curators, and artists have begun collaborating on developing contemporary art exhibitions installed within historical sites, projects referred to in related scholarship either as "museum interventions" or, more pointedly, "artist-history interventions." As Jim Drobnick and Jennifer Fisher, founders of the curatorial collaborative DisplayCult, explain, the term "museum intervention" describes "the collaboration between artists and institutions to transform the museum from a *container* of cultural artifacts to a *medium* of contemporary work. In this practice, the museum context becomes the raw material or 'cultural readymade' for artistic analysis, commentary and reconfiguration."[31] Artists' "museum interventions" thus provide innovative ways to satisfy cravings for uniquely novel and authentic experiences. They frequently implicate viewers in their own subjectivities by "tweaking" the expected conventions of installations.[32] What is more, they foster a taste for interaction that has been identified in the 2010 American Art Museums' report on diversity as a strategy of the future to capture new audiences.[33] While some interventions aim to reconfigure these places as destinations appealing to a global (or international) audience, others interrogate the theoretical bedrocks of museological and curatorial practice.

In terms of the former, consider the case of the Château de Versailles, an institution that I would characterize as *the* exemplary house museum, one quintessentially monumental in both nature and scale. For Nora, the museumification of Louis XIV's palatial residence of the French court and government demonstrated how the material legacy of France's historical monuments could be deployed to anchor the nation's collective memory, commemorating the cultural and political supremacy of the French monarchy, nation, and state.[34] Over the course of the last decade, however, the site has hosted exhibitions of, as France's former minister of culture and communication Jean-Jacques Aillagon puts it, "outstanding artists of our time" such as Jeff Koons (2008), Xavier Veilhan (2009), and Takashi Murakami (2010) so as to deliberately agitate the museum's temporal (and ethnic) cohesion.[35]

These exhibits demonstrate the degree to which historic sites strive, most notably in the twenty-first century, to foster a global citizenry, dissolving boundaries between ethnicity and nationalism while simultaneously underscoring connections between art and history, culture and politics, and past and present. Case in point – the *Jeff Koons Versailles* show. In 2003, when the French ministry of culture began contemplating ways to develop programs to reiterate Versailles' "outstanding historical and artistic significance," they brought on board Laurent Le Bon, curator at the Centre national d'art et de culture Georges Pompidou. Le Bon recommended to the Ministry that Versailles devote for a few months – the typical timespan allotted to an exhibition – rooms to showcase one artist's work. While the Ministry agreed to this proposition, it also determined that: the artist should be a "foreigner" one year and French the next; that they should have an established "international reputation"; and, finally, that their works should be "sympathetic to and even in tune with the château."[36] *Entrez* Jeff Koons.

Significantly, Koons' location of selected works aimed to activate the spaces, stimulating a dialogue between past and present. And while many complained about the temporal disjuncture – how the art obliterated the "historical accuracy" of the period rooms – the exhibition in fact called attention to the art-ifice of residential heritage sites. Not only was Koons the first contemporary artist to showcase his art in the State Apartments, this exhibit also constituted the artist's first public retrospective show in France, illustrating his career from the 1980s up to 2008. As a result, Koons decided to feature his sculptures in the palace, the curatorial principle being "one room, one sculpture."[37] Locating his sculptures in these spaces, according to Koons, aimed to not only "allow for what's present in the rooms" so as to not "cover[ ] up the decorative arts of Versailles" but also stimulate a "give-and-take" dialogue, a mutual complementarity and exchange so that his works might interact with and augment a respective room's design, arrangement, and purpose(s). For instance, his *Large Vase of Flowers* (1991) – a hyperrealistic polychrome wood sculpture of 100 spring flowers in a vase – sat on a table in the Queen's Bedchamber, thus calling attention to the femininity and fertility of both the sculpture and the space; it was in this chamber where the Crown Princes (*les Dauphins*) were born.[38] The room's historical artifacts include an elaborate bed and canopy, gilded balustrade, and the Schwedfeger jewel-casket, all situated to evoke for visitors an awareness of the various activities that were documented as having taken place within, such as the Queen's daily ablutions, dressing, and adornment. While numerous parties lamented the destruction of the "authentic experience," complaining the exhibition did not take into account Versailles' target demographic – tourists looking to experience "what it felt like to live back then" – it also forced many to confront the fact that the château's period rooms are also exhibitionary spaces, meticulously researched, artfully designed, and strategically deployed.[39] Such confrontations throw into sharp relief that which this study has made evident upon critical consideration – the artistry of heritage. Other artist-history interventions offer more pointed opportunities to critique interpretations of the past.

Artist-history exchanges can provoke an engaged spectatorship, drawing in both museum staff and the broader community and ultimately revealing new ways to think about local and, in the case of my work, national history. Undertaken by installation-based artists such as Michael Asher, Judith Barry, Andrea Fraser, Hans Haacke, Jamielee Hassan, and Mel Ziegler, among others, these ventures demonstrate how museum exhibition practices are entangled within a specific ideological framework.[40] They underscore how the institutional context informs an artwork's meaning, as well as the meaning of the museum visit, and so these artists, in their installation practice, critique the policies, practices, and power structures governing art galleries and historical museums.[41]

Artist interventions in heritage sites interrogate who actually possesses historical authority.[42] Heritage sites conventionally re-deploy the historic structure so that it functions as a representational sign, an artifactual object furnished with other objects that, cumulatively and by virtue of their provenance, conservation, and subsequent institutionalization, validate the institutionalized interpretation by reconceiving authority as so-called "historical authenticity." Historians, curators, and interpreters use the objects at hand, conducting extensive research and then offering interpretations designed to position the museum's representation as legitimate, credible, and ultimately authoritative.[43] Prior to the 1990s, the museum community remained staunchly resistant to issues raised by critical dialogue, preferring instead to remain isolated from critical art history. A crucial turn, however, was affected most notably in Fred Wilson's 1992 installation *Mining the Museum*. Wilson's intervention and others that followed encouraged *different* parties to critique interpretations of the past as well as the present.

In 1991, director George Ciscle and curator Lisa Corrin of the arts organization The Contemporary in Baltimore invited Wilson to create an installation using the permanent collection of one of the city's museums with the intention of having it installed during the city's hosting of the 1992 American Association of Museums conference. Ultimately, Wilson chose to assume a year-long post as an artist-in-residence at the Maryland Historical Society and created a "museum intervention," one deliberately appropriated from the "museum exhibition lexicon."[44] Given the entire third floor of the Society Building to work with, Wilson arranged objects so that they appeared to be within an extended installation of the Society's permanent collection (located on the lower two floors) and then disrupted the apparent uniformity with objects that raised questions about how museums (fail to) represent African Americans and Native Americans. For example, in one section, labelled "Metalwork 1793–1880," Wilson illustrated how museum classification can promote a "tidy structure of institutional denial."[45] He placed shackles used to manacle slaves during the auctioning of human beings alongside silverwork done in the Baltimore Repoussé style, also dating – like the shackles – to the early nineteenth-century, making the point that a luxury economy was built on the system of slavery.[46] The installation not only provoked discussions about slavery's legacy in the city and state, it also stimulated dialogue among African American employees at the Society, as the project stood on display for an eleven-month period. As Melissa Rachleff states, "Wilson's process *mined* curatorial practices, but the ultimate design of the installation did not provide closure; rather, it raised questions and critiques about historical interpretation generally, and about the Maryland Historical Society's presentation of the past in particular."[47] Twenty years later, the merit of unearthing untold histories in North American historic museums remains as salient as ever.

Wilson's project speaks to the ways in which the dialogue between museum curators, interpreters, artists, and audiences has shifted. Given the intervention's presence in the context of the American Association of Museums conference, curators throughout North America took note of Wilson's project. In its wake, both curators and artists have mounted similar interventions in select cities across the globe. In the summer of 2001, the curatorial collaborative DisplayCult, led by Drobnick and Fisher, mounted *Museopathy*, a multi-site exhibition in museums and heritage sites throughout Kingston, Ontario. Organized by Jan Allen and the Agnes Etherington Art Centre, the project entailed artist installations of site-specific works in museums as well as an object-based exhibition culled from collections of the city's museums displayed in the Art Centre. Featured in Bellevue House, Mel Ziegler's *Mail Order Authenticity* involved the introduction of contemporary and Victorian-style objects purchased from mail-order and electronic catalogues into the home's restored interior. Given the dearth of explanatory text panels in the house museum, as well as the relatively diminutive nature of some objects, such as the Post-it pad on the writing desk, visitors had to carefully scrutinize the validity of individual objects within the period landscape or, as the curators term it, the object's "authentic" character. This installation required visitors not only to appreciate but also interrogate the validity *and* discrepancies of the artifactual arrangements.[48]

Characterized by curator Meredith Malone, Wilson's and Ziegler's interventions function as site-specific projects or, more broadly, "site-oriented practices," the artists, in both cases, working with the respective institution's permanent collections.[49] Both depend primarily on the rearrangement of objects. Andrea Fraser's artistic practice, on the other hand, interrogates the politics of tour performances in the museum context. Arguably best known for her *Museum Highlights* performance (1989), in which the artist delivered parodic performances as a fictionalized volunteer docent named Jane Castleton giving guided tours of collection highlights at the Philadelphia Museum of Art, Fraser's formative practice methods aimed to mimic the "public face" of singular institutions while, at the same time, critiquing them.[50] She later went on to take into account seismic shifts in the global cultural economy, what with the introduction of virtual relationships ushered in by the Internet and globalization and, subsequent to that, with the prioritization of a service-based economy over a goods-based one. Accordingly, Fraser reoriented her practice so as to "effect change from within," working in private galleries, corporations with art collections, and American university art departments.[51] As she herself explains it, "If you want to transform relations ... the only chance you have is to intervene in those relations in their enactment, as they are produced and reproduced."[52]

Similarly, Iris Häussler's 2008 intervention – a staged archaeological excavation at the Grange, the nineteenth-century house attached to the Art Gallery of Ontario – provokes internal transformation, both structurally and cognitively. In light of the larger discussion brought about by this book, her work lays bare the extent to which heritage practitioners utilize and, by extension, depend upon a particular artistry.[53]

Entitled *He Named Her Amber*, Häussler's project depends upon the participation of volunteer interpreters who lead visitors throughout the site while identifying various "findings" planted by the artist in deliberately staged excavated sections of the house. The interpreters explain their supposed significance or implications to contemporary understandings of nineteenth-century domestic culture, based on a script composed by Häussler. As one guide, fiction writer Martha Baillie described it, "I had been asked to lie. I had been asked to tell a story ... Around me I could feel the tug and give of contradictory desires – a yearning for enchantment and a thirst for the factual, delight in discovery, hunger for the inexplicable and a longing for definition."[54] Interpreters nonetheless draw on Häussler's instructions, inviting visitors to critically analyze their seemingly inherent faith in "artifactual accuracy."

Ideally, such projects encourage the dissolution of boundaries between the commissioned work, the institutional voice, and the public. In the case of *He Named Her Amber*, from the outset, Häussler conceived of the house tour as an artwork. In 2007, then Curator of Contemporary Art at the Art Gallery of Ontario (hereafter AGO) David Moos commissioned Häussler to create a new work for the gallery's November 2008 reopening, following the completion of its expansion project led by "starchitect" Frank Gehry.[55] Born in Germany in 1962 and having studied at the Munich Academy of Fine Arts, Häussler developed an installation-based practice, compiling hyperrealistic lived-in settings in rented apartments and hotel rooms, supposedly occupied by reclusive fictional characters of the artist's design. In 2001, she moved to Toronto and continued this practice, putting together the "immersive narrative installation," entitled *The Legacy of Joseph Wagenbach*, at 105 Robinson Street, Toronto (curated by Rhonda Corvese).[56] Bringing this individual to life, Häussler conceived of Wagenbach as an elderly German immigrant born near the concentration camp Bergen-Belsen who attempted to cope with the trauma he experienced by creating 120 sculptures – produced by the artist herself – made from concrete, plaster, and wax, scattered throughout the rented house. Häussler herself posed as an archivist, wearing a white lab coat and gloves, taking people throughout the house, explaining her role in the assessment of the "cultural value" of the sculptures. The critical and public success of the project encouraged Moos to approach Häussler and curate *He Named Her Amber*.[57]

Notably, Häussler undertook the AGO-commissioned project in a state-sanctioned national historic site, a "living history" house museum – similar to those interrogated in this study – to which the Gallery has been appended. Built in 1817 for lawyer and merchant D'Arcy Boulton Junior, the Georgian residence reflects, according to the commemorative HSMBC plaque erected in 1984 and revised in 2010, "the conservative influence of 18th century British classical tradition" with its symmetrical five-bay façade and central pediment. Boulton's daughter-in-law, Harriet Dixon Boulton Smith bequeathed the Grange, upon her death, to the Ontario Society of Artists so that it might become the Art Museum of Toronto. Following Dixon's passing, in 1913, the Art Museum of Toronto held its first exhibition in the recontextualized residence. By 1966, the Art Museum of Toronto became the AGO and additions to the home were made to accommodate the institution's growing collection and display policies. Notably, in the early 1970s, the AGO's Junior Women's Committee raised over $500,000 to ultimately restore The Grange as a house museum, which opened in 1973. A paid staff of fifteen individuals offered guided tours of the historic interior re-furnished to reflect the year 1835. Notably, Häussler's project takes into account the necessity of interpreters and the role they play in the visitor's experience, as well as women's contribution to the preservation and study of Canada's material and visual culture located within restored domestic sites.

Entering into the Grange in 2008, visitors took the tour *He Named Her Amber*, an excursion devoted to displaying and discussing the life of a so-called "deranged scullery maid," a decisive inversion of the standardized "upstairs-downstairs" tour offered at The Grange for decades prior.[58] Volunteer interpreters take visitors throughout the house, pointing out different archeological excavations, seemingly in progress, all the result of an accidental discovery, so it was claimed. According to the interpreters, some letters had surfaced during the AGO's renovation, as well as a diary belonging to Henry Whyte, butler at The Grange from 1815–57, which contained a detailed map of the house indicating where an Irish maid named Mary O'Shea – a seventeen year-old "spinster" from Kilkenney who began working at the Grange household in 1828 – had secreted away wax parcels. In the course of his duties, the butler happened upon these specimens, which struck him as resembling pieces of fossil ambers. As a result, according to interpreters, the AGO brought in a professional team called Anthropological Services Ontario that proceeded to uncover larger objects. One such object sits in a glass cube on a plinth in the front hall where interpreters greet visitors and commence with the tour introduction. Interpreters call visitors' attention to the rotund mound of clay and beeswax, labelled with a detailed

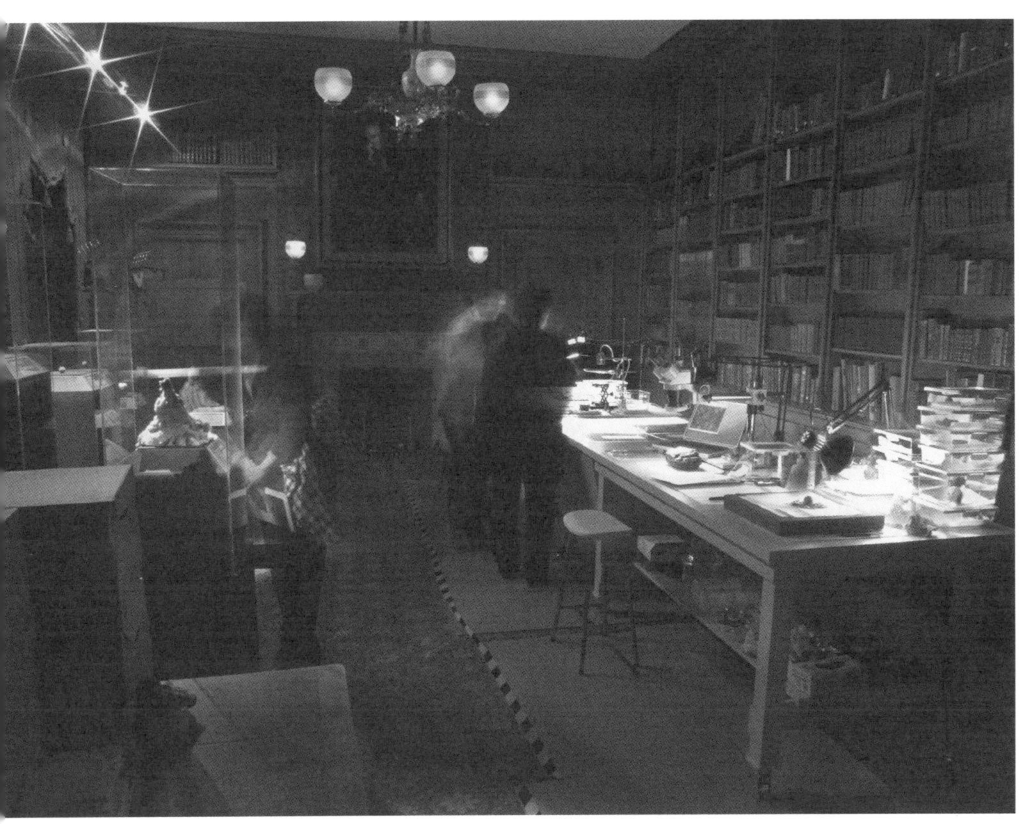

8.4 Iris Häussler, "View into the Goldwin Smith Library, used as staging area for the research the Anthropological Services Ontario undertook in 2008–9," *He Named Her Amber*, The Grange in the Art Gallery of Ontario, 2008. © Iris Häussler/sodrac (2014).

text panel, noting that it has been found – upon scientific investigation – to contain the dried human blood of an unknown person. They then proceed through the house's main floor and basement, pointing out what Moos characterizes as "distinct spheres of activity," such as the library, dominated by a monstrous assessment table, featuring microscopes, X-rays, computers, and numerous display cases cast about the space.

Significantly, Häussler leaves various signals throughout the house, such as strings of beads on a light box spelling out the letters ART, thereby calling attention to the arrangement's creativity and signalling its fictitious nature. Upon the tour's completion, interpreters give visitors "Excavation notes," a rather extensive missive signed by the artist herself that reveals the tour to be an artwork "created to be experienced as historic fact, as a method for direct and personal involvement of the visitor."[59] As such, all visitors only learn of the tour's fictive nature upon its completion, which in turn underscores the significance and merit of the artist's intervention, one intended to be definitively experiential *and* revelatory.

Häussler conceives of this project – and others like it that define her practice – as "haptic conceptual art," a practice that depends upon the visitor's "direct, immersive experience," one intended to provoke a meaningful experience that, upon revelation, encourages critical reflection. The onsite tours re-present historicized constructions of reality, followed by revealing the fictitiousness of the project, so that the work operates, in Häussler's words, in the "space between fiction and nonfiction."[60] Notably, the plethora of facts, dates, and details mimic the type of delivery, as well as the content, offered in the house museum tours considered in this study. As Gillian McKay recalls, following her visit, "Reflecting back, all of us marveled at the audacity of the ruse, at the brilliance of its execution, and most of all, at our eagerness to believe. Had the combined forces of validation – which included the tour guide, the team of scientists and the AGO itself – disabled our critical faculties?"[61] As the saying goes, the devil is in the details.

Deploying extensive measures to validate the so-called "reality" of the excavation, the entire project took Häussler approximately one year to design, construct, and produce. She wrote a script, invented a backstory, made artifacts, installed various sophisticated archeological dioramas throughout the house, and even hired a professional team from Historic Renovations Ltd. to open up the brick floors and jackhammer through the concrete slabs in the basement. While Häussler is quick to point out that the process does not change "the simple fact that the work as a whole is a fiction," it does speak to the artist's (and the curator's) respect for the sanctity of the historical structure. While Moos argues that it is the guided tour "which takes place within the frame of an art museum [that] creates the impression of plausibility,"[62] I would hasten to add that there is the artifactual accuracy offered by The Grange itself also to consider. Its attachment to the AGO, or rather the AGO's growth out of The Grange, informs its reception, but its structural and, by extension, historical integrity, restoration, and reanimation are equal – if not primary – contributors to the experience. As Häussler herself notes, *He Named Her Amber* allowed the artist to consider the "fundamental dilemma of immigration in [Toronto,] this city of immigrants."[63] Probing these issues through the narrative fictionalization of the life experiences and activities of Mary O'Shea, grounded in The

Grange, Häussler brings concerns pertaining to communal memory to the forefront.

Art historians, curators, and journalists are quick to point out how Häussler's interrogative installation practice references the work of German performance artist Joseph Beuys. As Moos explains, Häussler's materialized queries are "grounded in the so-called German problem – deep-rooted issues of communal identity and historical guilt." He goes on to point out how the post-Second World War context in Germany encouraged Beuys to develop a conceptual practice that probes the "horrors of the German passage through the twentieth century." Explaining further, he writes, "Drawing deeply on myths, fables and a shaman-like self-styled persona, Beuys offered an artistic model to Häussler that emphasizes direct encounter and performance, trading on the power of ephemeral experience. Understanding art as a means to healing, Beuys developed an inclusive idea of how art could become a salve for historical ills and social needs."[64] In a similar vein, Häussler sets up the house as a "central metaphorical predicate that requires a critical view."[65]

House museums in Canada offer poignant possibilities and venues for artists to promote a critically engaged public spectatorship. Ideally, such projects encourage the dissolution of boundaries between the commissioned work, the institutional voice, and the public; they allow for the introduction of critical voices that disrupt commonplace interpretive goals.[66] While art historians, curators, and theorists have long since recognized and promoted the importance of "history-infused artist projects," historians seem to refrain from doing so, possibly, according to Rachleff, because of the relative dearth of sustained analyses regarding such projects for the history community. While these engagements are as yet episodic (as was the case with *He Named Her Amber*) such projects, to my mind, merit sustenance, particularly in light of ideologies that shaped the preservation, restoration, and reanimation of Dundurn Castle, Mackenzie House, and the Cartier House as well as recent contradictory representations of Canada's history articulated by current Prime Minister Stephen Harper. In his address to attendees of the 2010 G-20 Summit, Harper proclaimed, "We also have no history of colonialism. So we have all of the things that many people admire about the great powers but none of the things that threaten or bother them." Significantly, he gave this speech less than a year after offering the historic public apology on behalf of the Canadian Government to all Aboriginal peoples for the Indian Residential School system. Capturing Harper's G-20 utterance in his vivid

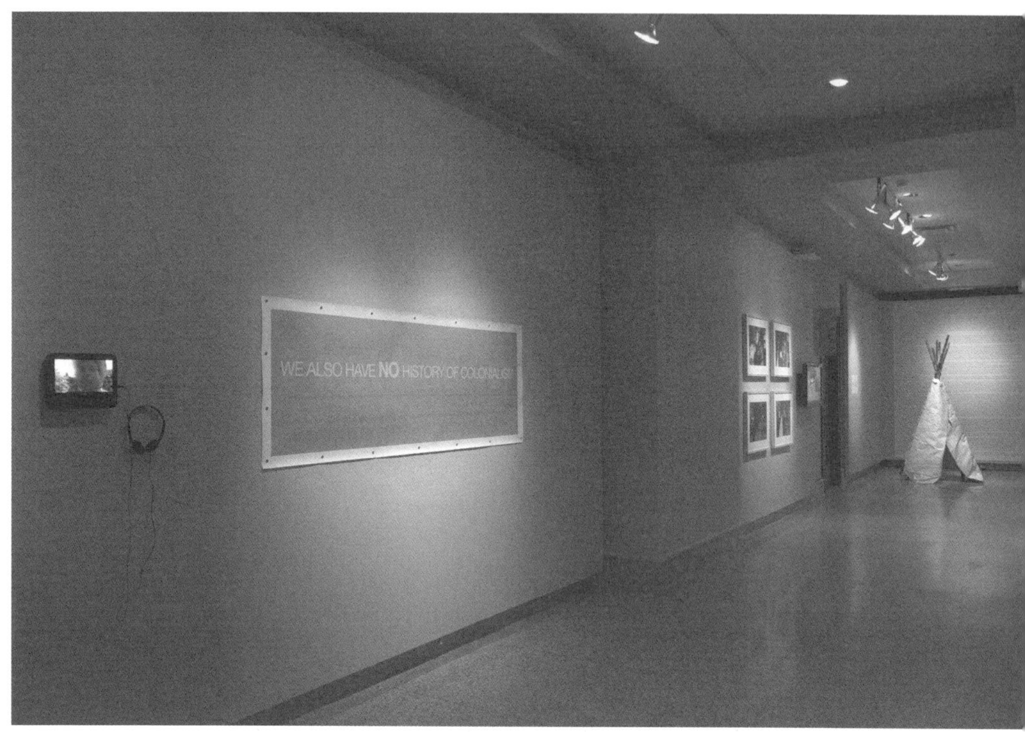

8.5 *Decolonize Me* installation at the Ottawa Art Gallery, 2011, including Sonny Assu, *Chief Speaker*, 2011, and Jordan Bennett, *Sovereignty Performance*, 2009.

turquoise text-based work *Chief Speaker* (2011), Sonny Assu (Ligwilda'x̱w [We Wai Kai] of the Kwakwaka'wakw Nations) reminds us of the selective nature of historical memory, ultimately ensuring it will not be forgotten.

Notes

Introduction

1 Cameron, "Spirit," 77.

2 Schwartz, *Copy*, 279; Mills, "Moving," 113, 114; Gable and Handler, "Public," 251.

3 West, *Domesticating*, xii.

4 Young, "Museum in the House?" 60.

5 Casey, "Museum Effect," 11.

6 Handler and Saxton, "Dyssimulation," 243–4.

7 Casey, "Museum Effect," 10–12; Timothy, "Introduction," xiii.

8 Osborne, "Landscapes," 10.

9 Church and White, "Toronto's." On 19 September 2011, the city's Executive Committee approved the manager's report, thereby ratifying the closure of museums with low attendance and revenues pending City Council's approval on 26 September 2011. City of Toronto, "Committee Recommendations."

10 McKay and Bates, *Province*, 377. See also Black, *Engaging*; and Conn, *Museums*.

11 In 2004, according to Statistics Canada, Canadians took the fewest number of domestic excursions between the months of October and December. The most popular months for travel were April, May, and June. A 2006 survey states that late fall and early winter "is typically the time of year in which

Canadians travel least in Canada, as they are likely more attracted by southern destinations or simply prefer staying in the comfort of their homes" (Statistics Canada, *Canadian Travel*, 21–2; quote from 21).

12 Vachhani and Pullen, "Home," 808; Holliday and Thompson, "Body"; Wajcman, *Feminism*.

13 Tracy, "Introduction," 1.

14 See, for example, Connelly, *Christmas*; Restad, *Christmas*; Nissenbaum, *Battle*.

15 Schwartz, *Culture*, 279.

16 Nesbitt interview, 2003.

17 Similarly, Australian historian and house museum curator Linda Young writes, "The challenge is for house curators to let go of received truth as the only vector of understanding. Conventional histories can be offered to visitors, but what they actually make out of a house museum visit is their own product ... [A] broad grasp of the [house museum's] tradition enlightens understanding of the possibilities that might be unleashed for visitors" (Young, "Museum in the House?" 76).

18 Prior to my recording both the tours and interviews, I secured interpreters' written consent to tape-record and transcribe the material; the names of the interpreters, however, have been removed from the discussion that follows to maintain confidentiality.

19 See, for example, Anderson, *Time*; Bruner, "Abraham Lincoln"; Donnelly, *Interpreting*; Leon and Rosenzweig, *History*; Levine, *Defining*; West, *Domesticating*. Some examples of Canadian living history studies include Campbell, "It was Canadian," 5–34; Macleod, "Decolonizing," 361–80; Peers, "Playing," 39–59.

20 John D. Rockefeller Jr., the first and primary benefactor of the Colonial Williamsburg restoration project, spoke of the purpose of the site, saying, "To those in search of a deeper understanding of our country Williamsburg offers tangible evidence that human freedom, self-government, and sovereignty of the individual have been the well-springs of our greatness. I believe that this nation can be better comprehended through knowledge of its roots and traditions" (quoted in Kammen, *Mystic*, 583).

21 Gable and Handler, *New*, 13.

22 Neal, *Trauma*, 23.

23 Stratton and Ang, "Imagined," 152.

24 Day, *Multiculturalism*, 9, emphasis in the original.

25 Mackey, *House*, 18; Harles, "Multiculturalism," 229.

26 Nora, "Between," 7–25.

27 Katriel, "Sites," 118.

28 Schwartz, *Culture*, 996, 279, emphasis in the original.

29 Smith, *Nationalism*, 133.

30 Smith, "Ethnoscapes," 11; Smith, *Chosen*, 258–9; Handler and Saxton, "Dyssimulation," 245; Casey, "Museum Effect," 12.

31 Smith, *Nationalism*, 71.

32 Macleod, "Decolonizing," 366–7.

33 West, *Domesticating*, xii.

34 As Macleod puts it, "Political rhetoric and popular myth celebrate the heterogeneity of Canada's population, but cultural institutions and social practices belie claims to multicultural identity" ("Decolonizing," 362).

35 Casey, "Museum Effect," 12, 11; Parks Canada, *Management Plan*, 2007, 31.

36 Kratz and Karp, "Frictions," 5.

37 Jenkins, "Renaissance," 173.

38 For example, in 1991, then-chairperson of the Toronto Historical Board Christine Caroppo Clarence wrote, "In Toronto, we have the special challenge to interpret the story of Toronto through our museums, which are largely Euro-Canadian in nature and date from the 19th and the late 18th century. In the context of a multi-cultural 20th century city, how do we make this heritage relevant to the current inhabitants of a city founded by the English with earlier occupation of the French and the presence of Native cultures thousands of years old?" (*1990 Annual Report*, 2).

39 Sassen, *Global*.

40 Toronto Historical Board, "Joint Meeting Museums Committee and the Historical Sites Committee, Monday 18 September 1961," *Toronto Civic Historical Committee*, 1.

41 Yúdice, *Expediency*.

42 Nora, "Between," 19.

43 West, *Domesticating*, 162.

Chapter One

1 Quoted in Desmond, *Rome*, 7.

2 Taylor, *Negotiating*. See also Pelletier, "Politics," and Symons, *Place*.

3 Strong-Boag, "Experts," 62.

4 Burgoyne, "Contested," 210.

5 Gable and Handler, "Public," 251.

6 Walkowitz and Knauer, *Memory*, 8.

7 Handler and Saxton, "Dyssimulation," 245.

8 See, for instance, Blatti, *Past*; Bodnar, *Remaking*; Carson, "Living"; Connerton, *Societies*; Frow, "Tourism"; Halbwachs, *Collective*; Kirshenblatt-Gimblett, *Destination*; Lowenthal, *Foreign*; Wallace, "Visiting"; Walsh, *Representations*; Warren and Rosenzweig, *History*.

9 Anderson, "Living," 291.

10 Anderson, *Time*, 19.

11 Bennett, "Museums," 70.

12 Gable, Handler, and Lawson, "Relativism," 794–5.

13 Ibid., 797.

14 Ibid., 796.

15 See Anderson, *Imagined Communities*; Bodnar, *Remaking*; Boyer, *City*; Bruner, "Abraham Lincoln"; Clifford, *Predicament*; Clifford, *Routes*; Duncan, *Civilizing*; Karp and Mullen Creamer, *Museums*; Karp and Levine, *Exhibiting*; Kirshenblatt-Gimblett, *Destination*; McClintock, *Imperial*; Norkunas, *Politics*; and Urry, *Tourist*. For a discussion of the Canadian context, see Martin, *Politics*.

16 Nora, "Between," 19. Similarly, Brian Osborne ("Native," 159) suggests that, while memorial structures might solidify ideas in both time and space, conveying messages in iron, marble, brick, or concrete, their permanence is "illusory." Memorial structures are, in fact, produced by historical, political, and aesthetic actualities that constantly evolve, shift, and change.

17 Nora, "Between," 19.

18 McKay suggests that the terms of reference of this particular moniker might be expanded to include the "subsequent elaboration and stabilization of a federal system down to 1896" ("Liberal Order," 633).

19 Silver, "Confederation (1867)," 57.

20 In his statement to the House of Commons, Prime Minister Trudeau outlined the purpose(s) of the multiculturalist policy: "A policy of multiculturalism within a bilingual framework commends itself to the government as the most suitable means of assuring the cultural freedom of Canadians ... National unity, if it is to mean anything in the deeply personal sense, must be founded on confidence in one's own individual identity; out of this can grow respect for that of others and a willingness to share ideas, attitudes and assumptions. A vigourous policy of multiculturalism will create this initial confidence. It can form the base of a society which is based on fair play for all. The government will support and encourage the various cultures and ethnic groups that give

structure and vitality to our society. They will be encouraged to share their cultural expression and values with other Canadians and so contribute to a richer life for us all." Canada, House of Commons, 1971, 8545; quoted in R. Breton, "Multiculturalism," 50. For further discussion of the adoption of multiculturalism in Canada in the interest of national unity, see Stratton and Ang, "Imagined," 124–9. The government created the Royal Commission on Bilingualism and Biculturalism in an effort to appease those involved in the independence movement in Quebec. Breton, "Multiculturalism," 38–9.

21 Ashworth and Graham, "Senses," 8.

22 Mills, "Moving," 111, 113.

23 Schwartz, *Copy*, 279.

24 Mills, "Moving," 113, 114.

25 Mills explains further, writing: "Seeing an artefact in its original location is not an interpretive process, but unmediated, unproblematic and straightforward, a perspective that extends to the surrounding assemblage." "Open," 83, 81.

26 Preziosi, "Seeing," 222. In a related vein, Steiner contends that art historical canon formation is founded on the belief that objective conditions not only guide but also dictate aesthetic judgements, ostensibly liberated from political, economic, and social influences. "Canonical art," Steiner suggests, "like divinity itself, is said to exist in a realm of its own" ("Canon," 217). Significantly, Ruth Phillips and Christopher Steiner note, "Far from being either produced or consumed without regard for matters of money or market, works of art, aesthetic valuations and judgments of taste are indeed highly dependent on an object's commodity potential and economic value" ("Art," 15).

27 For an early argument to this effect, see Baxandall, "Exhibiting," 33–41.

28 Preziosi, "Seeing," 218.

29 As James Clifford argues, "The history of collections (not limited to museums) is central to an understanding of how those social groups that invented anthropology and modern art have *appropriated* exotic things, facts and meaning. (Appropriate: 'to make one's own,' from the Latin *proprius*, 'proper,' 'property.') It is important to analyze how powerful discriminations are made at particular moments constitute the general system of objects within which valued artifacts circulate and make sense" (*Predicament*, 220–1). He argues that curators, collectors, and producers appropriate objects to identify and label them as property. Following Clifford, I consider the historic homes selected in this study to be objects that have been appropriated – by virtue of their preservation, restoration, and reanimation – as artifactual evidence of the nation's "material legacy of history" (Handler, *Nationalism*, 17).

Consequently, one must consider the nature, significance, and ramifications of "discriminating" decisions made regarding restoration and reanimation of these sites to effectively and critically analyze the socio-political significance of Canadian heritage sites and, more specifically, historic homes once owned by political figures from the pre-Confederation time period.

30 Preziosi, "Art," 521. As Preziosi puts it, in the past, the discipline of art history has been largely defined by the paradigm "everything about an object is meaningful in *some* way, while not everything about an object is meaningful in the *same* way" ("Seeing," 219).

31 Albano, "Displaying," 17.

32 Bruner, "Lincoln," 400.

33 Schwartz, *Copy,* 278–9. Quote from 279, emphasis in the original.

34 For a discussion of historical accuracy, see Bruner, "Lincoln," 399.

35 Katriel, "Sites of Memory," 107.

36 Ibid., 117–18; 126.

37 Smith, *Nationalism,* 133.

38 Smith, "Ethnoscapes," 11. He also characterizes "sites of memory" as "objects of the sacred" in that objects are often selected, constructed, or interpreted according to doctrines of civic virtue and national heroism. Legacies of religious heritage, as evidenced in Judeo-Christian beliefs, traditions, and practices that also have parallels in Islamic faith, he suggests, spawned these doctrinal beliefs and ideologies (Smith, *Chosen,* 220–1). Smith's assertion is echoed by Stephen Mills, who writes that the selection of commemorative sites places "a heavy responsibility upon the choice of artefacts, again verging into the domain of domestic relics. Paradoxically, [the selection of sites to be commemorated] indicates that just when artifacts are deemed most authentic and unique, they are equally deemed indicative of wider themes, metaphors for otherwise inaccessible processes" (Mills, "Moving," 114).

39 Here, Smith cites Nora's series *Lieux de Mémoire,* 1984–1992; Smith, "Ethnoscapes," 13.

40 Smith, *Chosen,* 258–9.

41 Boyer, *City,* 33–4; quoted in Osborne, "Native," 157.

42 Osborne, "Landscapes," 3; Handler and Saxton, "Dyssimulation," 243. See also Zelnisky's *Nation* and Lowenthal's *Possessed.*

43 Jessup, "Hard," xxi, emphasis in original. See also Casey, "Museum Effect," 11.

44 Gordon, *Making,* 7.

45 Handler and Saxton, "Dyssimulation," 243–4. See also Bennett, *Birth,* 147–8; McKay, "Liberal," 148.

46 Osborne, "Landscapes," 2–3; Anderson, *Imagined Communities*; Lefebvre,
    Production of Space; Conrad et al. *Canadians and Their Pasts*, ch. 5. See also
    Daniels' *Fields* for discussion of "patriotic landscapes"; Sullivan's *Drama* for
    "landscapes of sovereignty; and Hakli's "Cultures of Demarcation," 123–50, for
    "discursive landscapes."
47 The Pasts Collective, *Canadians*, 67–8.
48 Conrad, Létourneau, and Northrup, "Canadians," 29.
49 Ibid., 33.
50 The Pasts Collective, *Canadians*, 82–3.
51 Katriel, "Sites of Memory," 106–7.
52 Wang, *Tourism*, 66, 59.
53 Ibid., 58.
54 Ibid., 68.
55 McKay, "Liberal," 620; McKay, "After Canada," 76–97.
56 McKay, "Liberal," 76–7.
57 Stewart, *On Longing*, 23.
58 Macleod, "Decolonizing," 366–7.
59 Day, *Multiculturalism*, 9
60 Bennett, *Birth*, 147.

Chapter Two

 1 Mackey, *House*; Bannerji, *Dark Side*; Macleod, "Decolonizing," 366–7.
 2 Quoted in Nolan, "Royals 'Looking,'" A10.
 3 Nolan, "Duchess," http://www.thespec.com/news/local/
    article/269673--duchess-to-become-patron-of-castle.
 4 West, *Domesticating*, xii.
 5 Wright, *Architecture*, 8.
 6 Mackey, *House*, 58.
 7 Metcalfe File: "Canada's Birthday and Dundurn," *Spectator* (Hamilton), 21
    September 1961, 6. During the 1960s, this type of characterization became
    increasingly common both in the Hamilton press and among those directly
    involved in the restoration project. Interestingly, Anthony Adamson, the
    architectural consultant to the Dundurn Restoration project, refrained from
    even mentioning MacNab's ties to the Family Compact, writing simply, "The
    builder of Dundurn ranks as the most famous citizen of Hamilton and one of
    the most colourful men in Canadian history" (*Proposal*, 1).
 8 Gordon, *Making*, xv.

9 McCarthy, *Women's Culture*, xi.

10 Smith, *Chosen*, 258–9.

11 Stainton, *Nature*; quoted in Koval, *Framing Nature*, 2.

12 Ibid., 3.

13 Yallop, "Nash," 57.

14 Koval, 3.

15 Yallop, 73.

16 Picturesque buildings, such as Dundurn, were to be "viewed as an integral but subsidiary part of the overall scenic composition." Wright, *Architecture*, 7.

17 Ibid., 80, 8, 39.

18 Beers, *Sir Allan*, 404.

19 Ibid., ix. One other significant choice MacNab made in his personal life that reflected his affiliation with the Family Compact was his choice of second wife. On 29 September 1831, MacNab, a member of the Church of England, married Mary Stuart of the Stuart Family of Brockville, who, despite being a devout Roman Catholic, retained blood ties to the Family Compact. Ibid., 42.

20 Ibid., 402

21 As Beers explains, "[MacNab] demonstrated a considerable measure of skill in making use of the grey, uncertain areas of contemporary ethics, rather than outright dishonesty, to promote his own economic interests, and he was prepared on occasion to make considerable sacrifices to ensure the success of ventures with which he was associated" (ibid., 403–4).

22 Ibid., 404.

23 MacRae, *MacNab*, 188–90.

24 Badone, *Dundurn*, 45.

25 "Hamilton's Attic," 1. How and why the authorities chose this date to open the museum is made evident in a speech delivered at the opening celebrations by Sir John Bourinot of Ottawa, then a leading expert on Canadian history and government. He states, "It was a happy thought on the part of the mayor and civic authorities of Hamilton to defer the opening of this park until the Queen's Birthday, the true Empire day, the great holiday of all Canadians, irrespective of race and creed. This is the day above all others when we can best recall the memories of the loyal men who have made the old district of Gore famous in the annals of the Dominion" (Scrapbook, vol. 1 7r: "Sir John Bourinot's Speech," *Spectator* [Hamilton], 25 May 1900, 12). See also *Canadian Encyclopedia*, 261.

26 Coleman, *White Civility*, 20.

27 After three years of campaigning, in which she used her own money,

Fessenden celebrated the establishment of Empire Day, May 23rd, the day
before Queen Victoria's birthday. On Empire Day, the school children of
Canada celebrated the Queen's birthday. T. Melville Bailey and Charles
Ambrose Carter, *Hamilton Firsts* (Hamilton: W.L. Griffin Limited, 1973),
12. Schools in every province of the Dominion celebrated Empire day, as
did Commonwealth countries such as New Zealand and Australia. The
celebration of Empire Day slowly died out by the 1940s. See Manitoba
Education Archives, *Victoria Day and Empire Day: A Canadian Tradition*
(Manitoba Education, 1997), 7, 14.

28 Pulver Ungar, "Trenholme."

29 Fessenden, Curator, "Historic Dundurn," n.p.: Scrapbook, vol. 1, 7DD.

30 West, *Domesticating*, 1. In an important contribution to the growing body
of critical literature that examines links between the American house
museum movement and women's involvement in the public sphere, cultural
historian Patricia West argues that the house museum movement began in
the nineteenth-century as a public venue and was developed, administered,
and controlled by "disenfranchised though politically engaged women." The
book is based on her chronological analysis of the founding years, processes,
and people involved in the restoration of historical sites, such as: George
Washington's Mount Vernon; Louisa May Alcott's family home, Orchard
House; Thomas Jefferson's Monticello, and the replica birthplace of Booker T.
Washington. West stipulates that the process of establishing a house museum
operated as a vehicle for women to negotiate the shifting relationship between
women's customary power base (the home) and the public realm (the state).
West, *Domesticating*, 159–60.

31 "Dundurn Park and Castle," 11.

32 Feminist historian Amanda Vickery writes that, in the nineteenth century, elite
mistresses managed their households "like a museum curator administering
to her collection." These mistresses oversaw the order of the house and
furniture, which were too reflective of character to be left to the care of
servants. Vickery, *Gentleman's Daughter*, 145.

33 Pulver Ungar, "Trenholme."

34 Scrapbook, vol. 1, 7z: "Dundurn and Its Memories," *Globe and Mail* (Toronto),
11 July 1901.

35 Wright, *Domesticating*, 8. In the early twentieth-century, various politicians,
cultural producers, and historians took note of the increasing numbers of
non-British immigrants coming to Canada and, as a result, came to regard
commemorative endeavours as tools through which to instill and enhance

a sense of developing nationalistic pride and patriotism. For instance, as President of the Canadian Club, A.A. Manning explained at the opening of Dundurn Park, "In a country so young as Canada, with a population drawn from such varied sources, with a population which, however rich in energy, intelligence and industry, is as yet absorbed in the production of wealth and the development of our natural resources, national and patriotic feeling must of necessity be in its infancy ... History should ever be held in grateful remembrance. It is our duty to see that the names of these men and women are plucked from oblivion; that the memory of their great and heroic deeds are handed down to posterity, to teach our children that the liberty of thought, speech and conscience which we enjoy is not ours as are the God-given light and air, but is the priceless heritage secured to us by the tears and blood of the founders of our country; and, above all, to see that these liberties are handed unimpaired to the generations who follow us" (Scrapbook, vol. 1, 7d–7f: "Who the Canadian Club Honoured the Occasion in the Early Morning," *Spectator* [Hamilton], 25 May 1900, 2–3). Concrete examples of "Britishness," such as Dundurn, "represented the most advanced form of political and social life in the world, it was therefore assumed as the civil norm to which non-British Canadians should assimilate" (Coleman, *White Civility*, 19).

36 Coleman, *White Civility*, 10, 6–7.

37 McCarthy, *Women's Culture*, xi.

38 HPL, Gwen Metcalfe Files (hereafter GMF), personal letter from Metcalfe to the Iowa State Department of History and Archives, Des Moines, Iowa, USA, 14 July 1971.

39 HPL, GMF, personal letter from Metcalfe to Fred Mann of Rous and Mann Press Limited, 12 January 1961.

40 HPL, GMF, personal letter from Metcalfe to Dr W.S.T Connell, Chairman of the [Dundurn] Museum Committee, Hamilton, 13 November 1958.

41 Because Mundie, upon announcing her intention, criticized "the fact that Dundurn Castle and its contents of antiques and pictures are not sufficiently advertised so that visitors to the city can find it more easily," I would argue that she wanted to refurbish the site to increase visitor attendance. HPL, DCS, vol. 1, 57: "Dundurn Castle: Show Little Interest in Own History," *Spectator* (Hamilton), 8 November 1952.

42 Scrapbook, vol. 1, 81: Joyce Goodman, "Sir Allan's Ghost Still in Castle?" *Spectator* (Hamilton), 13 April 1957.

43 The article also reported that most visitors were from the Hamilton district; see "1,400 Visitors a Week."

44 Scrapbook, vol. 1, 84: "A Bedroom of 1850's is Dundurn Attraction," *Globe and Mail* (Toronto), 16 September 1957.

45 Scrapbook, vol. 1, 129: "Check Ordered: Face Lift Suggested For Castle," *Spectator* (Hamilton), 12 January 1961.

46 McCarthy, *Women's Culture*, xi.

47 Cameron, "Spirit," 78.

48 Mackey, *House*, 58.

49 Ibid., 59.

50 Cameron, "Spirit," 80–1.

51 Adamson was considered an expert consultant not just because he was an architect; he was also an associate professor of town planning in the School of Architecture at the University of Toronto and had been awarded a United Nations fellowship for the study of town planning and municipal government. Adamson suggested that the $167,000 could be raised through public subscription and government grants. See Scrapbook, vol. 1, 133: "$167,000 Dundurn Castle Development urged," *Spectator* (Hamilton), 20 September 1961. Additionally, Adamson had been credited as being "instrumental in the restoration of Upper Canada Village" (Scrapbook, vol. 1, 135: "Dundurn Castle Pageant: Challenge for City," *Spectator* [Hamilton], 1961, 29). He also co-authored the book, *The Ancestral Roof: Domestic Architecture of Upper Canada* with Marion MacRae, an instructor of design and museum research at the Ontario College of Art. The book details the styles of architecture that became prevalent in Ontario during the nineteenth century, and the authors included a brief study of Dundurn.

52 Adamson, *Proposal*, 6.

53 Adamson, *Undeveloped Asset*, 3; Adamson, *Proposal*,13. Adamson stipulated that the collection to date, containing "objects of interest and documents," detracted from the formation of a cohesive institutional policy. Adamson, *Undeveloped Asset*, 2. As far as programming was concerned, Adamson believed that what he termed the "historical value" of the objects related to MacNab's life and lifestyle would be greatly increased if they were placed in a dramatic context. Adamson, *Undeveloped Asset*, 12. It is significant that, in this particular context, he states that the "director," presumably Metcalfe, has "with remarkable skill arranged the displays which are available to her." As Metcalfe was the acting curator and business administrator, and Adamson refers specifically to a woman in this position, this assumption seems most reasonable. Adamson, *Undeveloped Asset*, 1.

54 Adamson's approach, as a result, linked achievements that some historians

suggest "contradict" each other. While MacNab's election as Prime Minister solidified his place in Canada's national narrative, in the early years of his political career, MacNab favoured British culture, a preference that manifested itself in the style and design of his home. "Belief in the British connection," Beers explains, "implied ... support for a 'British' type of society, especially a hierarchical social system. In his own life, MacNab expressed that support as powerfully as any man in Upper Canada. Dundurn was the symbol of it" (*Sir Allan*, 71).

55 Metcalfe File: "Ottawa Approves Dundurn Project," *Spectator* (Hamilton), 18 August 1964.

56 Finding such sources proved to be a difficult task. In 1965, Adamson himself wrote, "Our searches into the field of [MacNab's taste] have been unsuccessful. All we can say about Sir Allan is that he was as conservative in his cooking and heating methods as he was in his politics ... He was a romantic, a Scot, and a man who was trying to build a seat for his family in Upper Canada. He was proud of his ancestry and without doubt felt the importance of a baronetcy and the prime ministership. He was a spendthrift and alternated between periods of wealth and poverty. In interpreting his house, these things should be kept in mind" (Metcalfe File: Anthony Adamson, "Preliminary consideration for the furnishing of the ground and second floors of Dundurn – March 30, 1965" [Hamilton, 30 March 1965] 1).

57 MacRae, *Dundurn*, 211.

58 For a discussion of historical accuracy, see Bruner, "Abraham Lincoln," 399.

59 Metcalfe File: Personal letter to Metcalfe from Scott Symons, Sigmund Samuel Canadiana Gallery, Royal Ontario Museum, 7 September 1961, emphasis in original.

60 Coleman, *White Civility*, 5.

61 The generous recharacterization of MacNab in the interests of promoting the cultural status of Hamilton is illustrated by a writer for the Hamilton *Spectator* who, in 1962, characterized MacNab as "the most controversial figure in Hamilton history. He was distrusted by many as a member of that Upper Canadian 'Tory' group the Family Compact; he played an enthusiastic part in suppressing the rebellion led by William Lyon Mackenzie ... But one thing is sure, Sir Allan's impact on the early Canadian and local scene will outlive the opinions of those who assess his role in disparaging terms ... [The] restoration of Dundurn is wisely planned as the big local feature of Canada's centennial celebration in 1967" (Scrapbook, vol. 1, 148: "Renewed Interest in Dundurn," *Spectator* [Hamilton], 10 April 1962).

62 Within its first month of operation following the restoration, Dundurn
    Castle attendance averaged about 1,000 visitors per day. Scrapbook, vol. 2,
    299: "Dundurn Castle Packs 'em In. Averages 1,000 People Daily," *Spectator*
    (Hamilton), 17 July 1967.

63 Scrapbook, vol. 2, 292: "Dundurn Opens in Blaze of Colour," *Spectator*
    (Hamilton), 19 June 1967.

64 Duncan, *Civilizing*, 44.

65 Vickers, "Feminism," 137–8.

66 Barry, "What's in a Name?" 99.

67 Transcribed from the actual plaque located on the grounds of Dundurn
    National Historic Site.

68 Freeman, *Hamilton*, 31.

69 Beers, ix.

70 McIver, *End*.

71 Romney, *Getting*, 253.

72 McKay, "Solid Melts," xiv.

73 Transcribed from the actual plaque located on the grounds of Dundurn
    National Historic Site.

74 Transcribed from the actual plaque located on the grounds of Dundurn
    National Historic Site.

75 Duncan, *Civilizing*, 26.

76 Parks Canada, "Pioneers."

77 Wright, *Architecture of the Picturesque in Canada*, 68.

78 Ibid., 8.

79 Strong-Boag, "Experts," 66.

80 Osborne, "Landscapes," 10.

81 Tourism Hamilton, *2004 Experience Hamilton Visitor's Guide*.

82 Ibid., 40.

83 Ministry of Economic Development, *Hamilton*, 1.

84 City of Hamilton, *New Directions*, 14; City of Hamilton, *Open*, 16.

Chapter Three

1 Schwartz, *Culture*, 278–9.

2 Handler and Saxton, "Dyssimulation," 245.

3 Wright, *Architecture*, 8, 39; quote from 8.

4 Preziosi, *Brain*, 147.

5 Because the restoration allowed the museum to operate year-round, Metcalfe

believed that some type of programming might be offered to draw people during the winter. For inspiration, she looked to the Christmas program mounted at the William Lyon Mackenzie House in Toronto. In 1965, Metcalfe wrote to Lord Albermarle, Sir Allan's great-grandson, about a planned visit to the Mackenzie House in Toronto to examine their Christmas festivities: "With a program for Dundurn in mind, I'll be down to see what happens in a historic house" (Metcalfe File: Personal letter from Gwen Metcalfe, curator, to Lord Albermarle, 1 December 1965). This historic home, which displayed Mackenzie's life during the 1850s, was already portraying a "Victorian Christmas." According to an advertisement in the Toronto *Globe and Mail* dated 3 December 1965, the same year in which Metcalfe expressed her intention to visit the site, the program included Victorian cookies, cranberry punch, evergreens, an open wood fire, candles, decorated boughs, and a Kissing bough. Christmas music was played on an 1830 piano. "Things to do," 14. For further discussion of the development and content of the Mackenzie House's Christmas program, see Chapters 6 and 7 of this study.

6 Nesbitt interview, 2003.

7 Kuper, "English Christmas," 169.

8 Nesbitt states that there is a hierarchy of primary sources – primary documents related to Dundurn at the top, followed by sources related to Hamilton, Ontario, and finally English and American sources. Nesbitt interview, 2003.

9 Belk, "Materialism," 82–4.

10 George L. Parker records that first serialized publication of Dickens's *A Christmas Carol* (1843) in the nearby vicinity of the United Canadas took place in Charlottetown in 1844. The publication was issued in *The Palladium* (*Beginnings*, 58).

11 Kuper, "English Christmas," 160. In addition to the work of scholars, the mass media has distinguished the Victorian era as the time when contemporary Christmas traditions were invented.

12 Katriel, "Sites," 107.

13 Gable and Handler, *New*, 221.

14 Lowenthal, "Fabricating," 12.

15 Katriel, "Sites," 107.

16 In considering themes, activities, and facts repeatedly discussed by interpreters, I examine what aspects or ideologies interpreters construct as being predominantly associated with the historical celebration. My analysis does not aim to produce a generalized impression of content discussed

by interpreters; rather, I examine commonalities to provide insight into interpretive execution, performance, and content.

17 Michael Kammen uses the example of Martin Luther King Jr's birthday to explain what he terms the "depoliticization of memory." Martin Luther King Jr Day has been established as a national holiday so that the historical figure enjoys heroic status. As a result, the historical figure "has been depoliticized so that he is a charismatic advocate of civil rights rather than a more broadly based critical conscience who sought social change for oppressed people at home and abroad ... [The penchant for amnesia] is a matter of degree and is a function of yet another phenomenon that we have now encountered repeatedly: namely, the American inclination to depoliticize the past in order to minimize memories (and causes) of conflict. That is how we healed the wounds of sectional animosity following the Civil War; and that is how we *selectively remember* only those aspects of heroes' lives that will render them acceptable to as many people as possible" (*Mystic*, 662, 701, emphasis added).

18 18 December 2004.

19 The interpreters explain that the reason that both the drawing room and dining room are so impressive is that they have high ceilings – the highest in the house. This architectural feature, along with the furniture choices, has also been linked to architectural tastes then prevalent in the British Empire. One interpreter explains, "MacNab is knighted in 1838 for helping to put down the Rebellion of William Lyon Mackenzie in 1837. So he travels to England, and, while he's there, he looks at the furniture, the fashion, the styling, and when he comes back, he upgrades the house by raising the ceilings in here and the kinds of furniture in here" (10 December 2004).

20 11 December 2004.

21 16 December 2004; 12 December 2004.

22 16 December 2004.

23 The candelabrum bears an inscription that reads, "Presented to Colonel the Honourable Sir ALLAN NAPIER MACNAB, Prime Minister of Canada, who has represented the City of Hamilton for twenty-five years, by the citizens of Hamilton, as an acknowledgement of his valuable services and untiring efforts in promoting the material interest of that City and of the Province generally; but more especially for the important aid he has rendered in the Construction of the Great Western Railway, which has conferred the most important and lasting benefits – moral, fiscal, and political – upon Hamilton and upon Canada, 1855" (Bailey, *Laird*, 24).

24 The interpreters all explained that the table can actually be extended to

host a dinner party for 24 people, but one interpreter informed me that the institution's collection holds complete settings of flatware and silverware only for 12 people.

25 12 December 2004.

26 11 December 2004.

27 In addition, those in a position to give to the poor during the Christmas season did so ostensibly to exercise their class authority. As Stephen Nissenbaum explains, the act of charitable giving in the mid-nineteenth century preserved "the structure of an older Christmas ritual, in which people occupying positions of social and economic authority offered gifts to their dependents" ("Revisiting," 62).

28 12 December 2004.

29 Walsh, *Representation*, 53–5, 65–9.

30 Other modern amenities include the gasolier in the drawing room, central heating, gas lights, a bell system to signal the servants to go to specific rooms, and the dumbwaiter.

31 11 December 2004. Out of the eight tours I attended and transcribed, only two interpreters explained the reasoning behind this interpretation, which took into account the ages of the MacNab daughters. One interpreter stated that the nursery "would be the room for Minnie and Sophia. But, of course, Sophia's moved out, she's 23 and married, but Minnie's still in residence. So she'd be in one of the rooms, aged 21, and it would probably fall to her to supervise some of the children, the nieces and nephews, and some of the other cousins, the cousins that would be staying here because, for some of the young children, they would be sleeping here, they would be living here, they would also be taking most of their meals up here in the nursery. They would not be joining the adults downstairs" (16 December 2004).

32 11 December 2004.

33 Casey, "Museum Effect," 11.

34 Pustz, *Voices*.

35 11 December 2004. The servants also received three square meals a day, clothing, shoes, and a small beer ration. The scullery maid, the lowest paid servant of the house, would receive a minimum of three small rations of beer per day.

36 Blair, "Life Below," 23.

37 Ibid., 26.

38 Golby and Purdue, *Making*, 9. For further discussion of how the family dinner evolved from Victorian times into a distinguishing feature of the

contemporary celebration, see Nissenbaum, *Battle*; Brewis and Warren, "Merry Little Christmas?" 747–62; and Vachhani and Pullen, "Home," 807–21.

39 11 December 2004.

40 Wang, *Tourism*, 58–9; Casey, "Museum Effect," 11; Handler and Saxton, "Dyssimulation."

41 As Richard Day explains, "Before it thought about connecting itself to what it saw as a multiplicity of cultures and ethnic groups within its territories, the Canadian state first tried to solidify and clarify its articulation with the Two Founding Races. In theory, Canada had been a two-nation state since 1774, when the French of Quebec were granted the right to maintain certain aspects of their social, legal, and religious particularity. While this was undoubtedly a *gift* from the British, the deal struck at the time of Confederation implied that the two peoples were coming together as equals, to form ... 'the headstones of the entire edifice' of Canada" (*Multiculturalism*, 179–80).

42 Abu-Laban and Gabriel, *Selling Diversity*, 105.

43 Mackey, *House*; Bannerji, *Dark Side*; Macleod, "Decolonizing."

44 Bennett, *Birth*; Casey, "Museum Effect"; Handler, *Nationalism*; Katriel, "Sites"; Kirshenblatt-Gimblett, *Destination*.

45 Mackey, *House*, 153.

46 Day, *Multiculturalism*, 9.

47 Mackey, *House*, 53; Breton, "Multiculturalism," 42.

48 Stratton and Ang, "Imagined," 152.

49 Day, *Multiculturalism*, 9.

50 Mackey, *House*, 17.

51 Ibid., 18.

52 Ibid., 163.

53 Eric Breton points out that the Act stipulates that every individual is a Canadian first and communal attachments remain a private matter ("Canadian Federalism," 157–8). The Act states, "The Government of Canada ... is committed to a policy of multiculturalism designed to preserve and enhance the multicultural heritage of Canadians while working to achieve the equality of all Canadians in the economic, social, cultural and political life of Canada." The full title of the Act is *An Act for the Preservation and Enhancement of Multiculturalism in Canada* (R.S., 1985, c. 25 (rth Supp.) [C-18.7] [1988, c.31. (21 July 1988)]); quoted in Breton, 158.

54 Kamboureli, "Technology," 215.

55 Ibid.

56 Kallen, "Multiculturalism," 57–8. In public institutions, "ethnic minorities are

expected to acculturate linguistically to one of Canada's official languages." The rhetoric of the policy supports the notion that to attain social mobility, Canadians should become bilingual; the multiculturalism policy, as a result, supports the "somewhat contradictory notion" of individual equality regardless of ethnic classification (Kallen, "Multiculturalism," 56). Similarly, in her examination of how multiculturalism functions in the workforce and associated rhetoric demonstrates, Angela Davis asserts that the policy allows people to look, act, eat, and talk differently, but, in the end, it is expected that "other" peoples will be more productive if they act "as if" they were all the same or, rather, white. Davis's analysis makes evident that the promotion of heterogeneity or multiculturalism is intended to convey the fact that one can be different but should perform and, by extension, adopt a homogenous way of life, modeled on that of the middle-class white man. "Gender," 46.

57 On 9 July 1969, the Canadian House of Commons first adopted the Official Languages Act, which stipulated that "the English and French languages are the official languages of Canada for all purposes of the Parliament and Government of Canada and possess and enjoy equality status and equal rights and privileges as to their use in all institutions of the Parliament and Government of Canada" (Office of the Commissioner of Official Languages, *Two Official Languages*, 15–16).

58 Kamboureli, "Technology," 212, 216.

59 Kallen, "Multiculturalism," 58.

60 Ibid., 53.

61 Ibid., 53–4.

62 Kamboureli, "Technology," 218. In a similar vein, Himani Bannerji contends that multiculturalism negates capacity for resistance. The policy, with its deliberately politicized and normalizing rhetoric, obscures socio-political processes of racialization and organizes people as raced ethnicity; this "discourse of diversity" thus fuses cultural classification with politics, ostensibly to thereby conceptualize the discourse as a power neutral indicator of difference and multiplicity when it is actually anything but. *Dark Side*, 29, 47, 37.

63 Bennett, "Exhibition," 62.

64 Macleod, "Decolonizing," 366–7; quote from 367.

65 Anthony D. Smith, *Nationalism*, 133; Smith, "Ethnoscapes," 11.

66 Smith, "Ethnoscapes," 11–12.

67 Ibid., 12.

68 Ibid., 12.

69 Gordon, *Making*, 163. Similarly, Owen Dwyer writes, "Conceived of as 'materialized discourses' – built environments that embed and conduct meanings through their representation of social identities and their politics – memorial landscapes are shaped by and in turn influence the society that produces them. The narrative content of … memorials reflects the types of archival materials that survive, the intentions of their producers, and contemporary politics" ("Interpreting," 661).

70 McKay, "Liberal," 622.

Chapter Four

1 Parks Canada, *Development Concept*, 15–16.

2 As Richard Handler explains, the Quiet Revolution brought about the creation of Quebec's Ministère des Affaires culturelles (1961), which allowed the provincial government to develop its own heritage legislation, such as Quebec's "new" Historic Monuments Act (1963). "On Having," 196–7.

3 Ibid., 200; Létourneau, "'Remembering," 15–16; Oakes and Warren, *Language*, 27.

4 Handler, 196.

5 As Ian McKay explains, "the two nationalisms have been constructed against, but also in collaboration with, each other – they have rarely been 'two solitudes' in reality" ("After Canada," 94).

6 Casey, "Museum Effect," 10–11.

7 Kammen, *Mystic*, 662, 701.

8 Timothy, "Introduction," xiii.

9 Casey, "Museum Effect," 12.

10 As Handler explains, "the repatriation of heritage objects … establishes ownership, but only by reinterpreting cultural things in terms of the ideas of those who plundered them" ("On Having," 194).

11 Young, *Cartier*, 136, xiii.

12 "Extraits des procès-verbal de la réunion de la CLMHC tenue du 27 au 29 octobre 1964," quoted in Parcs Canada, *Énoncé*, 23.

13 Parks Canada, *Development Concept*, 16.

14 Dickinson and Young, *Short History*, 327.

15 Parks Canada, *Public Consultation*, 31.

16 Young, *Cartier*, xiii.

17 Parks Canada, *Management Plan*, 17.

18 In 1849, government officials instituted a "perambulating system" in which

the seat of government rotated every four years between Toronto and Quebec City. In 1857, Queen Victoria, having been petitioned by government officials to exercise "Royal Prerogative," selected Ottawa as the permanent seat of government. Schwartz, "Photographs," 164.

19 He held his first post as a member for the Vèrcheres riding from 1848 until 1863, and then sat for Montreal-East from 1863–67. Young, *Cartier*, 56.

20 Parks Canada, *Management Plan*, 17.

21 Ibid., 17–18.

22 Silver, "Confederation (1867)," 57.

23 Young, *Cartier*, xiii, 48.

24 As Jean-Claude Marsan explains, in Montreal during the Victorian era, residential design and construction allowed for the expression of "the Victorian man's strengths and virtues, his eccentricities, his individuality, or his wealth. For the first time, perhaps, architecture would not be regarded as a form of art subjected to its own rules but rather as a symbol of an admired and coveted reality" (*Montreal*, 189).

25 Sutcliffe, "Montreal Metropolis," 22. Similarly, architectural historian Leslie Maitland explains that "French architects of Quebec typically borrowed Neoclassical ideas from both the English-speaking architects with whom they shared the building worlds of Montreal and Quebec, and from more direct contacts with France ... From English Neoclassicism French architects borrowed the toned-down Palladian elevation, a linear treatment of the façade, and antique details" (*Neoclassical Architecture*, 32).

26 Parks Canada, *Management Plan*, 17–18; Maitland, *Neoclassical Architecture*, 24, 27.

27 Parks Canada, *Management Plan*, 18; Parcs Canada, *Énoncé*, 2004, 10.

28 London townhouses typically contained a courtyard, a space that oftentimes sank into the ground and separated the house from the street. Given that smaller plot sizes in nineteenth-century urban Montreal could not accommodate this inclusion, Cartier's houses sit directly adjacent to and in alignment with Notre Dame Street. *Énoncé*, 2004, 10.

29 Parks Canada, *Management Plan*, 17–19.

30 Rocher, "Introduction," 73, 80.

31 Breton, "From Ethnic," 99; Turgeon, "Interpreting," 62.

32 Dickinson and Young, *Short History*, 319; Rocher, "Introduction," 206; Handler, *Nationalism*, 173.

33 Handler, "On Having," 196–7, 200.

34 Ibid., 213.

35 "Extraits du procès-verbal de la réunion de la CLMHC tenue du 24 au 28 juin 1967"; quoted in *Énoncé*, 23.

36 Gillis, *Commemorations*, 5.

37 Furthermore, the Board stipulated that the graves of those listed be maintained by the Board "at the expense of the nation" ("Extraits des procès-verbal de la réunion de la CLMHC tenue du 25 au 29 mai 1959"; quoted in *Énoncé*, 22).

38 Parks Canada, *Management Plan*, 9.

39 It was also suggested that the program include the preservation of a house of Sir John A. Macdonald's. "Extraits des procès-verbal de la réunion de la CLMHC tenue du 27 au 29 octobre 1964"; quoted in *Énoncé*, 23.

40 Parks Canada, *Management Plan*, 2007, 10; Des Rochers and Roy, "Old Montreal," 252.

41 Parks Canada, *Management Plan*, 1985, 9.

42 Pierre Elliott Trudeau, "The Federation Stands," *Globe and Mail* (Toronto) 6 November, 1981, 6; quoted in Desruisseaux, Fortin, and Ignatieff, "Patriation," 255, 258.

43 Parks Canada, *Development Concept*, 15.

44 Ibid., 16, 17.

45 Ibid., 13, 17.

46 Ibid., 17.

47 Ibid., 15.

48 Ibid., 16.

49 Pierre Elliott Trudeau, "The Federation Stands," *Globe and Mail* (Toronto) 6 November, 1981, 6; quoted in Desruisseaux, Fortin, and Ignatieff, "Patriation," 255, 258.

50 Conrad and Finkel, *Canada*, 516–17. The Act sought to promote "the principle of equalization between richer and poorer provinces" (Desruisseaux et al., "Patriation," 254). Unanimous consent of all provinces and both houses of Parliament, however, "would continue to be required for amendments affecting representation in the House of Commons, Senate, and Supreme Court and for changes affecting the use of the French and English languages" (Conrad and Finkel, *Canada*, 517).

51 Desruisseaux et al., "Patriation," 260.

52 Pelletier, "Politics," 135.

53 Mackey, *House*, 58.

54 Parks Canada, *Guiding Principles*, 26, 49, 84.

55 Neufeld, "Indigenous peoples," 185.

56 Parks Canada, *Public Consultation*, 7.

57 Twelve agencies not only participated in the program but also submitted
comments and suggestions, groups including L'Association des propriétaires
du Vieux Montréal, Le Conseil des monuments et sites du Québec, La
Fédération des sociétés d'histoire du Québec, Héritage Montréal and,
le ministère des Affaires culturelles du Québec. Ibid., 9–10.

58 Ibid., 26.

59 Parks Canada, *Public Consultation*, 32.

60 Brian Young, "Letter from historian Brian Young"; quoted in the *Public
Consultation*, 27, 31.

61 Parks Canada, *Public Consultation*, 46.

62 Ibid., 31.

63 Ibid., 31, 46.

64 Ibid., 31.

65 Parks Canada, *Influential Politician*, 1.

66 According to the 2006 Canadian Census, 80 per cent of Quebec residents
are francophone, while 8 per cent are anglophone. Pasts Collective,
Canadians, 97.

67 According to the Act, "the English and French languages are the official
languages of Canada for all purposes of the Parliament and Government of
Canada and possess and enjoy equality status and equal rights and privileges
as to their use in all institutions of the Parliament and Government of
Canada" (Office of the Commissioner of Official Languages, *Our Two Official
Languages over Time*, rev. ed. [May 1994] 15–16).

68 Hustak, "Vanishing brass plaques."

69 Ibid.

70 Parks Canada, "Cartier, Sir George-Étienne."

71 McKay, "Tourist Gaze," 138.

72 Parks Canada, *Management Plan*, 2007, 29.

73 The west house also contains two exhibition areas smaller than those located
in the east house, which display artifacts and information pertaining to
themes explored in the site's guided tours. Significantly, these exhibitions
are temporary in that they are set up to compliment the content or concepts
discussed in the period rooms, such as "the bourgeois lifestyle, Cartier's built
heritage, and some of his Montreal haunts" (ibid., 20, 29–30).

74 Parks Canada, *Public Consultation*, 47.

75 Canadian Press, "Parks Canada."

76 Ledoyen, personal communication.

77 Parks Canada, "Explora."

78 Ibid.

79 Ledoyen.

80 Parks Canada, "Learning Experiences."

81 Ibid.

82 Author's translation: "The 'Victorian Christmas' event allows the site to increase and diversify its clientele, increase income, diversify activities that use elements of the permanent exhibition and, finally, increase the visibility and attractiveness of the site." Bélanger, *Le Noël victorien*, 2.

83 McKay and Bates, *Province*, 377. See also Black, *Engaging*; and Conn, *Museums*.

Chapter Five

1 Parks Canada, *2008 Schedule*, n.p.

2 Handler, "On Having," 213.

3 *2008 Schedule*. Notably, the west house also contains two "smaller" exhibitions on the first floor, which display both artifactual arrangements and text panels designed to complement the theme showcased in the period rooms. Entering into the west house, visitors first go through one of the first two temporary exhibitions to reach the period rooms. This first exhibition explores the origins of the decorated Christmas tree and greeting card exchange. The second exhibition, into which visitors move after having toured the period rooms on the first floor, examines how Christmas festivities developed from a commemoration of the birth of Jesus Christ to incorporate gift exchange. Parks Canada, *Management Plan*, 2007, 29. My analysis of the tour content, however, focuses on the interpreter content because the site offers guided tours to "create an experience with visitors." As one interpreter explains, the guided tours "enhance" the object-based exhibitions, but it is the interpreters who relay information to visitors so that visitors might experience what it "felt like to live back then" (Parks Canada, *Management Plan*, 2007, 31; Handler and Saxton, "Dyssimulation," 245). As I explain below, the site's performative elements are believed to be more memorable than their encounters with object-based exhibitions.

4 Casey, "Museum Effect," 10–11; Timothy, "Introduction," xiii.

5 Casey, "Museum Effect," 11; Parks Canada, *Management Plan*, 2007, 31.

6 Parks Canada, *Management Plan*, 2007, 20.

7 Ibid., 20, 31.

8 Ibid., 31.

9 In order to prove his point, Léonidoff recorded the annual visitation rates of certain historic sites in Montreal, comparing the number of visitors these sites brought in during the summer months with the number of visits generated in December. For example, in 1980–81, the Du Calvet House received 50,361 visitors; 10,295 visitors came in July while only 903 people visited the site in December. In 1981, La Château Ramesay received 60,537 visitors; 9,584 people attended the site in August whereas far fewer visitors came in the month of December, 670 to be exact. Léonidoff, *Concept-Plan*, 48–9.

10 Young, *Cartier*, 136. Parks Canada conservators also provided research and mounted a temporary exhibition in the two exhibition rooms in the west house, entitled "*Nos Noël d'antan*/Our Christmas of Old," which displayed various nineteenth-century toys and games with accompanying text panels. Bélanger, *Le Noël victorien*, 2.

11 Bélanger, *Le Noël victorien*, 2.

12 Parks Canada, *Management Plan*, 2007, 21.

13 Casey, "Museum Effect," 12. A 1996 visitor survey found that a quarter of the site's clientele came from Montreal, half from outside the Quebec region, and less than a quarter from the United States. Leith, *Étude*, 1. In 2000, a study of 421 visitors surveys completed at the site in the summer and fall of that year found that 42 per cent of visitors came from the Montreal region and 16 per cent from the province of Quebec; 65 per cent of the surveys were completed in French. Rainville, *Étude*, 2. The latest survey, conducted in the summer of 2007, found that, based on analysis of 356 completed surveys, 21 per cent of visitors came from the Montreal region, 13 from Quebec, and 14 from elsewhere in Canada; 55 per cent of the surveys were completed in French, a 15 per cent decrease from 2000. Service de la recherche en science sociales, *Étude*, 20. Based on these statistics, the site's primary demographic continues to be francophones living in the Montreal region, although this trend seems to be decreasing, as the rate of Canadians attending the site – those living either in Quebec or other provinces – has been steadily increasing. Furthermore, while the percentage of francophone speakers attending the site also seems to be proportionally decreasing, it is still the primary language of choice among visitors.

14 Kammen, *Mystic*, 662, 701.

15 Ibid., 25.

16 Ibid., 25; Bélanger, *Le Noël victorien*, 6.

17 Alexander, *Museums in Motion*, 5.

18 Parks Canada translation, "I am a sort of lawyer engaged in politics and business."

19 Baudelaire, *Painter of Modern Life.*

20 Magnuson, "Public School Myth," 32; Hamelin and Poulin, "Chauveau," n.p.; Dennison and Gallagher, *Community Colleges,* 38.

21 The Pasts Collective, *Canadians,* 100. They go on to state that, "In a remarkably short time span, education levels skyrocketed, the average income of francophones rose from near the bottom to the top of Quebec's ethnic hierarchy, the birth rate and marriage rate dropped from the highest to the lowest in Canada, and the movement for independence gained widespread support."

22 Author's translation: "the collaborative spirit associated with the reforms." Design + Communication Inc., *Extrait,* n.p. Similarly, in an interview with the author, one interpreter points out that Sir George-Étienne Cartier is not only a politician but also "one of the founders of Canada ... George-Étienne Cartier is not the only politician included in that mission."

23 Young, *Cartier,* 40–1, 43.

24 Restad, *Christmas,* 63.

25 Parks Canada, *2008 Schedule.*

26 Handler and Saxton, "Dyssimulation," 245; Kammen, *Mystic,* 662, 701.

27 Parks Canada, *Management Plan,* 1985, 30

28 14 December 2008.

29 Ibid.

30 Ibid.

31 Ibid.; 7 December 2008.

32 14 December 2008.

33 Parks Canada, "Noël au Coeur de la religion/Christmas and Christianity," text panel.

34 Interpreters explain that Jesus Christ could be considered a "donator or gift giving character" because a lamb appears in the image. "The lamb is an allegorical figure of himself, that's why it's in the image and also [why he could] be seen as a donator" – because he gave himself to the world (14 December 2008).

35 14 December 2008. While interpreters do not state this, the second exhibition on the first floor of the west house contains an informational placard showing each of the three Santa figures that are projected in the drawing room. According to the information on the placard, illustrator Henri Julien produced the 1875 version, which appeared in the December 1875 issue of the *Canadian Illustrated News.* The 1884 image, in contrast, comes from the French illustrated serial *Le Monde illustré.*

36 13 December 2008; 6 December 2008.

37 6 December 2008.

38 She also cites the literary works of Charles Dickens, the "great British author," who wrote short stories in which he oftentimes described the Christmas tree as "that pretty German toy" (6 December 2008).

39 6 December 2008; 13 December 2008. Similarly, in the French tours, the interpreter states, "La chandelle est en fait la décoration la plus ancienne dans la maison" (14 December 2008). Author's translation: "The candle is the oldest decoration in the house."

40 6 December 2008.

41 Ibid.

42 Ibid.

43 13 December 2008. Likewise, in the French tour, an interpreter explains, "Donc le réveillon, voici une tradition bien française. Le réveillon au départ consistait en une collation qu'on prenait après la messe de minuit, au moment où la famille se réunissait autour du foyer pour rouler la bûche de Noël" (14 December 2008). Author's translation: "Thus *le réveillon* [the midnight supper] is quite a French tradition. The midnight supper originally consisted of a snack had after midnight mass, when the family comes together around the fire to roll the bûche de Noël (yule log)."

44 13 December 2008. Similarly, during the French tours, interpreters characterize the turkey's location, saying, "Et la place d'honneur sur la table est réservée pour la dinde" (14 December 2008). Author's translation: "And the place of honour on the table is reserved for the turkey." Based on these similar characterizations, it is evident that interpreters work to relay the same core information to both anglophone and francophone visitors.

45 Parks Canada, *Information Bulletin*, 30.

46 Handler and Saxton, "Dyssimulation," 245; Casey, "Museum Effect," 11.

47 Kammen, *Mystic*, 662, 701.

48 Ibid., 701.

49 Macleod, "Decolonizing," 366.

50 Gordon, *Making*, 177.

51 Parks Canada, *Development Concept*, 15.

52 Gable and Handler, *New*, 251.

53 "Both museum and mysteries," Preziosi writes, "teach us how to solve things; how to think; and how to put two and two together. Both teach us that things are not always as they seem at first glance. They demonstrate that the world

needs to be coherently pieced together (literally, re-membered) in a fashion that may be perceived as rational and orderly: a manner that, in reviewing its steps, seems by hindsight to be natural or inevitable. In this respect, the present of the museum (within the parameters of which is also positioned our identity) may be staged as the inevitable or logical outcome of a particular past (this is our heritage and origins), thereby extending identity and cultural patrimony back into a historical or mythical past, which is thereby recuperated and preserved, without appearing to lose its mystery" ("Art," 511).

54 Preziosi, "Art," 509.

55 Ibid., 511.

56 Ibid., 511.

57 Parks Canada, *Development Concept*, 15.

58 This adoption signalled a "shift from a pan-Canadian to a Quebec definition of the boundaries of the collectivity – a second reversal so to speak; that is a reversal to the view that prevailed at the time of Confederation" (Breton, "From Ethnic," 94).

59 Breton, "From Ethnic," 89–90; quote from 90.

60 More specifically, the Québécois felt that this type of linguistic assimilation encouraged the impression that Canada was primarily an English-speaking country. Ibid., 90.

61 Warren and Oakes, *Language*, 27.

62 Létourneau writes, "Stuck in an inconsolable sadness resulting from their supposed situation as 'failed rebels,' they are unable, or barely able, to escape from the imaginary of a victim and the mentality of a person owed a debt. To grow up, they have been told and are still being told, you have to suffer" ("Remembering," 15).

63 Létourneau, "Remembering," 15.

64 Breton, "From Ethnic," 94. For example, those involved in the Quiet Revolution worked to bring the Parti Québécois to power in 1976, after which time they announced their intention to implement legislation that would make the French language the langue publique commune/common language of public life for all those living in Quebec. Accordingly, in 1977, they passed the Charter of the French Language, qualifying Quebec as a unilingual French-speaking society. Handler, *Nationalism*, 173; Oakes and Warren, *Language*, 28–9. This legislation thus represented Quebec's efforts and subsequent achievement of "national affirmation in the face of pan-Canadian attempts at nation-building" (Gagnon and Iacovino, "Interculturalism," 373).

65 Létourneau, "Remembering," 16.
66 Ibid., 17.
67 Ibid., 18.
68 Ibid., 19.
69 Stewart, On Longing, 23.
70 McKay, "Liberal," 76–7.
71 Gable and Handler, *New*, 237.
72 Macleod, "Decolonizing," 366–7.
73 Parks Canada, *Management Plan*, 2007, 31.

Chapter Six

1 Jenkins, "Cultural Renaissance," 169–86.
2 Sassen, *Global City*.
3 Dissanayake, "Globalization," 41.
4 Ibid.
5 Frank, *Mackenzie Panels*, 2; quoted in Duffy, "Sideways," 132.
6 Abu-Laban and Gabriel, *Selling Diversity*, 105.
7 Gregorovich, "Chairman's Report," 2.
8 Jenkins, "Cultural Renaissance," 173; City of Toronto, *Culture Plan*, 8–9, 14.
9 In so doing, I draw on the work of Preziosi, who characterizes art museums as cultural institutions that typically function as instruments of a "historiographic practice" or "civic instrument[s] for *practicing* history" (Preziosi, "Art," 509).
10 The community organizations, including the Kwanzaa Committee of Toronto, the Holy Blossom Temple Archives, the Toronto Native Community History Project at the Native Canadian Centre of Toronto, and the Chinese Cultural Centre of Greater Toronto provided letters, images, and research material related to the events, which was then written up by in-house staff. Lucas, 17 December 2007.
11 Toronto Historical Board, "Joint Meeting Museums Committee and the Historical Sites Committee, Monday 18 September 1961," *Toronto Civic Historical Committee*, 1.
12 Here I draw on the work of George Yúdice, who states that, in the current global age, the management of cultural institutions has not only identified but also come to privilege "the *usefulness of the claim to difference* as a warrant." The possibility for economic gains therefore trumps the nature or significance of the content. See *Expediency*, 23.

13 Steiner, "Canon," 213.

14 Duffy, "Grandfathering," 591.

15 While Mackenzie withdrew from political affairs, he continued to act as
a newspaper editor and publisher, issuing the *Message* in the late 1850s,
but this endeavour proved to be, as Nancy Luno describes it, "more of a
financial burden than an asset." Despite the fact that, over the course of the
next two years, the number of subscribers consistently declined, Mackenzie
managed to keep publishing the paper doing all of the work himself. He
finally shut down production on 15 September 1860. See Nancy Luno,
Genteel, 62.

16 Coutu, "Vehicles," 187; Conrad and Finkel, *Canada*, 205.

17 Ajzenstat, *Political Thought*, 3–4, 44, 114 n8.

18 Darke and Karadi, *Mackenzie*, 12.

19 *The Mackenzie Homestead, Minutes of Proceedings ... With the Address of the
Central Committee*, 1856, BR; quoted in Nesbitt, *Mackenzie*, 1.

20 Typical exterior details of the Greek Revival style evident in the house
include a tall rectangular façade, a garden front, recessed doorway, and a
Greek key frieze. Interior details include the support arch in the front hall
with decorative corbels, the high ceilings in the parlour and dining room,
and the pocket doors dividing the dining room from the parlour. Nesbitt,
Mackenzie, 4–5.

21 Lindsey, *Life*, 298–9, 12–13; quote from 13.

22 Silver, *Lost*, 128; Luno, *Genteel*, 99.

23 The Committee in fact purchased the house for 887 pounds and 10 shillings
"of lawful money of Canada." Deed of Sale, No. 666, W.&V. Rogers to
William Lyon Mackenzie, Registered 9 August 1859, Toronto Land Registry
Office; quoted in Luno, *Genteel*, 96.

24 Luno, *Genteel*, 103–4. As architectural historian Peter Ward explains, row
house floor plans, which typically included the parlour and dining room
on the ground floor and bedrooms on the upper floor, were not only
standardized but "almost universal" in design (*Domestic Space*, 31).

25 In January 1861, a city-wide census records that there were seven people
living in the house at that time. Along with Mr and Mrs Mackenzie lived
the couples' three daughters, Helen, 29, Elizabeth, 24, Isabel Grace, 17, and
twenty-year old George, the family's youngest son. The oldest son, William
Lyon Jr., lived on his own at this time. The family also employed a live-in
servant named Catherine Byrns, a nineteen-year old Irish Catholic woman.
Luno, *Genteel*, 104; Lindsey, *Life*, 1st vol., 13.

26 Luno, *Genteel*, 111.

27 Duffy, "Sideways," 139. Such texts include John Charles Dent's *Story of the Upper Canadian Rebellion* (1885), W.H.P. Clement's *The History of the Dominion of Upper Canada* (1897), and W.L. Grant's *Ontario High School History of Canada* (1914).

28 Duffy, "Sideways," 140.

29 For example, in 1936, Mackenzie King commissioned Canadian sculptor Walter Seymour Allward, designer of the Vimy Memorial, to create a monument dedicated to the actions and memory of his grandfather to stand in Queen's Park, the west side of the Ontario legislature in Toronto. Evidence suggests, however, that the intention to erect this monument might have been inspired by contemporaneous plans to preserve the Mackenzie House. According to Duffy, in August 1936, Senator Frank P. O'Connor told Prime Minister Mackenzie King that a Mackenzie Homestead Committee had gathered funds to purchase his grandfather's Bond Street residence; O'Connor suggested that a memorial sculpture might *also* be appropriate to celebrate the centenary of the Rebellion. See Duffy, "Grandfathering," 589. For an in-depth examination of the allegorical representation and commemorative purpose of the sculpture based on a formal analysis of the Queen's Park monument, see Duffy, "Complexity," 189–206. Other monuments mounted to honour Mackenzie include the restoration of his house in Queenston, ON, in which he lived and published the *Colonial Advocate* newspaper. A commemorative arch decorated with relief sculptures depicting various episodes related to the rebellion, known as the Clifton Gate Pioneer Memorial Arch, was also ordered by Thomas Baker McQuesten, Member of Parliament for Hamilton and minister of Highways and Public Works. Designed by Toronto-based architect William Lyon Somerville, the arch was originally located at the convergence of the Queen Elizabeth Way, the Niagara Parkway, and the Honeymoon Bridge. In 1976, however, a Niagara Parks Commission labelled the arch a "traffic hazard," and it was taken down. On 6 September 1984, the restored panels were unveiled in the garden of the Mackenzie House. See Coutu, "Vehicles," 185, 189; Frank, *Mackenzie Panels*, vi–vii, 4.

30 Between 1933 and 1937, the houses on either side of Mackenzie House had been demolished. An article published in the *Toronto Star Weekly*, dated 27 November 1937, showed photographs of the house "before the bordering houses were torn down" and "as it is today" ("After One Hundred Years," *Star* (Toronto) 27 November 1937; quoted in Nesbitt, *Mackenzie*, 8).

31 Nesbitt, *Mackenzie*, 8.

32 According to a pamphlet advertising the site, the dates of the representation
   spanned from 1820–60. See William Lyon Mackenzie Homestead Foundation,
   Addresses.

33 Leslie M. Frost, K.C., "Address," *Addresses*, 2.

34 Transcribed from the actual plaque located on the Mackenzie House Museum
   grounds.

35 An article from the *Globe and Mail* newspaper, entitled "Hemmed In:
   Landmark Doom Looms," reported that the Mackenzie House was "one
   step away from destruction" as the owners of properties adjacent to the
   house – Revere Electric and Macmillan Publishing – refused to part with any
   part of their property to save the site. The article also quoted a municipal
   officer identified as City Controller Newman who advocated that the house
   be preserved, stating, "As the home of our first mayor, [Mackenzie House]
   represents a unique link with an important era in our history ... At the rate
   we're going we soon will have nothing to remind us of our early settlers. We
   have so little now in the way of original housing it just seems too bad to lose
   this site" ("Hemmed In," 5).

36 One particular episode that inspired the public's interest in and concern for
   Toronto's historic sites was the municipal government's 1958 decision to erect a
   new city hall building, thus abandoning the original city hall building, erected
   in 1844, located at the corner of Queen and Bay Streets. See Arthur, *Toronto*,
   208, 232–6.

37 In addition to overseeing the operations of Mackenzie House, the Board also
   produced "new and special displays" at Fort York and the now-closed Marine
   Museum of Upper Canada, originally located in the historic Stanley Barracks
   at Exhibition Place. See Dr John W. Scott, "Chairman's Report," *1977 Year
   Book*, 1; Toronto Historical Board, "Museums," *1989 Annual Report*, 9.

38 Luno, *Genteel*, 115.

39 Later that same year, in 1960, it also took over the responsibility of operating
   and overseeing Colborne Lodge in High Park. In 1978, the Board, in
   conjunction with the Ontario Heritage Foundation acquired Spadina House,
   the Austin estate at 285 Spadina Road, and opened the house as a museum in
   1984. See Toronto Historical Board, *New Direction*, Appendix A.

40 Board members elected that the museum have a terminal date of 1861, the
   year of Mackenzie's death. See Toronto Historical Board, "Director's Report
   for the year 1960" *Toronto Civic Historical Committee, 1958–1960*, 9; Toronto
   Historical Board, "Joint Meeting Museums Committee and the Historical
   Sites Committee, Monday, 18 September 1961," *Toronto Civic Historical*

Committee, 1. Decisions regarding the museum policy were made after "considerable discussion." The Museum Committee Meeting Minutes of the Toronto Historical Board records "it was moved ... that (a) Mackenzie House be restored as a domestic dwelling house during the Mackenzie family occupation from 1859–1861 (b) a print shop be erected to house the Mackenzie press and suitable objects of a functioning print shop of the period (c) the connecting link between the house and shop be designed to accommodate material dealing with the life of William Lyon Mackenzie, with a particular emphasis placed on his publishing and political life ... The motion was carried" (Toronto Historical Board, "Museums Committee Meeting Minutes, 1 May 1962," *Toronto Civic Historical Committee*, 1).

41 Toronto Historical Board, "Coming Events," *Toronto Civic Historical Committee*, 1. The program, mounted by the Board in cooperation with the Provisional Class of the Junior League of Toronto, was first offered in 1962 as a six-day long program, which included baking demonstrations, decorations, and music. Research into "authentic" nineteenth-century recipes and decorations, such as a kissing ball, yule log, and decorated fir tree, was conducted "under the guidance of the Toronto Reference library" ("1862 Christmas Open to Public," *Star* [Toronto] 3 December 1962, 49). According to Board records, the event proved to be a "success"; over 2,000 people visited the site for the event, 1,403 of which were paid admissions. The event earned a net profit of approximately $500. See Toronto Historical Board, "Information and Education Committee Meeting Minutes, 19 December 1962," *Toronto Civic Historical Committee*, 1.

42 While Mackenzie did own and operate print shops at various times and places throughout his life, he never owned one connected to his house. See Toronto Historical Board, "Joint Meeting Museums Committee and the Historical Sites Committee, Monday 18 September 1961," 1.

43 In 1966–7, the Board applied for funds to construct an addition offered under Winter Works Incentive Program; grants were awarded based on the condition that the Board, the municipal government, and "higher levels of Government" contribute the funds required for the project. See J.A. McGinnis, "Report on Operations for 1967," *Annual Report 1967* (Toronto: Toronto Historical Board, 1967) 2; Toronto Historical Board, *Centennial Project* (Toronto: Stanley Barracks, 1965).

44 McGinnis, 1967, 2.

45 To cultivate a "closer relationship" between cultural administrators and the city's residents, the Board instituted a "Community Relations Programme."

This program required cultural administrators to encourage and work with various ethnic communities in the Toronto area to preserve the architectural structures and layouts of their existing neighbourhoods. See J.A. McGinnis, "Managing Director's Report," *Toronto Historical Board Year Book 1978* (Toronto: Toronto Historical Board, 1978), 6; Shirley McManus, "Working Toward Twenty Years: 1971–1980," *History of the Toronto Civic Historical Committee and the Toronto Historical Board 1949–1985* (Toronto: Toronto Historical Board, 31 January 1986), 29.

46 McManus, *History*, 29.

47 Ibid., 29.

48 The Board hired a student from the University of Toronto's museology program who curated the program as part of her internship. The panels were first displayed at Nathan Phillips Square in August 1979. See J.A. McGinnis, "Managing Director's Report," *Year Book 1980* (Toronto Historical Board: Toronto, 1980) 9, 20 [image on 20]; McManus, 29.

49 McManus, *History*, 28.

50 In 1980, Chairman Gregorovich asserted that the Board alone determined what monuments might be erected in the Toronto region, writing, "I regret to report ... that some monuments have been erected without our consultation, for example the Portuguese Monument (1978) and the Katyn Memorial (1980). We have recommended changes to the procedures in City Hall in the hopes that we can, in future, properly fulfill our responsibility in this area ... We are concerned that all Torontonians, whether natives or immigrants, whether from an older or newer ethnic group, have the opportunity to share in the history and past culture of Toronto through the facilities and programmes of the Board" (See Gregorovich, "Chairman's Report," *Year Book 1980*, 3).

51 James, "Managing Director's Report," *Annual Report 1984*, 11.

52 The exhibition travelled to libraries, schools, and community halls throughout Toronto; it was also set up at public events, including Toronto-based festivals. See Toronto Historical Board, "Outreach Programs: Serving the Community," *Annual Report 1984*, 34; Toronto Historical Board, "Community Relations," *Annual Report 1986*, 23; Toronto Historical Board, *Multicultural*, n.p.

53 According to McManus, the Board wanted to look into setting up a location where "a collection of sculptures relating to individual ethnic groups" might be housed (McManus, *History*, 29–30, emphasis added).

54 In the early 1990s, the City imposed a "series of severe belt-tightening measures," which forced the Board to reduce the number of staff members employed at historic sites, shorten the museums' operating hours, and

terminate the museums' costume program (Burnside and James, "From the Chairman and Managing Director," *1991 Annual Report*, 2).

55 As part of its reorganization, City Council created the Culture Division, which is part of the Economic Development, Culture and Tourism Department. This particular department has four operating divisions: Culture, Economic Development, Parks and Recreation, and Special Events. Toronto Culture, *Workprint*, 2.

56 Ibid., 3.

57 Ibid., 15. The city's heritage sites "all tell *a portion* of the Toronto story" (ibid., 4, emphasis added).

58 Abu-Laban and Gabriel, *Selling Diversity*, 12.

59 Yúdice, *Expediency*, 23.

60 Interestingly, Toronto Culture sought to increase both short- and long-term outlooks. In terms of the short-term outlook, Toronto Culture determined that, by branding its historic sites as culturally diverse, this particular initiative would not only require but also merit a funding increase for municipal cultural institutions. It also determined, drawing on the work of Richard Florida, that such "branding" would attract tourists and mobile, educated newcomers – referred to by Florida as those members of the "Creative Class" – who might be integrated into the "whole fabric of the city's cultural life" and, based on their residency, actively contribute to the development of the city's economic infrastructure. See Jenkins, "Cultural Renaissance," 178; Toronto Culture, *Workprint*, 14–5; City of Toronto, *Culture Plan*, 6–9; quote from City of Toronto, *Culture Plan*, 8. See also Florida, *Flight* and *Rise*.

61 City of Toronto, *Culture Plan*, 1. While the *Culture Plan* does not use the term "brand" per se, it does call for the city's historic sites to represent various ethnic communities that live and work in the Toronto region in order to "distinguish Toronto from any other city in the world" (14). Elsewhere, the plan stipulates that Toronto, by and large, needs to "[focus] on cultural diversity as a theme for advocacy, by reminding cultural institutions ... to welcome newcomers" (8). Barbara Jenkins explains that such moves, particularly those that aim to use the concept of multiculturalism or cultural icons – or, in the case of my work, an amalgamation of the two – to draw attention to and to promote regions or cities as international cultural destinations, are "branding" exercises. See Jenkins, "Cultural Renaissance," 173.

62 City of Toronto, *Culture Plan*, 14.

63 Ibid., 15.

64 Jenkins, "Cultural Renaissance," 170.

65 Wood and Gilbert, "Multiculturalism," 685.

Chapter Seven

1 Bennett, "Introduction," 5.

2 Handler and Saxton, "Dyssimulation," 245.

3 For example, in 1852 and 1857, Mackenzie published the *Message* on 25 December. He also, in 1839, docked an office employee's pay for being "absent Chris & new year [sic]" (*Gazette* Account Book, p. 2097, MLP; quoted in Luno, 167). Mackenzie's view of this particular day fit with the conception of the time; in fact, it was not until 1872 that the Canadian government declared Christmas a "legal holiday," in which financial transactions were prohibited. What is more, that particular legislation applied solely to the provinces of Ontario, New Brunswick, and Nova Scotia. Canada, *Statutes of Canada* (M. Cameron, Law Printer to the Queen's Most Excellent Majesty, 1872), 33. Furthermore, according to Françoise Noël, in mid-nineteenth century Canada, the Legislative Assembly often stayed in session during the Christmas season; many members, as a result, spent time in a boarding house, which, in Noël's words, "suggests that being home for the occasion was not a high priority" (*Family Life*, 94). Luno records, however, that Mackenzie did, on occasion, attend Catholic Christmas Masses. The Christmas mass represented, in Mackenzie's words, a "novelty to us" – "us" referring to both him and family members he himself characterized as "[n]ot being of that denomination of Protestant who consider Yule a religious festival" (*Colonial Advocate*, 1 January 1829; quoted in Luno, *Genteel*, 168).

4 Russell, 21 February 2007. All quotations attributed to Russell are taken from this interview.

5 Preziosi, "Seeing," 222.

6 As Russell puts it, "we can't do it specifically with the Mackenzies."

7 For example, Russell states that she made a "conscious choice" not to put up a Christmas tree. While she acknowledges that upper-class mid-Victorian society had incorporated the decoration of the Christmas tree into their holiday celebration following its introduction to Britain by Queen Victoria's consort, Prince Albert, Russell states that, based on what she refers to as the "trickle-down effect," this particular tradition "hadn't [yet] become a part of the common celebration" in Toronto.

8 In other words, the site depicts the type of celebration that might have been

put on by those poor, yet notably educated and thus civilized members of society. As one interpreter explains, Mackenzie House, when decorated in the guise of a "Victorian Christmas," reflects the "genteel poverty of the middle class" (13 December 2006).

9 Toronto Historical Board, "Joint Meeting Museums Committee and the Historical Sites Committee, Monday 18 September 1961," *Toronto Civic Historical Committee*, 1.

10 Toronto Culture, *Workprint*, 14.

11 Lucas, 27 November 2007.

12 "Joint Meeting Museums Committee," 1960, 1.

13 Luno, *Genteel*, 103–4.

14 According to one interpreter, these panels "[give] you a sense of the true history of our Christmas celebration" (24 December 2006). Again, these banners are not historical artifacts but contain explanatory texts with illustrations and receive little attention in terms of live interpretation. In fact, over the eight tours attended and observed, only one interpreter refers to the banners, stating, "Of course, in Toronto, we have various communities celebrating different holidays, so we have Hanukkah, First Nations, and Chinese New Year's coming up" (24 December 2006). For the most part, over the course of the other seven tours, visitors are invited to peruse the exhibition(s) in the hall and read the panels themselves.

15 24 December 2006.

16 Ibid.

17 Ibid.

18 13 December 2006. Another interpreter states, responding to a visitor's enquiry if Mackenzie was in fact rich, "Mackenzie wasn't wealthy at all. He actually died bankrupt. He would have been considered, I guess, middle-class. A lot of people think that he was a politician, he had his own newspaper, he would have been well-off, but politicians didn't really get paid that much money, compared to today" (16 December 2008).

19 21 December 2006.

20 13 December 2006. As one interpreter explains, "Christmas trees start becoming popular in Canada sort of in the years following the 1870s, 80s, because of trends from England. Queen Victoria, the English Queen married Prince Albert, who was German. And Christmas trees were more popular in Germany, so, when they married, he brought that tradition over and people would see images. They'd make Christmas cards showing the Royal family, the Queen and the Prince and their children, around a tree, opening presents, so

that started to catch on. So if this house was a couple of decades later, they would have had a Christmas tree" (21 December 2006).

21 For instance, one interpreter states, "In 1860, for a Presbyterian Scottish family living in Toronto, they would not have had a Christmas tree" (21 December 2006). In so doing, interpreters frequently refer to Mackenzie's documented perceptions regarding the Christmas season to further justify the Christmas tree's absence from the portrayal. As one interpreter explains, "Mackenzie really didn't celebrate Christmas much, but being a politician, we have a writing that he did go down to attend a Catholic Mass down in St [Michael's]. But he wasn't Catholic himself, but he wanted to let those Catholic people that voted for him know that he supported them" (13 December 2006). Another interpreter says, "Christmas wasn't really a big deal for Mr Mackenzie ... He actually used to go to work on Christmas day" (14 December 2006). In addressing Mackenzie's perceptions regarding the Christmas season, interpreters' comments recall for visitors the fictionalized nature of the program. On the other hand, however, they also refer to particular artifacts to convey the "historical accuracy" of the representation.

22 14 December 2006.

23 24 December 2006. Another interpreter explains that in order to produce candied orange peels, one would eat the orange and cut the peel into strips, boil the pieces with sugar and water and produce a candied fruit (14 December 2006).

24 16 December 2006.

25 What is interesting to note is that, while the interpreters characterize this type of porcelain as that which the middle-classes would have purchased in the nineteenth-century, they are quick to point out that flow blue china, because it was considered to be a mistake and not produced again, is currently considered rare and, as a result, valuable (13 December 2006).

26 In Mackenzie's daughters' bedroom, interpreters call attention to another family artifact, the slipper chair in the daughters' bedroom, a piece embroidered with both wool and coloured beads by daughter Janet Mackenzie. Toronto Culture, *Self-Guided Tour*, 3.

27 21 December 2006.

28 Interpreters also use reproductions of hoop skirts, petty coats, and historical advertisements, as well as modern-day pictures of corsets, to discuss clothing and dressing procedures of the nineteenth-century in this particular space.

29 24 December 2006. Similarly, another interpreter says, "here's the master bedroom. This is the room that William died in in 1861. Unfortunately, we

don't have his bed, but sleigh beds were popular at this time, so we have a sleigh bed in here. The bed's from 1845 … and Mackenzie, I think the cause of death that [the doctor] actually wrote down was 'softening of the brain,' but I think we probably think it was a stroke. They just didn't necessarily understand it at the time" (21 December 2006).

30 Schwartz, *Culture,* 279.

31 One might also surmise that because, as discussed above, the house is often labelled Mackenzie's "retirement house," this type of factual narrative further reinforces the idea that this was ultimately, as one interpreter puts it, "Mackenzie's last house" (21 December 2006).

32 14 December 2006. Overall, interpreters consistently relay the same story to visitors. For example, one interpreter explains, "In here we just have a study. Originally, in the house … we don't know if this was actually a box room or an extra bedroom. But again it just reflects that some people did have studies. This is not original to Mackenzie but it's something that you could find in the late 1860s" (16 December 2006). Similarly, another interpreter states, "The room … is restored to look like Mackenzie's study. More likely, it was probably used as a storage room" (21 December 2006).

33 Casey, "Museum Effect," 11.

34 24 December 2006.

35 Ibid.

36 Interpreters also point out the desk and chair as well as the map of the city from 1857, the year when the house was built, that hangs on the wall opposite to the one with the proclamation (13 December 2006).

37 24 December 2006.

38 21 December 2006.

39 31 December 2006. Similarly, another interpreter states, "It's a living basement … And it's not as fancy as the rooms upstairs, but it's sort of much more comfortable" (14 December 2006).

40 21 December 2006.

41 When describing the operations of the oven, they are quick to point out the fact that the built-in cook stove is "not original to the house" because, when the City of Toronto acquired the house in 1960, the stove had been removed. During the restoration, however, interpreters explain that workers found an American model, dating to the 1840s, in a house located nearby on Sherbourne Street that was due for demolition. It fit into the vacant space left by the original model, as one interpreter puts it, "like a hand in a glove" (28 December 2006). Another interpreter suggests, based on this evidence, that

"it's very, very likely that we've got the right model here" (24 December 2006).

42 As one interpreter puts it, "So, besides being mayor and leader of the Rebellion, Mackenzie was also a printer and publisher of newspapers ... [His print shop] wasn't here in the house, that would have been way too neat, it was on King Street" (31 December 2006).

43 24 December 2006.

44 20 December 2006. Significantly, while in the print shop, interpreters consistently describe Mackenzie as a political activist and newspaper publisher who sacrificed his financial security for his ideologies; in so doing, they recall the type of characterization offered at the beginning of the tour when interpreters first welcome visitors to the site. As one interpreter explains in the context of the print shop, Mackenzie "was more of a publisher and journalist but never made a lot of really wise business decisions, because he always seemed a little short on money. That's probably one thing we always think of him ... He gave up a lot for his art, which was his newspapers and his writings" (24 December 2006).

45 Handler and Saxton, "Dyssimulation," 245; Casey, "Museum Effect," 11.

46 Mackey, *House*, 102.

47 Ibid., 102.

48 Steiner, "Canon," 214.

49 Bennett, "Introduction," 5.

50 Jessup, "Hard Inclusion," xxi, emphasis in original.

51 Bennett, "Introduction," 6.

52 Stratton and Ang, "Imagined," 152.

53 Bennett, "Introduction," 6.

54 Day, *Multiculturalism*, 9.

55 Steiner, "Canon," 217.

56 Hage, *White*, 87–9.

57 Mackey, *House*, 163.

58 Canadian Multiculturalism Act, 835; quoted in Smaro Kamboureli, "Technology," 215; Bissoondath, *Selling*, 218.

59 Bannerji, *Dark Side*, 35–7.

60 Kamboureli, *Scandalous*, 105.

61 Bissoondath, *Selling*, 211.

62 Bannerji, *Dark Side*, 37.

63 Ibid., 36.

64 Mackey, *House*, 157.

65 Yúdice, "Translator's Introduction," xxxviii.

66 Rogoff, "Hit," 72–3.
67 McKay, "Liberal," 622.

Conclusion

1 Romney, *Getting It Wrong*, 253.
2 Schwartz, "Photographs," 164.
3 Sixty per cent of the interior was restored in the 1980s to represent the year 1864. Currently, the site operates under the purviews of both Parks Canada and the provincial government in that it not only acts as a historic site offering guided tours, displays and an audio-visual presentation for visitors, it also houses the legislative assembly.
4 According to Statistics Canada, in 1998/99, those who made "culture/heritage visits" most often visited Nova Scotia and frequented sites such as the Fortress of Louisbourg and the Alexander Graham Bell Museum in Cape Breton. The study also found that between 1996 and 1999, "culture/heritage visits" increased more rapidly than other types of visits, including visiting family members and sight-seeing. It ultimately concluded that "Canadians are participating increasingly in culture/heritage travel" (Statistics Canada, "Canadians," 6).
5 Statistics Canada, "Heritage Institutions."
6 Along with George-Étienne Cartier and George Brown, Macdonald formed a coalition government in 1864 in order to achieve confederation of the United Canadas. Conrad and Finkle, *Canada*, 246. Given that, following the achievement of Confederation, Macdonald went on to become Canada's first Prime Minister, certain parties have made a concerted effort to characterize Macdonald as, to use historian Christopher Moore's conceptualization, the "single hero in the confederation wars" (*1867*, 246). For example, Canadian historian Donald Creighton, writing in 1952, championed Macdonald's role in Confederation, describing 1 July 1867 as Macdonald's "day, if it was anybody's." Creighton goes on to state that Macdonald, "above all others, had ensured its coming, and he had prescribed the order of its celebration ... Others would expatiate eloquently upon [the significance of Confederation] – after he had done the work of bringing it about." (*Macdonald*, 466). As Moore points out, however, the achievement of Confederation represented the "success of a parliamentary process rather than a leader-driven, quasi-presidential one" (Ibid., 247).
7 Designed in the style of the Italian villas located in the region of Tuscany,

Bellevue's architectural style is defined by its stuccoed limestone walls, shuttered windows, numerous balconies, and the square Italianate tower located in the middle of the structure. See Angus, *Old Stones*, 86–7.

8 "Historic sites and Monuments: Suggested Acquisition of Residence of Sir John A. Macdonald at Kingston, 18 March 1964," in *Debates*, 1229.

9 Significantly, the Architectural Conservancy of Ontario, writing in 1967, characterized Dundurn as Hamilton's "best known monument" and the "most conspicuous mansion of [MacNab's] time" (*Victorian Architecture*, 2, 4). Similarly, architectural historian Janet Wright refers to Dundurn as "the most comprehensive statement of the Picturesque values of Canadian architecture" (*Architecture*, 78).

10 Casey, "Museum Effect," 10–12; Timothy, "Introduction," xiii.

11 Smith, *Chosen*, 258–9.

12 The funds for the restoration project had been awarded through *National Centennial Projects Act* grant, a grant that awarded federal money to projects that would garner domestic tourism during Centennial celebrations and be of a "lasting nature" (Adamson, *Proposal*, 4).

13 Hamilton Public Library, *Metcalfe*, 7 September 1961, emphasis in original.

14 Canadian historian and then-Board member Donald Creighton conducted extensive research and subsequently produced a list of names of those both present and active in both the Quebec (1864) and London conferences, which he presented to the Board advocating that his list be considered "official and correct" as well as "authoritative." "Extraits des procès-verbal de la réunion de la CLMHC tenue du 25 au 29 mai 1959"; quoted in Parcs Canada, *Énoncé*, 2004, 22.

15 Parcs Canada, *Énoncé*, 2004, 23.

16 Leslie M. Frost, K.C., *Addresses*, 2–3.

17 Toronto Historical Board, "Director's Report for the year 1960" *Toronto Civic Historical Committee*, 9.

18 As historian Paul Stern explains, people have the strongest and "most primordial ties" to the family unit so that these relations typically "arouse the strongest empathy, and exact the most stringent obligations from members – it is for [this group] that people are most likely to sacrifice their lives" ("Why," 115).

19 Smith, *Nationalism*, 71.

20 Macleod, "Decolonizing," 366–7.

21 Parks Canada, "Management Plan Newsletters."

22 Pannekoek, "Riel House," 255. Historian Robert J. Coutts explains that the Red

River frame style tended to be the "building style of choice" among settlers in what is now the southern region of Manitoba. Designed using tongue-and-groove log construction with relatively "simple" layouts and exteriors "devoid of stylistic embellishments," these houses "represented an affordable and functional adaptation to the environment for farmers, hunters, and traders. Stone houses, on the other hand, were costlier and more labour-intensive and were generally built by the wealthy members of the red river society, such as the retired chief factors of the Hudson's Bay Company" (*Road*, 116).

23 Osborne, "Corporeal," 319.

24 Parks Canada, "Management Plan Newsletters."

25 Osborne, "Corporeal," 307.

26 Parks Canada, "Cultural Heritage."

27 Nora, "Between," 12.

28 Ibid., 19.

29 Mills, "Moving," 111.

30 Stokes Sims, "Introduction," 12.

31 Drobnick and Fisher, *Museopathy*, 15.

32 Ibid., 14.

33 Stokes Sims, "Introduction," 16.

34 Goldstein, *Vaux*, 20.

35 Aillagon, "Introductory."

36 Ibid., "Preface," 8–9.

37 Le Bon and Koons, "Interview," 108; Geuna and Le Bon, "Celebration," 128.

38 Le Bon and Koons, "Interview," 154–5.

39 Handler and Saxton, "Dyssimulation," 245; Rychen, "Abundance," 8.

40 Corrin, *Wilson*, 49; Rachleff, "Peering," 219. As curator Lisa G. Corrin explains, "To speak of the ideological apparatus underlying museum practices is to peak of the relation between power, representation, and cultural identity; of how history is written and communicated; of whose history is voiced and whose is silenced" ("Mining," 45).

41 Corrin, "Mining," 49

42 Rachleff, "Peering," 209.

43 Ibid.

44 Ibid., 217

45 Corrin, "Mining," 64.

46 Ibid.

47 Rachleff, "Peering," 218.

48 Fisher and Drobnick, *Museopathy*, 56.

49 Malone, *Fraser*, 16.

50 Trainor, "Andrea Fraser," n.p.

51 Malone, 16.

52 Fraser, "Interview?"; quoted in Malone, 16.

53 The Grange has hosted other artist interventions such as the 2001–02 exhibition *House Guests: Contemporary Artists in The Grange*, conceived of by Christina Ritchie and Jessica Bradley and organized by Jenny Reiger. Toronto based artists Luis Jacob, Robert Fones, Rebecca Belmore, and Christy Thompson, New York artists Elaine Reichek and Josiah McElheny, and London based (UK) artist Elizabeth LeMoine all produced contemporary art installations in particular areas of the house so as to "intervene" and, as Bradley puts it, "unsettle and reinterpret histories that, in the shifting of old hierarchies … make room for new voices" (Bradley, "House Guests: Contemporary Artists in The Grange," 77).

54 Baillie, "Memoir of a Tour Guide," 91–2.

55 Robertson, "Titanium," 202. Other artists invited included Shary Boyle, Tim Whiten, Willie Cole, Kent Monkman, Frank Stella, and Kara Walker. Notably, Boyle's "grotesque" figurines inspired by Royal Doulton collectible statuettes resided for a time in the historic European galleries.

56 McKay, "Häussler."

57 Ibid.

58 Ibid.

59 Häussler, "Disclosure."

60 Häussler, "Artist's Statement."

61 McKay.

62 Moos, *Amber*, 112.

63 Häussler, "Disclosure."

64 Moos, *Amber*, 108.

65 Ibid., 110.

66 Rachleff, "Peering," 221–2.

Bibliography

Archival Sources

Special Collections, Hamilton Public Library, Hamilton, on.
Dundurn Castle Scrapbook of Clippings, vol. 1, 1849–1964
Dundurn Castle Scrapbook of Clippings, vol. 2, 1965–1968.
Dundurn Castle Scrapbook of Clippings, vol. 3a, February 1974–1981 Gwen
  Metcalfe File Boxes.

City of Toronto Archives
McManus, Shirley. History of the Toronto Civic Historical Committee and the
  Toronto Historical Board 1949–1985. 31 January 1986.

Heritage Toronto Archives
Toronto Historical Board. Toronto Civic Historical Committee, 1958–1960;
  Toronto Historical Board, 1960–1962.

Interviews and Communications

Ledoyen, David. Team Leader, Visitor Experience (interpretation and education),
  The Sir George-Étienne Cartier and the Fur Trade at Lachine National

Historic Sites, Montreal, QC. Personal communication with author.
21 February 2014.

Lucas, Fiona. Site Administrator, Mackenzie House, Toronto, ON. Interview with
author. 17 December 2007; 27 November 2007.

Nesbitt, Bill. Curator, Dundurn Castle, Hamilton, ON. Interview with author. 26
November 2003.

Russell, Rita. Programs Officer, Mackenzie House, Toronto, ON. Interview with
author. 21 February 2007.

Published Sources

"1862 Christmas Open to Public." *Star* (Toronto), 3 December 1962, 49.

Abu-Laban, Yasmeen, and Christina Gabriel. *Selling Diversity: Immigration,
Multiculturalism, Employment Equity and Globalisation*. Peterborough:
Broadview Press, 2002.

Adamson, Anthony. *Dundurn Castle: An Undeveloped Asset*. Toronto, Ontario,
Submission to Parks Board of Hamilton, 12 September 1961.

– *A Proposal for the Restoration of Dundurn as the Core of a Centennial Project for
the City of Hamilton*. Hamilton: 10 February 1962.

– and Marion MacRae. *The Ancestral Roof: Domestic Architecture of Upper Canada*.
Toronto: Clarke and Irwin, 1963.

– "Preface." In *Jeff Koons Versailles* [exhibition catalogue], 7–10. Éditions Xavier
Barral, 2008.

Ajzenstat, Janet. *The Political Thought of Lord Durham*. Montreal and Kingston:
McGill-Queen's University Press, 1988.

Albano, Caterina. "Displaying Lives: The Narrative of Objects in Biographical
Exhibitions." *Museum and Society* 5.1 (March 2007): 15–28.

Alexander, Edward, and Mary Alexander. *Museums in Motion: An Introduction to
the History and Function of Museums*, 2nd edition. Plymouth, UK: AltaMira
Press, 2008.

Anderson, Benedict. *Imagined Communities*. London: Verso, 1991.

Anderson, Jay. *Time Machines: The World of Living History*. Nashville: The
American Association for State and Local History, 1984.

– "Living History: Simulating Everyday Life in Living Museums." *American
Quarterly* 34.3 (1982): 290–306.

Angus, Margaret. *The Old Stones of Kingston: Its Buildings Before 1867*. Toronto:
University of Toronto Press, 1989.

Architectural Conservancy of Ontario. *Victorian Architecture in Hamilton*.

Hamilton: Architectural Conservancy of Ontario, 1967.

Arthur, Eric. *Toronto: No Mean City*. Toronto: University of Toronto Press, 1964.

Ashley, Susan. "The Changing Face of Heritage at Canada's National Historic Sites." *International Journal of Heritage Studies* 13.6 (2007): 478–88.

Ashworth, G.J., and Brian Graham. Introduction to *Senses of Place: Senses of Time*, edited by G.J. Ashworth and Brian Graham, 3–12. Aldershot, Hants, UK; Burlington, VT: Ashgate, 2005.

AuthentiCity. *Creative City Planning Framework*. City of Toronto: AuthentiCity, February 2008.

Bailey, T. Melville. *The Laird of Dundurn*. Hamilton: W.L. Griffin Limited, 1968.

Bailey, T. Melville, and Charles Ambrose Carter. *Hamilton Firsts*. Hamilton: W.L. Griffin Limited, 1973.

Baldone, Donalda. *Dundurn Castle*. Erin: Boston Mills, 1990.

Bannerji, Himani. *The Dark Side of the Nation: Essays on Multiculturalism, Nationalism and Gender*. Toronto: Canadian Scholars Press, 2000.

Barry, Sandra. "What's in a Name? The Gilbert Stuart Newton Plaque Error." *Acadiensis* 25.5 (Autumn 1995): 99–116.

Baudelaire, Charles. *The Painter of Modern Life and Other Essays*. Phaidon Press, 1995.

Baxandall, Michael. "Exhibiting Intention: Some Preconditions of Visual Display of Culturally Purposeful Objects." In *Exhibiting Cultures: The Poetics and Politics of Museum Display*, edited by Ivan Karp and Steven Lavine, 33–41. Washington: Smithsonian Press, 1991

Beers, Donald. *Sir Allan Napier MacNab*. Hamilton: W.L. Griffin Limited, 1984.

Bélanger, Diane. *Lieu Historique National de Sir-George-Étienne-Cartier: Le Noël victorien de la maison George-Étienne Cartier*. Parcs Canada: Service Ethnologiques, Avril 1999.

Belk, Russell. "Materialism and the Making of the Modern American Christmas." In *Unwrapping Christmas*, edited by Daniel Miller, 75–104. Oxford: Clarendon Press, 1993.

Bennett, David. "Introduction." In *Multicultural States: Rethinking Difference and Identity*, edited by David Bennett, 1–25. New York: Routledge, 1998.

Bennett, Tony. *The Birth of the Museum: History, Theory, Politics*. London: Routledge, 1995.

– "Exhibitions, Difference and the Logic of Culture." In *Museum Frictions: Public Cultures/Global Transformations*, edited by Ivan Karp, Corinne A. Katz, Lynn Szwaja, and Tomás Ybarra-Frausto, 46–69. Durham and London: Duke University Press, 2007.

– "Museums and 'The People.'" In *The Museum Time Machine: Putting Cultures on Display*, edited by Robert Lumley, 63–84. London: Routledge, 1988.

Bissoondath, Neil. *Selling Illusions: The Cult of Multiculturalism in Canada*. Toronto: Penguin, 2002.

Blair, Louisa. "Life Below Stairs." *Beaver* 85.3 (June/July 2005): 18–27.

Black, Graham. *The Engaging Museum: Developing Museums for Visitor Involvement*. Abingdon: Routledge, 2005.

Blatti, Jo, ed. *Past Meets Present: Essays about Historical Interpretation and Public Audiences*. Washington: Smithsonian Institution, 1987.

Bodnar, John, ed. *Remaking America: Public Memory, Commemoration, and Patriotism in the Twentieth Century*. Princeton, NJ: Princeton University Press, 1992.

Boswell, David, and Jessica Evans, eds. *Representing the Nation: A Reader. Histories, Heritage and Museums*. Princeton: Princeton University Press, 1999.

Boyer, M. Christine. *The City of Collective Memory: Its Historical Imagery and Architectural Entertainments*. Cambridge: Massachusetts Institute of Technology Press, 1994.

Bradley, Jessica. "House Guests: Contemporary Artists in The Grange." In *House Guests: The Grange 1817 to Today*, edited by Jessica Bradley and Gillian MacKay, 75–81. Toronto: Art Gallery of Ontario, 2001.

Breton, Eric. "Canadian Federalism, Multiculturalism and the Twenty-First Century." *International Journal of Canadian Studies* 21 (2000): 155–98.

Breton, Raymond. "From Ethnic to Civic Nationalism: English Canada and Quebec." *Ethnic and Racial Studies* 11.1 (January 1988): 85–102.

– "Multiculturalism and Canadian Nation-Building." In *The Politics of Gender, Ethnicity and Language in Canada*, edited by Alan Cairns and Cynthia Williams, 27–66. Toronto: University of Toronto Press, 1986.

Brewis, Joanna, and Samantha Warren. "Have Yourself a Merry Little Christmas? Organizing Christmas in Women's Magazines Past and Present." *Organization* 18.6 (November 2011): 747–62.

Bruner, Edward. "Abraham Lincoln as Authentic Reproduction: A Critique of Postmodernism." *American Anthropologist* 96.2 (1994): 397–415.

Bruner, M. Lane. *Strategies of Remembrance: The Rhetorical Dimensions of National Identity Construction*. Columbia, South Carolina: University of South Carolina Press, 2002.

Burgoyne, Robert. "From Contested to Consensual Memory: The Rock and Roll Hall of Fame and Museum." In *Memory, History, Nation: Contested Pasts*, edited by Katharine Hodgkin and Susannah Radstone, 208–20. New

Brunswick: Transaction Publishers, 2006.

Burnside, David, and R. Scott James. "From the Chairman and Managing Director." *Toronto Historical Board 1991 Annual Report*, 1–2. Toronto Historical Board, 1991.

Cameron, Christina. "The Spirit of Place: The Physical Memory of Canada." *Journal of Canadian Studies* 35.3 (Spring 2000): 77–94.

Campbell, Claire. "'It was Canadian, then, typically Canadian': Revisiting Wilderness at Historic Sites." *British Journal of Canadian Studies* 21.1 (2008): 5–34.

Canada. "Historic sites and Monuments: Suggested Acquisition of Residence of Sir John A. Macdonald at Kingston, 18 March 1964." *House of Commons Debates: Official Report. Second Session – Twenty Sixth Parliament*. Vol. 2, 1224–31. Ottawa: Queen's Printer and Controller of Stationary, 1964.

– Statutes of Canada. *M. Cameron, Law Printer to the Queen's Most Excellent Majesty*, 1872.

The Canadian Press. "Parks Canada buildings in worse shape than claimed: Internal report." 11 February 2014: n.p. *CBC News: Politics*. Accessed 4 March 2014. http://www.cbc.ca/news/politics/parks-canada-buildings-in-worse-shape-than-claimed-internal-report-1.2531987.

Canclini, Néstor García ed. *Consumers and Citizens: Globalization and Multicultural Conflicts*. Minneapolis, University of Minnesota Press, 2001.

Carmichael, Barbara. "Global Competitiveness and Special Events in Cultural Tourism: The Example of the Barnes Exhibit at the Art Gallery of Ontario, Toronto." *Canadian Geographer* 24.4 (2002): 310–24.

Carson, Cary. "Living Museums of Everyman's History." *Harvard Magazine* 83 (July – August 1981): 22–32.

Casey, Valerie. "The Museum Effect: Gazing from Object to Performance in Contemporary Cultural-History Museum." ICHIM, www.ichim.org 3 (September 2003): 2–20.

Chui, Tina, Kelly Tran, and Hélène Maheux. *Immigration In Canada: A Portrait of Foreign-Born Population*. Ottawa: Minster of Industry, Statistics Canada, 2007.

Church, Elizabeth, and Patrick White. "Toronto's Cost-Cutting Plan Puts Subsidized Daycare, Zoos on the Block." *Globe and Mail* (Toronto). 14 September 2011: n.p. Accessed 14 September 2011. http://www.theglobeandmail.com/news/national/toronto/torontos-cost-cutting-plan-puts-subsidized-daycare-zoos-on-the-block/article2162261/.

City of Hamilton. *Open for Opportunity: Hamilton Economic Development Review, 2001*. Hamilton, 2001.

City of Hamilton. *New Directions: Economic Development Review, 2000*. Hamilton, 2000.

City of Toronto. "Committee Recommendations." Toronto [City Council] Item. Accessed 22 September 2011. http://app.toronto.ca/tmmis/ viewAgendaItemHistory.do?item=2011.EX10.1.– "Culture Plan for the Creative City. Toronto: Department of Economic Development, Culture and Tourism Division," 2003.

Clarence, Christina C. "Chairman's Report." *Toronto Historical Board 1990 Annual Report*, 1–2. Toronto: Toronto Historical Board, 1990.

Clifford, James. *Routes: Travel and Translation in the Late Twentieth Century*. Harvard University Press, 1997.

– *The Predicament of Culture: Twentieth-Century Ethnography, Literature and Art*. Cambridge: Harvard University Press, 1988.

Coleman, Daniel. *White Civility: The Literary Project of English Canada*. Toronto: University of Toronto Press, 2006.

Conn, Steven. *Do Museums Still Need Objects?* Philadelphia: University of Pennsylvania Press, 2010.

Connelly, Marc, ed. *Christmas at the Movies: Images of Christmas in American, British and European Cinema*. London: I.B. Tauris Publishers, 2000.

Connerton, Paul. *How Societies Remember*. Cambridge: Cambridge University Press, 1989.

Conrad, Margaret, and Alvin Finkel. *Canada: A National History*. Toronto: Pearson Education Canada Inc., 2003.

– Jocelyn Létourneau, and David Northrup. "Canadians and Their Pasts: An Exploration in Historical Consciousness." *Public Historian* 31.1 (Winter 2009): 15–34.

Corrin, Lisa G. "Mining the Museum: Artists Look at Museums, Museums Look at Themselves." In *Fred Wilson: A Critical Reader*, edited by Doro Globus, 45–74. Ridinghouse, 2011.

Coutts, Robert J. *The Road to the Rapids: Nineteenth-Century Church and Society at St. Andrew's Parish, Red River*. Calgary: University of Calgary, 2000.

Coutu, Joan. "Vehicles of Nationalism: Defining Canada in the 1930s." *Journal of Canadian Studies* 37.1 (Spring 2002): 180–203.

Creighton, Donald. *John A. Macdonald: The Young Politician, the Old Chieftain*. Toronto: University of Toronto Press, 1952, 1998.

Daniels, Stephen. *Fields of Vision: Landscape Imagery and National Identity in England and the United States*. Princeton: Princeton University Press, 1993.

Darke, Eleanor, Gabriella Karadi, and Chris Raible. *William Lyon Mackenzie and the 1837 Rebellion*. Toronto: Toronto Historical Board, n.d.

Davis, Angela Y. "Gender, Class and Multiculturalism: Rethinking 'Race' Politics."
In *Mapping Multiculturalism*, edited by Avery F. Gordon and Christopher
Newfield, 40–8. Minneapolis: University of Minnesota Press, 1996.

Day, Richard. *Multiculturalism and the History of Canadian Diversity*. Toronto:
University of Toronto Press, 1999.

Dennison, John D., and Paul Gallagher. *Canada's Community Colleges: A Critical
Analysis*. Vancouver: University of British Columbia Press, 2011.

Des Rochers, Jacques, and Alain Roy. "Old Montreal, Place and Time
Rediscovered, 1950–21st Century." In *Old Montreal: History through Heritage*,
edited by Gilles Lauzon and Madeleine Forget, 247–90. Sainte-Foy, QC: Les
Publications du Québec, 2004.

Design + Communication Inc. *Parc Historique National de Sir-George-Étienne
Cartier: Extrait du Cahier de Réalisation Préliminaire*. Québec: Parcs Canada,
Mars 1984.

Desmond, Jerry R. *Georgia's Rome*. Charleston, SC: History Press, 2008.

Desruisseaux, Alain, Sarah Fortin, and Nicholas Ignatieff. "The Patriation of
the Constitution (1982)." In *As I Recall/Si Je Me Souviens Bien: Historical
Perspectives*, edited by the Institute for Research on Public Policy, 253–60.
National Library of Canada, Quebec, 1999.

Dick, Lyle. "Public History in Canada: An Introduction." *Public Historian* 31.1
(Winter 2009): 7–14.

Dickinson, John, and Brian Young. *A Short History of Quebec*, 3rd ed. Montreal:
McGill-Queen's University Press, 2003.

Dissanayake, Wimal. "Globalization and the Experience of Culture: The Resilience
of Nationhood." In *Globalization, Culture Identities and Media Representation*,
edited by Natascha Gentz and Stefan Kramer, 25–44. New York: State
University of New York Press, 2006.

Donnelly, Jessica Foy, ed. *Interpreting Historic House Museums*. Walnut Creek, CA:
Altamira Press, 2002.

Drobnick, Jim, and Jennifer Fisher. *Museopathy* [exhibition catalogue]. Kingston:
Agnes Etherington Art Centre, 2002.

Duffy, Dennis. "Complexity and Contradiction in Canadian Public Sculpture: The
Case of Walter Allward." *American Review of Canadian Studies* 38.2 (Summer
2008): 189–206.

– "The Grandfathering of William Lyon Mackenzie King." *American Review of
Canadian Studies* 32.4 (Winter 2002): 581–608.

– "The Sideways March: Mackenzie King's Monumental Quest, 1893–1940."

Ontario History 100.2 (Autumn 2008): 130–49.

Duncan, Carol. *Civilizing Rituals: Inside Public Art Museums*. New York: Routledge, 1995.

– and Allan Wallach. "The Universal Survey Museum." *Art History* 3.4 (December 1980): 448–69.

Dwyer, Owen. "Interpreting the Civil Rights Movement: Place, Memory and Conflict." *Professional Geographer* 52.4 (2000): 660–71.

Edwards, Elizabeth, Chris Gosden, and Ruth B. Phillips, eds. *Sensible Objects: Colonialism, Museums and Material Culture*. Oxford: Berg, 2006.

Fessenden, Clementina. "Historic Dundurn." *Globe and Mail* (Toronto). 20 July 1901.

Fitzpatrick, Ashley. "Royal Welcome; Diminished Crowds, but Warm Reception for Royal Couple." *The Telegram* (St. John's, NFLD). 3 November 2009, A1.

Florida, Richard. *The Flight of the Creative Class: The New Global Competition for Talent*. New York: Harper Business, 2005.

– *The Rise of the Creative Class: And How It's Transforming Work, Leisure, Community and Everyday Life*. New York: Basic Books, 2002.

Frank, Marc. *The Mackenzie Panels: The Strange Case of Niagara's Fallen Arch*. Toronto: Red Robin Press, 1987.

Fraser, Andrea, interview by Andrew Hunt. "Is This a Site-specific Interview?" *Untitled* 32 (Summer 2004), n.p.

Freeman, Bill. *Hamilton: A People's History*. James Lorimer Company, 2006.

Frow, John. "Tourism and the Semiotics of Nostalgia." *October* 57 (1991): 123–51.

Gable, Eric, and Richard Handler. "The Authority of Documents at some American History Museums." *The Journal of American History* 81.1 (1994): 119–36.

– *The New History in an Old Museum: Creating the Past at Colonial Williamsburg*. Durham, NC: Duke University Press, 1997.

– "Public History, Private Memory: Notes from the Ethnography of Colonial Williamsburg, Virginia, USA." *Ethnos* 65.2 (2000): 237–52.

– and Anna Lawson. "On the Uses of Relativism: Fact, Conjecture, and Black White Histories at Colonial Williamsburg." *American Ethnologist* 19.4 (1992): 791–805.

Gagnon, Alain-G., and Raffaele Iacovino. "Interculturalism: Expanding the Boundaries of Citizenship." *Québec: State and Society*, 3rd ed., edited by Alain-G. Gagnon, 369–88. Peterborough, ON: Broadview Press, 2004.

Geuna, Elena, and Laurent Le Bon. "A Celebration of Statuary In Situ, Contemporaneity, Luxury and Banality." *Jeff Koons Versailles* [exhibition catalogue], 127–9. Éditions Xavier Barral, 2008.

Gillis, John, ed. *Commemorations: The Politics of National Identity*. Princeton: Princeton University Press, 1994.

Glassberg, David. *Sense of History: The Place of the Past in American Life*. Amherst: University of Massachusetts Press, 2001.

Goldstein, Claire. *Vaux and Versailles: The Appropriations, Erasures and Accidents That Made Modern France*. University of Pennsylvania Press, 2008.

Gordon, Alan. *Making Public Pasts: The Contested Terrain of Montreal's Public Memories, 1891–1930*. Montreal: McGill-Queen's University Press, 2001.

Gregorovich, Andrew. "Chairman's Report." *Year Book*, 1–2. Toronto: Toronto Historical Board, 1982.

– "Chairman's Report." *Year Book* 1980, 3–4. Toronto: Toronto Historical Board, 1980.

Hage, Ghassan. *White Nation: Fantasies of White Supremacy in a Multicultural Society*. New York: Routledge, 2000.

Hakli, Jouini. "Cultures of Demarcation: Territory and National Identity in Finland." In *Nested Identities: Nationalism, Territory, and Scale*, edited by Guntrum H. Herb and David H. Kaplan, 123–50. Lanham: Rowman and Littlefield, 1999.

Halbwachs, Maurice. *The Collective Memory*. London: Harper and Row, 1980.

Hamelin, Jean, and Pierre Poulin, "Chauveau, Pierre-Joseph-Olivier." Dictionary of Canadian Biography, vol. 11, University of Toronto/Université Laval, 2003. Accessed December 15, 2014. http://www.biographi.ca/en/bio/chauveau_pierre_joseph_olivier_11E.html.

Hamilton, Roberta. *Gendering the Vertical Mosaic: Feminist Perspectives on Canadian Society*. Toronto: Copp Clark Ltd., 1996.

Handler, Richard. *Nationalism and the Politics of Culture in Quebec*. Madison, WI: University of Wisconsin Press, 1988.

– "On Having a Culture: Nationalism and the Preservation of Quebec's Patrimoine." In *Objects and Others: Essays on Museums and Material Culture*, edited by George Stocking, 192–217. Madison, WI: University of Wisconsin Press, 1985.

Handler, Richard, and William Saxton. "Dyssimulation: Reflexivity, Narrative, and The Quest for Authenticity in 'Living History.'" *Cultural Anthropology* 3.3 (August 1988): 242–60.

Harles, John. "Multiculturalism, National Identity, and National Integration: The Canadian Case." *International Journal of Canadian Studies* 17 (1998): 217–45.

Häussler, Iris. "Artist's Statement: Fact and Fiction," *He Named Her Amber – The*

Artist's View. Accessed 24 February 2014. http://haeussler.ca/amber/artist.
html.

– "Disclosure – Excavation notes 01/2009." *He Named Her Amber – The Artist's
View*. Accessed 24 February 2014. http://haeussler.ca/amber/artist.html.

– and David Moos, Sarah Milroy, and Martha Baillie. *He Named Her Amber – The
Artist's View* [exhibition catalogue]. Art Gallery of Toronto, 2011.

"Hemmed In: Landmark Doom Looms." *Globe and Mail* (Toronto). 1 April 1960, 5.

Holliday, R., and G. Thompson. "A Body of Work." In *Contested Bodies*, edited by
R. Holliday and J. Hassard, 117–34. London: Routledge, 2001.

Hustak, Alan. "Vanishing brass plaques to be replaced by Parks Canada." *The
Gazette* (Montreal). 14 April 2006, A6.

James, R. Scott. "Managing Director's Report." *Annual Report 1984*, 10–11. Toronto:
Toronto Historical Board, 1984.

Jenkins, Barbara. "Toronto's Cultural Renaissance." *Canadian Journal of
Communication* 30 (2005): 169–86.

Jessup, Lynda. "Hard Inclusion." In *On Aboriginal Representation in the Gallery*,
edited by Lynda Jessup and Shannon Bagg, xiii–xxx. Hull, QC: Canadian
Museum of Civilization, 2002.

Kallen, Evelyn. "Multiculturalism: Ideology, Policy and Reality." *Journal of
Canadian Studies* 17.1 (1982): 51–63.

Kamboureli, Smaro. *Scandalous Bodies: Diasporic Literature in English Canada*.
Don Mills, ON: Oxford University Press Canada, 2000.

– "The Technology of Ethnicity: Canadian Multiculturalism and the Language
of Law." In *Multicultural States: Rethinking Difference and Identity*, edited by
David Bennett, 208–19. London; New York: Routledge, 1998.

Kammen, Michael. *Mystic Chords of Memory: The Transformation of Tradition in
American Culture*. New York: Knopf, 1991.

Karp, Ivan, and Christine Mullen Kreamer, eds. *Museums and Communities: The
Politics of Public Culture*. Washington: Smithsonian Press, 1992.

– and Steven Levine, eds. *Exhibiting Cultures: The Poetics and Politics of Museum
Display*. Washington: Smithsonian Press, 1991.

Katriel, Tamar. "Sites of Memory: Discourses of the Past in Israeli Pioneering
Settlement Museums." In *Cultural Memory and the Construction of Identity*,
edited by Dan Ben-Amos and Liliane Weissberg, 99–135. Detroit: Wayne State
University Press, 1999.

Kratz, Corinne A., and Ivan Karp. "Introduction: Museum Frictions: Public
Cultures/Global Transformation." In *Museum Frictions: Public Cultures/
Global Transformations*, edited by Ivan Karp, Corinne A. Katz, Lynn Szwaja,

and Tomás Ybarra-Frausto, 1–34. Durham: Duke University Press, 2007.

Kirshenblatt-Gimblett, Barbara. *Destination Culture: Tourism, Museums, and Heritage*. Berkeley: University of California Press, 1998.

Koval, Anne. *Framing Nature: The Picturesque Tradition in Landscape* [exhibition catalogue]. Sackville, NB: Owens Art Gallery, 2003.

Kuper, Adam. "The English Christmas and the Family: Time Out and Alternative Realities." In *Unwrapping Christmas*, edited by Daniel Miller, 157–75. Oxford: Clarendon Press, 1993.

Le Bon, Laurent, and Jeff Koons. "Interview with Jeff Koons by Laurent Le Bon – Versailles, July 2008." *Jeff Koons Versailles* [exhibition catalogue], 106–12. Éditions Xavier Barral, 2008.

Lee, Jo-Anne, and Linda Cardinal. "Hegemonic Nationalism and the Politics of Feminism and Multiculturalism in Canada." In P*ainting the Maple: Essays on Race, Gender, and the Construction of Canada*, edited by Veronica Strong-Boag, Sherrill Grace, Avigail Eisenberg, and Joan Anderson, 215–41. Vancouver: UBC Press, 1998.

Lefebvre, Henri. *The Production of Space*. Oxford: Blackwell, 1991.

Leith, Marie-Andrée. *Lieu Historique National de Sir-George-Étienne-Cartier: Étude sur les clientele actuelles individuelles*. Québec: Service du Marketing et des affaires du program, Parcs Canada, March 1996.

Leon, Warren, and Roy Rosenzweig, eds. *History Museums in the United States: A Critical Assessment*. Chicago: University of Illinois Press, 1989.

Léonidoff, Georges-Pierre. *Parc Historique National Sir George-Étienne-Cartier: Concept – Plan d'Ameublement Historique*. Québec: Parcs Canada, Service au Publique, Mars 1983.

Létourneau, Jocelyn. *A History for the Future: Rewriting Memory and Identity in Quebec*, translated by Phillis Aronoff and Howard Scott, 3–29. Montreal: McGill-Queen's University Press, 2004.

Levine, Amy K., ed. *Defining Memory: Local Museums and the Construction of History in America's Changing Communities*. Rowman Altamira, 2007.

Lindsey, Charles. *The Life and Times of William Lyon Mackenzie and the Rebellion of 1837–38*, 2nd vol. Toronto: P.R. Randall, 1862.

Lowenthal, David. "Fabricating History." *History and Memory* 10.1 (1998): 5–24.

– *Possessed by the Past: The Heritage Crusade and the Spoils of History*. New York: Free Press, 1996.

– *The Past is a Foreign Country*. Cambridge, New York: Cambridge University Press, 1985.

Luno, Nancy. *A Genteel Exterior: The Domestic Life of William Lyon Mackenzie*

King and His Family. Toronto: Toronto Historical Board, 1990.

Macdonald, Sharon. *Difficult Heritage: Negotiating the Nazi Past in Nuremberg and Beyond*. New York: Routledge, 2009.

Mackey, Eva. *The House of Difference: Cultural Politics and National Identity in Canada*. London and New York: Routledge, 1999.

Macleod, Erna. "Decolonizing Interpretation at the Fortress of Louisbourg National Historic Site." In *Canadian Cultural Poesis: Essays on Canadian Culture*, edited by Garry Sherbert, Annie Gérin, and Sheila Petty, 361–80. Waterloo: Wilfrid Laurier University Press, 2006.

MacRae, Marion. *MacNab of Dundurn*. Toronto: Clarke, Irwin and Co. Ltd., 1971.

Maginnis, J.A. "Managing Director's Report." *Year Book 1980*, 8–10. Toronto: Toronto Historical Board, 1980.

– "Managing Director's Report." *Toronto Historical Board: Year Book 1978*, 6. Toronto: Toronto Historical Board, 1978.

– "Report on Operations for 1967." *Annual Report 1967*, 1–5. Toronto: Toronto Historical Board, 1967.

Magnuson, Roger. "The Public School Myth: Quebec Education 1875–1960." McGill Journal of Education 22.1 (Winter 1987): 29–40.

Maitland, Leslie. *Neoclassical Architecture in Canada*. Ottawa: Minister of the Environment, 1984.

Malone, Meredith and Andrea Fraser, *"What do I, as an artist, provide?"* [exhibition catalogue]. St. Louis, MO: Mildred Lane Kemper Art Museum, 2007.

Manitoba Education Archives. *Victoria Day and Empire Day: A Canadian Tradition*. Manitoba Education, 1997.

Marson, Jean-Claude. *Montreal in Evolution: Historical Analysis of the Development of Montreal's Architecture and Urban Environment*. Montreal: McGill-Queen's University Press, 1981.

Martin, Lee-Ann. *The Politics of Inclusion and Exclusion: Contemporary Native Art and Public Art Museums in Canada*. A Report Submitted to the Canada Council. Ottawa: Canada Council, 1991.

McCarthy, Kathleen D. *Women's Culture: American Philanthropy and Art*, 1830–1920. Chicago: University of Chicago Press, 1991.

McClintock, Anne. *Imperial Leather: Race, Gender and Sexuality in the Colonial Context*. New York: Routledge, 1995.

McIver, Don. *End of the Line: The 1857 Train Wreck at the Desjardins Canal Bridge*. Dundurn, 2013.

McKay, Gillian. "Iris Häussler: Brilliant Disguise," *Canadian Art*

(1 December 2009). Accessed 24 February 2014. http://www.canadianart.ca/features/2009/12/01/iris-haussler-brilliant-disguise/.

McKay, Ian. "After Canada: On Amnesia and Apocalypse in the Contemporary Crisis." *Acadiensis* 28.1 (1998): 76–97.

– ed. *The Challenge of Modernity: A Reader on Post-Confederation Canada*. Toronto: McGraw-Hill Ryerson, 1992.

– "History and the Tourist Gaze: The Politics of Commemoration in Nova Scotia, 1935–1964," *Acadiensis* 22.2 (Spring 1993): 102–38.

– "The Liberal Order Framework: A Prospectus for a Reconnaissance of Canadian History." *Canadian Historical Review* 81.4 (2000): 617–45.

– and Robin Bates. *In the Province of History: The Making of the Public Past in Twentieth-Century Nova Scotia*. Montreal: McGill-Queen's University Press, 2010.

Mills, Stephen F. "Moving Buildings and Changing History." In *Heritage, Memory and the Politics of Identity: New Perspectives on the Cultural Landscape*, edited by Niamh Moore and Yvonne Whelan, 109–20. Aldershot, England: Ashgate, 2007.

– "Open Air Museums and the Tourist Gaze." In *Visual Culture and Tourism*, edited by David Crouch and Nina Lübbren, 75–88. Oxford and New York: Routledge, 2003.

Ministry of Economic Development, Trade and Tourism, Ontario. *Hamilton Wentworth's Travel Markets – 1994*. Toronto: Queen's Printer for Ontario, 1996.

Morgan, Niles, and Annette Pritchard. *Tourism, Promotion, and Power: Creating Images, Creating Identities*. Chichester: John Wiley and Sons, 1998.

Moore, Christopher. *1867: How the Fathers Made the Deal*. Toronto: McClelland & Stewart Inc., 1997.

Moore, Niamh, and Yvonne Whelan, eds. *Heritage, Memory, and the Politics of Identity: New Perspectives on the Cultural Landscape*. Aldershot, England: Ashgate, 2007.

Neal, Arthur G. *National Trauma and Collective Memory: Extraordinary Events in the American Experience*. 2nd ed. M.E. Sharpe, 2005.

Nesbitt, Kelly. *The Mackenzie Homestead: A Brief History from 1858 to Present Day, Including Room Descriptions of the Restored Museum*. Adapted from *The Genteel Exterior*, by Nancy Luno. City of Toronto: Mackenzie House, Museum and Heritage Services, Culture Division, 2001.

Neufeld, David. "Indigenous peoples and protected heritage areas: Acknowledging cultural pluralism." *Transforming Parks and Protected Areas: Policy and Governance in a Changing World*, edited by Kevin S. Hanna, Douglas A. Clark, and D. Scott Slocombe, 181–99. London: Routledge, 2008.

Nissenbaum, Stephen. *The Battle for Christmas: A Cultural History of America's Most Cherished Holiday.* New York: Vintage Books, 1996.
– "Revisiting 'A Visit from St. Nicholas': The Battle for Christmas in Early Nineteenth-Century America." In *The Mythmaking Frame of Mind: Social Imagination and American Culture*, edited by James Gilbert, Amy Gilman, Donald M. Scott, and Joan W. Scott, 25–70. Belmont: Wadsworth Publishing, 1993.
Nöel, Françoise. *Family Life and Sociability in Upper and Lower Canada, 1780–1870: A View from Diaries and Family Correspondence.* Montreal: McGill-Queen's University Press, 2003.
Nolan, Daniel. "Duchess to become patron of Castle." *The Spectator* (Hamilton). 10 October 2010. Accessed 6 January 2012. http://www.thespec.com/news/local/article/269673-duchess-to-become-patron-of-castle.
– "Royals 'looking forward' to Hamilton Visit." *The Spectator* (Hamilton). 3 November 2009, A10.
Nora, Pierre. "Between Memory and History." *Representations* 26 (Spring 1989): 7–25.
– *Les Lieux de Mémoire*, 3 vols. Paris: Gallimard, 1984–1992.
Norkunas, Martha. *The Politics of Public Memory: Tourism, History and Ethnicity in Monterey, California.* Albany: SUNY Press, 1993.
Oakes, Leigh, and Jan Warren. *Language, Citizenship and Identity in Quebec.* New York: Palgrave Macmillan, 2007.
Office of the Commissioner of Official Languages. *Our Two Official Languages over Time.* Rev. ed. Ottawa: Office of the Commissioner of Official Languages, May 1994.
Osborne, Brian. "Corporeal Politics and the Body Politic: The Re-presentation of Louis Riel in Canadian Identity." *International Journal of Heritage Studies* 8.2 (December 2002): 303–22.
– "From Native Pines to Diasporic Geese: Placing Culture, Setting Our Sites, Locating Identity in a Transnational Canada." *Canadian Journal of Communication* 31 (2006): 147–75.
– "Landscapes, Memory, Monuments, and Commemoration: Putting Identity in its Place." *Canadian Ethnic Studies* 33.3 (2001): 39–77.
Pannekoek, Fritz. "Riel House: A Critical Review." *Archivaria* 18 (Summer 1984): 255–62.
Parker, George L. *The Beginnings of the Book Trade in Canada.* Toronto: University of Toronto Press, 1985.
Parks Canada. *Sir George-Étienne Cartier National Historic Site of Canada: Lower Canada's Most Influential Politician Lived Here.* Ottawa: Parks Canada, n.d.

– "Cartier, Sir George-Étienne, National Historic Person, Montréal, Quebec." *Directory of Federal Designations*. 3 March 2014. Accessed at http://www. pc.gc.ca/apps/dfhd/page_nhs_eng.aspx?id=1563.

– "Cultural Heritage – On-line Tour." *Riel House National Historic Site of Canada*. Accessed 13 July 2010. http://www.pc.gc.ca/eng/lhn-nhs/mb/riel/ natcul/guide.aspx.

– *Énoncé d'Intégrité Commémorative: Lieu Historique du Canada de Sir-George-Étienne-Cartier*. Québec: Parcs Canada, Unité de l'Ouest du Québec, 2004.

– "Explora Guided Tour App." *Sir George-Étienne Cartier National Historic Site*. 3 March 2014. Accessed at http://www.pc.gc.ca/eng/lhn-nhs/qc/ etiennecartier/activ/explora.aspx

– *Information Bulletin: "A Victorian Christmas" at the Elegant Victorian House of Sir George-Étienne Cartier*. Ottawa: Parks Canada, 3 September 2008.

– "Learning Experiences." *Sir George-Étienne Cartier National Historic Site*. Accessed 3 March 2014. http://www.pc.gc.ca/eng/lhn-nhs/qc/ etiennecartier/edu.aspx

– "Management Plan Newsletters." *Riel House National Historic Site of Canada*. Accessed 13 July 2010. http://www.pc.gc.ca/eng/lhn-nhs/mb/riel/ plan/bulletin01.aspx#a1.

– *National Historic Sites of Canada System Plan*. Ottawa: Parks Canada, 2000.

– *Parks Canada Guiding Principles and Operational Policies*. Ottawa: Ministry of the Environment, 1994.

– "Pioneers in Architectural History at Parks Canada!" *Canada's Historic Places*. Accessed 20 Feb. 2014. http://www.historicplaces.ca/en/pages/23_ architectural_history.aspx.

– *Report on the Public Consultation Program: The Residences of Sir George-Étienne Cartier National Historic Park*. Quebec: Parks Canada, March 1983.

– *Sir George-Étienne Cartier National Historic Site of Canada: 2008 Schedule*. Ottawa: Parks Canada, 2008.

– *Sir George-Étienne Cartier National Historic Park: Development Concept*. Quebec: Parks Canada, May 1982.

– *Sir George-Étienne Cartier National Historic Site of Canada: Management Plan*. Ottawa: Parks Canada, March 1985.

– *Sir George-Étienne Cartier National Historic Site of Canada: Management Plan*. Parks Canada: Western Quebec Field Unit, Quebec, 2007.

The Pasts Collective. *Canadian and their Pasts*. Toronto: University of Toronto Press, 2013.

Peers, Laura. "'Playing Ourselves': First Nations and Native American Interpreters at Living History Sites." *Public Historian* 21.4 (Fall 1999): 39–59.

Pelletier, Yves. "The Politics of Selection: The Historic Sites and Monuments Board of Canada and the Imperial Commemoration of Canadian History." *Journal of the Canadian Historical Association* 17.1 (2006): 125–50.

Phillips, Ruth, and Christopher Steiner. "Art, Authenticity, and the Baggage of Colonial Encounter." *Unpacking Culture: Art and Commodity in Colonial and Post-Colonial Worlds*, edited by Ruth Phillips and Christopher Steiner, 3–19. Berkeley: University of California Press, 1999.

Preziosi, Donald. "The Art of Art History." In *The Art of Art History: A Critical Anthology*, edited by Donald Preziosi, 507–25. Oxford: Oxford University Press, 1998.

– *Brain of the Earth's Body: Art, Museums, and the Phantasms of Modernity.* Minneapolis: University of Minnesota Press, 2003.

– "Seeing Through Art History." In *Knowledges: Historical and Critical Studies in Disciplinarity*, edited by Ellen Messer-Davidow, David Shumway, and David Sylan, 215–31. Charlottesville: University of Virginia Press, 1993.

Pulver Ungar, Molly. "Trenholme, Clementina (Fessenden)." *Dictionary of Canadian Biography Online*, vol. XIV (1911–1920). Accessed 24 March 2013. http://www.biographi.ca/009004-119.01-e.php?BioId=41864.

Pustz, Jennifer. *Voices from the Back Stairs: Interpreting Servants at Historic House Museums.* Northern Illinois University Press, 2009.

Rachleff, Melissa. "Peering behind the curtain: Artists and questioning historical authority." In *Letting Go?: Sharing Historical Authority in a User-Generated World*, edited by Bill Adair, Benjamin Filene, and Laura Koloski, 208–24. Left Coast Press, 2012.

Rainville, Alain. *Lieu Historique National de Sir-George-Étienne-Cartier: Étude sur la satisfaction des visiteurs été/automne 2000.* Québec: Service du Marketing et des affaires du program, Parcs Canada, October 2001.

Restad, Penne L. *Christmas in America: A History.* New York: Oxford University Press, 1995.

Robertson, Kirsty. "Titanium Motherships of the New Economy: Museums, Neoliberalism, and Resistance." In *Imagining Resistance: Visual Culture and Activism in Canada*, edited by J. Keri Cronin and Kirsty Robertson, 197–214. Waterloo: Wilfrid Laurier University Press, 2010.

Rocher, Guy. "Introduction: Beyond the Quiet Revolution." In *As I Recall/Si Je Me Souviens Bien: Historical Perspectives*, edited by the Institute for Research on Public Policy, 203–9. National Library of Canada, Quebec, 1999.

Rogoff, Irit. "Hit and Run – Museums and Cultural Difference." *Art Journal* 61.3 (Autumn 2002): 63–73.

Romney, Paul. *Getting It Wrong: How Canadians Forgot Their Past and Imperilled Confederation*. Toronto: University of Toronto Press, 1999.

Rychen, Jailee. "Abundance and Banality." *Shift: Graduate Journal of Visual and Material Culture* 4 (2011): 1–11.

Sassen, Saskia. *The Global City: New York, London, Tokyo*. Princeton: Princeton University Press, 1991.

Schwartz, Hillel. *The Culture of the Copy: Striking Likenesses, Unreasonable Facsimiles*. New York: Zone Books, 1996.

Schwartz, Joan. "Photographs from the Edge of Empire." In *Cultural Geography in Practice*, edited by Alison Blunt, 154–71. New York: Oxford University Press, 2003.

Scott, John W. "Chairman's Report." *Toronto Historical Board: 1977 Year Book*, 1–2. Toronto: Toronto Historical Board, 1977.

Service de la recherche en science sociales. *Lieu Historique National de Sir-George-Étienne-Cartier: Étude sur la satisfaction des visiteurs 2007*. Québec: Centre de services du Québec, Parcs Canada, Avril 2008.

Shaffer, Marguerite. *See America First: Tourism and National Identity*. Washington: Smithsonian Institute Press, 2001.

– "Selling the Past/Co-opting History: Colonial Williamsburg as Republican Disneyland." *American Quarterly* 50 (September 1998): 875–84.

Shields, Rob. *Places on the Margin: Alternative Geographies of Modernity*. London: Routledge, 1991.

Silver, Arthur. "Confederation (1867)." In *As I Recall/Si Je Me Souviens Bien: Historical Perspectives*, edited by the Institute for Research on Public Policy, 55–64. National Library of Canada, Quebec, 1999.

Silver, Nathan. *Lost New York*, 2nd ed. New York: Houghton Mifflin Company, 1967.

Smith, Anthony D. *Chosen People: Sacred Sources of Identity*. Oxford: Oxford University Press, 2003.

– *The Ethnic Origins of Nations*. Oxford: Blackwell, 1986.

– *Nationalism: Theory, Ideology, History*. Malden, MA: Polity Press, 2001.

– "Nations and Ethnoscapes." *Oxford International Review* 8.2 (1997): 11–18.

Stainton, Lindsay. *Nature into Art: English Landscape Watercolours* [exhibition catalogue]. London: British Museum Press, 1991.

Statistics Canada. *Analysis in Brief. Christmas: Consumers' Season*. Distributive Trades Division, Statistics, Canada: Ottawa, December 2003.

– *Canadian Travel Survey: Domestic Travel, 2004*. Ottawa: Minister of Industry, 2006.

– "Canadians' Participation in Culture/Heritage Travel in Canada." Travel-log: Catalogue no. 87-003-XIE 20. 3 (Summer 2001): 1–12.

– "Heritage Institutions." *The Daily* (Ottawa). 26 March 2008: n.p. Accessed 2 June 2009. http://www.statcan.gc.ca/daily-quotidien/080326/dq080326d-eng.htm.

Steiner, Christopher. "Can the Canon Burst?" *Art Bulletin* 78 (1996): 213–17.

Stern, Paul C. "Why Do People Sacrifice for Their Nations?" In *Perspectives on Nationalism and War*, edited by John L. Comaroff and Paul C. Stern, 99–121. Amsterdam: Gordon and Breach Publishers, 1995.

Stewart, Susan. *On Longing: Narratives of the Miniature, the Gigantic, the Souvenir, the Collection*. Baltimore: Johns Hopkins University, 1984.

Stokes Sims, Lowery. "Introduction – Fred Wilson: Musings on and Mining of Museums." In *Fred Wilson: A Critical Reader*, edited by Doro Globus, 11–26. Ridinghouse, 2011.

Stratton, Jon, and Ien Ang. "Imagined Multicultural Communities: Cultural Difference and National Identity in Australia and the USA." *Continuum* 8 (1994): 124–58.

Strong-Boag, Veronica. "Experts on Our Own Lives: Commemorating Canada at the Beginning of the 21st Century." *Public Historian* 31.1 (Winter 2009): 46–68.

– and Sherrill Grace, Avigail Eisenberg, and Joan Anderson, eds. *Painting the Maple: Essays on Race, Gender, and the Construction of Canada*. Vancouver: UBC Press, 1998.

Sullivan, Garrett A. *The Drama of Landscape: Land, Property, and Social Relations on the Early Modern Stage*. Stanford, California: Stanford University Press, 1998.

Sutcliffe, Anthony. "Montreal Metropolis." *Montreal Metropolis, 1880–1930*, edited by Isabelle Gournay and France VanLaethem, 19–24. Montreal: Centre for Canadian Architecture and Stoddart Publishing, 1998.

Symons, Thomas, ed. *The Place of History: Commemorating Canada's Past*. Royal Society, 1997.

Taylor, C.J. *Negotiating the Past: The Making of Canada's National Historic Parks and Sites*. McGill-Queen's University Press, 1990.

"Things to Do and See During the Weekend." *Globe and Mail* (Toronto). 3 December 1965, 4.

Timothy, Dallen, ed. *The Political Nature of Cultural Heritage and Tourism, Critical Essays*, 3rd vol. Burlington, VT: Ashgate, 2007.

Toronto Culture. *The Creative City: A Workprint*. Toronto: Toronto Culture, April 2001.

– *Mackenzie House: Self-Guided Tour*. Toronto: Toronto Culture, n.d.

Toronto Historical Board. *1989 Annual Report*. Toronto: Toronto Historical Board, 1989.

– *Annual Report 1984*. Toronto: Toronto Historical Board, 1984.

– *Annual Report 1986*. Toronto: Toronto Historical Board, 1986.

– *Centennial Project*. Toronto: Stanley Barracks, 1965.

– *A New Direction for Heritage*. Toronto: Toronto Historical Board, 1996.

– *Toronto's Multicultural Heritage*. Toronto: Toronto Historical Board, 1982.

Tourism Hamilton. *Experience Hamilton: Visitor's Guide 2004*. Hamilton, 2004.

Tracy, James. "Introduction." In *Christmas Unwrapped: Consumerism, Christ, and Culture*, edited by Richard Horsley and James Tracy, 1–8. Harrisburg, PA: Trinity Press International, 2001.

Trainor, James. "Andrea Fraser: Pat Hearn Art Gallery/Friedrich Petzel Gallery, New York." *Frieze Magazine* 66 (April 2002). Accessed 12 September 2014. http://www.frieze.com/issue/review/andrea_fraser/.

Turgeon, Luc. "Interpreting Québec's Historical Trajectories: Between La Société Globale and the Regional Space." In *Québec: State and Society*, 3rd ed., edited by Alain-G. Gagnon, 51–68. Peterborough, ON: Broadview Press, 2004.

Urry, Jonathan. *Consuming Places*. New York: Routledge, 1995.

– *The Tourist Gaze: Leisure and Travel in Contemporary Societies*. London: Sage, 1990.

Vachhani, Sheena J., and Alison Pullen. "Home is Where the Heart is? Organizing Women's Work and Domesticity at Christmas." *Organization* 18.6 (November 2011): 807–21.

Vickers, Jill. "Feminism and Nationalism in English Canada." *Journal of Canadian Studies* 35.2 (2000): 128–48.

Vickery, Amanda. *The Gentleman's Daughter: Women's Lives in Georgian England*. New Haven: Yale University Press, 1998.

– "Golden Age to Separate Spheres? A Review of the Categories and Chronology of English Women's History." *Historical Journal* 36 (1993): 383–414.

Wajcman, J. *Feminism Confronts Technology*. Cambridge: Polity, 1991.

Walkowitz, Daniel J., and Lisa Maya Knauer, eds. *Memory and the Impact of Political Transformation in Public Space*. Durham, NC: Duke University Press, 2004.

Wallace, Michael. "Visiting the Past: History Museums in the United States." *Radical History Review* 25 (1981): 63–96.

Walsh, Kevin. *The Representation of the Past: Museums and Heritage in the Post-Modern World*. New York: Routledge, 1992.

Wang, Ning. *Tourism and Modernity: A Sociological Analysis*. New York: Pergamon, 2000.

Ward, Peter. *A History of Domestic Space: Privacy and the Canadian Home*. Vancouver: University of British Columbia Press, 1999.

West, Patricia. *Domesticating History: The Political Origins of America's House Museum*. Washington: Smithsonian Press, 1999.

William Lyon Mackenzie Homestead Foundation. *Addresses Delivered by the Honourable Leslie M. Frost, K.C. and Leonard W. Brockington in Connection with the Opening of Mackenzie House, 82 Bond Street, Toronto*. Toronto: William Lyon Mackenzie Homestead Foundation, 1950.

Wood, Patricia K., and Liette Gilbert. "Multiculturalism in Canada: Accidental Discourse, Alternative Vision, Urban Practice." *International Journal of Urban and Regional Research* 29.3 (September 2005): 679–91.

Wright, Janet. *Architecture of the Picturesque in Canada*. Ottawa: Minister of the Environment, 1984.

Yallop, Rosemary. "Nash and the villa rustica." In *John Nash: Architect of the Picturesque*, edited by Geoffrey Tyack, 57–74. Swindon: English Heritage, 2013.

Young, Brian. *George-Etienne Cartier: Montreal Bourgeois*. Montreal: McGill-Queen's University Press, 1981.

Young, Linda. "Is There a Museum in the House? Historic Houses as a Species of Museum." *Museum Management and Curatorship* 22. 1 (2007): 59–77.

Yúdice, George. *The Expediency of Culture: Uses of Culture in the Global Era*. Durham NC: Duke University Press, 2003.

– "Translator's Introduction." In *Néstor García Canclini, Consumers and Citizens: Globalization and Multicultural Conflicts*, trans. George Yúdice, ix–xxxviii. Minneapolis: University of Minnesota Press, 2001.

Zelinsky, Wilbur. *Nation into State: The Shifting Symbolic Foundations of American Nationalism*. Chapel Hill: North Carolina Press, 1988.

Index